LEADERSHIP
AND THE
COMPUTER

How to Order:

Quantity discounts are available from the publisher, Prima Publishing, P.O. Box 1260MB, Rocklin, CA 95677; telephone (916) 624-5718. On your letterhead include information concerning the intended use of the books and the number of books you wish to purchase.

U.S. Bookstores and Libraries: Please submit all orders to St. Martin's Press, 175 Fifth Avenue, New York, NY 10010; telephone (212) 674-5151.

LEADERSHIP

AND THE

COMPUTER

Mary E. Boone

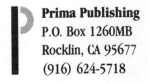

Prima Publishing
P.O. Box 1260MB
Rocklin, CA 95677
(916) 624-5718

This research was supported in part by grants from:

Comshare Inc.
Digital Equipment Corporation
Lotus Development Corporation
N. Dean Meyer and Associates Inc.

The author appreciates the generous support of these corporations in making this research possible.

Typography by Dharma Enterprises
Production by Carol Dondrea, Bookman Productions
Copyediting by Toni Murray
Interior Design by Renee Deprey
Cover Design by Kirschner-Caroff Design

Prima Publishing
Rocklin, CA

Library of Congress Cataloging-in-Publication Data

Boone, Mary E.
    Leadership and the computer : top executives reveal how they personally use computers to communicate, coach, convince, and compete / by Mary E. Boone.
        p.   cm.
    Includes index.
    ISBN 1-55958-080-1
    1. Management—Data processing.   2. Information technology.
    3. Chief executive officers.   I. Title.
    HD30.2.B66   1991   90-49111
    658.4'0C285—dc20   CIP

91 92 93 94 RRD 10 9 8 7 6 5 4 3 2 1

Printed in the United States of America

*This book is dedicated to
Dean Meyer and Charles Boone.*

CONTENTS

TABLE OF FIGURES

AUTHOR'S NOTE

Among my family, friends, and business associates, I am a renowned optimist. However, when it comes to research, a strong dose of skepticism is healthy, and a bit of cynicism (particularly about computers) seems fashionable.

I have made every attempt to remain objective and not overly enthusiastic. Nonetheless, I leave the experience of this research unquestionably biased: I believe that, when properly applied, the computer can serve as one of the most powerful leadership tools ever invented. The compelling evidence presented by the leading executives profiled in this book supports this belief.

Up to this point in history, executives have functioned with a variety of intellectual tools: meetings, speeches, books and periodicals, pens and paper, and telephones. The computer is a relatively new addition to this list. It provides tools that can significantly increase the capacity of the executive brain to deal with complexity—a capacity that is sorely needed in an age of globalization and rapid change.

But top executives, for the most part, are not using computers. The majority of those executives who do have computers are using them simply for reviewing routine operating reports. They often treat the computer as just a fancy version of what they used to receive on paper. This is hardly worth the time or expense.

There are a variety of reasons why executives are not using computers in more interesting and significant ways. The most important one is that *executives simply don't know what computers can do for them personally.*

I decided to find out what computers can do for executives by talking to some of the pioneering executives who actually use computers. When I selected the interviewees, I was interested only in those who use computers themselves, hands-on. Why did I insist on hands-on use? I believe that executives who have actually rolled up their sleeves have greater insights into the power of computers as leadership—as opposed to administrative—tools. These executives, who have taken the time to apply computers to their critical business needs, have experienced the headiness, the freedom, and the boost to intellectual power that computing and communications tools can provide. In fact, a European executive once said to me, "Taking my computer away would be like taking my car away."

The slow, steady evolution of executive computing has begun. What I have captured in this book are the ideas and the feelings of people who are at the forefront of this evolutionary process—innovators in executive computing who are using a variety of information tools to think and communicate clearly and creatively and to lead people more effectively. These are executives who recognize the inherent power of new leadership tools, and they shared with me their insights, their concerns, and their excitement.

Because of the benefits that they have personally experienced, all these executives agree that other executives should be exposed to information tools in a meaningful way so that the uninitiated can see the connections between the functions of an executive and the functions of a computer. That is the purpose of this book.

I'm sure most authors have impossibly high hopes for their books. I am certainly no exception. My greatest ambition is that it will have a positive influence on speeding and shaping the evolution of executive computing, thereby contributing to the increased intelligence of both executives and organizations.

Mary Boone
Ridgefield, Connecticut

ACKNOWLEDGMENTS

Writing a book is rewarding, but it is also arduous. It is arduous not only for the author, but even more so for those who are in the unfortunate position of *knowing* the author.

I'm grateful to all my friends for their indulgence of my seemingly endless need to "work on the book." They never interfered when I was busy, and they were always there when I needed them.

I thank also the sixteen executives who generously gave their time to be included in this book. I must single out one of them: Ron Compton of Aetna. He was the first executive to agree to be interviewed. It is notoriously difficult to get time with busy corporate executives, and Ron's name lent credibility to the project. I truly appreciate his early confidence in this work.

Ben Dominitz, president of Prima, was one of the precious few who understood from the start that this is a *management* book rather than a *computer* book. His input to the project has been invaluable.

My friend Tom Lodahl gave me excellent feedback and encouragement in the critical early stages of the writing. Also, he bravely provided detailed feedback on successive drafts of the manuscript. Sandy Kyrish made many astute comments on the future of executive computing. Thanks go also to John Shulman for his helpful comments on the manuscript. Toni Murray did a superb job of editing.

For many years, I've wanted an opportunity to publicly thank two people who are responsible for teaching me to write and giving me the confidence to do it: Bill Pell and Germaine Brée.

The entire staff at NDMA assisted and sheltered me to give me time to do this project. Each and every one of them took on more responsibility so that I could focus on the book.

My parents and my sister, Wende, lent moral support every step of the way. Having a terrific family is a good basis for any endeavor. This is certainly not the first time they have come through for me.

The most important thanks of all go to my partner, Dean Meyer, who went to Herculean lengths to help me edit this book. In many ways, I feel the book is as much his as mine. His structured, logical approach to expressing ideas is a perfect foil to my intuitive, creative one. As a reader you will directly benefit from his efforts—he helped make the manuscript infinitely more readable. I am deeply, abidingly grateful to him for the months of work he contributed.

ORGANIZATION OF THE BOOK

Part I provides the backdrop for the book. It gives a detailed account of the relationship between executive intellect and computers.

Parts II through V present profiles of top executives from medium and large corporations who are using computing and communications systems. But the information tools they use are meaningless out of context. Each profile tells a story of one executive's goals, objectives, challenges, and obstacles. I describe their management styles and leadership strategies and how tools for thinking enhance their leadership abilities.

The ways in which executives approach their business challenges are influenced by their distinctive leadership styles. Therefore, I have placed the executives I interviewed into four different categories, based on leadership styles:

- Commander
- Communicator
- Coach
- Culture change agent

It is important to note that I place no value judgment on these leadership styles. Different situations call for different leadership roles. In fact, savvy executives know when a situation calls for a switch in styles.

Because executives switch styles, sorting the executive profiles in Parts II through V was not an easy task. The profiles tell stories that are rich in diversity. Each executive's style may contain some aspects of the other three. None fits neatly into a single category. Nonetheless, I have grouped the profiles according to what I consider to be the *prevalent* leadership style.

Not only have I tried to avoid value judgments on leadership styles, I have also tried to avoid value judgments on leadership strategies. I was very impressed by this group of executives, and my writing reflects my respect. However, I don't want the reader to misinterpret my enthusiasm as a prescription for how to lead a company.

This is not another management book about "ideal" leaders. The executives I interviewed would probably be among the first to tell you that they aren't perfect. In fact, I'm sure you'll agree with some of their leadership strategies and disagree with others. Whether or not history brands these people as successes is not important for the purposes of this book. The executives I present here *are* exceptional in at least one regard: They are personally using a wide variety of information tools, hands-on, before most of their peers.

Whether or not you agree with *what* they are doing as leaders, I think you will be intrigued by *how* they are using computers to do it better. I am certain you will identify with many of the leadership challenges that these executives face, and I hope you will take away some new insights into how to approach your own challenges and opportunities.

Also, this is not a book about technology. I don't dwell on the details of the computer systems that executives use. Rather, the focus of this book is on the way in which readily available technologies are being applied to real business challenges. It is about innovative ways to use computers to leverage executive effectiveness.

Part VI examines the benefits of hands-on computer use in detail, and explores how to achieve them. If, indeed, computers are important to top executives, then what's been delaying executive computing? Chapter 18 examines myths that have arisen regarding computers and executives, and it shows how executives who use computers have refuted the myths. Chapter 19 distills the benefits of executive information tools in detail and includes some examples not discussed in the profiles. Chapter 20 provides practical guidelines for analyzing one's unique information needs, and it helps the reader to think about his or her own potential high-payoff applications.

Part VII contains speculations about the future of executive computing, anticipating the exciting promise of continued evolution.

I

THE
CONTEXT

Part I

An executive once said to me, "I'd stand on my hands two hours a day if I were convinced that it would make this company more successful." He, like many other sincere corporate leaders, works long hours, makes personal sacrifices, and puts a lot of heart and soul into building an effective organization. If running a corporation is so difficult, and if the computer offers an important source of assistance, why haven't executives flocked to it? "Computers can't help me with the kinds of things I do," they say. However, when I describe my research to them, executives are surprised to hear that computers can help with issues they care about as corporate leaders.

The executives' surprise is natural. For many years, computers were used as administrative tools and, in fact, were not all that relevant to executives. But now, computers are indeed pertinent to the issues that worry top executives. Perhaps those who have been reticent about using computers should take a look at what is available now.

The primary function of an executive is to think and to communicate thoughts effectively. Chapter 1 describes the evolution of information systems as thinking tools, and the basis for their relevance to today's executives. Part I provides a context for the profiles contained in Part II.

Computers, Human Intellect, and Organizational Nervous Systems

An executive provides vision and direction, makes decisions, diagnoses and solves problems, negotiates, convinces, and selects and coaches people. All these actions depend on the executive's ability to think creatively and communicate clearly; clear communication and creative thinking can be enhanced by the use of computers.

Unfortunately, most people don't realize this. The computer's role as a valuable thinking tool seems to be a secret. Instead, many intelligent people, even today, believe that computers are best suited to clerical and administrative tasks. They see the computer as only a convenience or an operational necessity. I see the computer as an extension of the human brain.

An understanding of the connection between the evolution of the human mind and computers takes us back in time.

The Relationship Between Tools and Thinking

For the human species, survival depends on intellect. We cannot depend on sheer strength or speed when confronting other species or the forces of nature. We are physically small and ungainly. Our only hope for successfully dealing with a complex environment is to out-smart our competitors.

Likewise, the organizations humans construct cannnot depend on magnitude or external attributes. Successful organizations are not built on sheer size (economies of scale) or riches (raw materials). If any-thing, size is proving to be a detriment. Modern technologies are diminishing the economies of scale, permitting small plants to be as efficient and productive as large ones. Meanwhile, small plants are inherently more flexible and able to respond to the market's drift away from mass production and toward niche-tailored specialty products.

Similarly, raw materials alone are no longer a healthy basis for a business. In our ecologically conscious world, we are finding inno-vative ways to make far better use of increasingly scarce materials—putting technology in competition with control of resources. Fur-thermore, those who depend for their success on control of resources are under increasing pressure from environmental constraints (natural and social), and they are poorly positioned for growth. In the informa-tion age, organizations must outsmart their competitors and overcome the reality of environmental constraints through creativity, flexibility, and responsiveness. In other words, organizations must find ways of increasing their "intelligence."

Thus, a seminal question for corporate leaders is: How do we make our organizations "smarter"? At least part of the answer lies in a corollary: How do we make our leaders smarter?

In answering this corollary, we have to consider whether or not intelligence is innate. Can it be that executives are born with a certain amount of brainpower and that they are destined to attain only that level of intelligence throughout their lifetimes? The answer is no. Intelligence depends not only on the power of a person's mind, but also on the tools and methods he or she uses to extend the thinking process.

Occasionally in the evolution of the human species, intellectual development has experienced quantum leaps. With a broad-brush view of the history of human intellect, Dr. Douglas C. Engelbart, a seminal thinker and inventor in the field of computing, tells of the link between tools and intelligence:

> Roughly 20,000 to 30,000 years ago, humans developed spoken lan-guage abilities. This allowed people to pass knowledge along from generation to generation. Thus, the species was able to accumulate more

knowledge than one person could learn in a lifetime, and hence people were able to deal effectively with more complexity.

But the amount of information the species could accumulate was bounded by the memory capacity of individuals. Myths and ballads made memorization easier, and somewhat extended the intellectual capacity of the species. Nonetheless, the limits of memory constrained the evolution of intellect.

Over 6,000 years ago, humans developed the ability to write—not just ideograms (pictures that represent whole ideas), but logograms (pictures that represent simple nouns and verbs which were the components of ideas).

In 3100 B.C., the Sumerians in southern Mesopotamia began combining logograms with syllabograms (pictures that represented phonetics— i.e., sounds) to represent abstract ideas. This phonetization, called the rebus principle, represented a massive leap in human ability to express complex thoughts in writing. As a result, human beings were able to be more and more specific in their communication of complex, abstract ideas.

Writing developed into an infinitely recombinant structured symbology that matched spoken language in its richness. This allowed the species to save exponentially more information than could be remembered in stories and songs, and in turn expanded by orders of magnitude our ability to deal with a complex world.

However, it remained difficult to disseminate information—hand copying was tedious, books were rare. Tribes and states tended to be relatively isolated, accumulating knowledge in parallel. The intellect of the species was, at this point, bounded by what each separate group of people could learn and understand.

Just over 500 years ago, Gutenberg developed the movable-type printing press, permitting the widespread dissemination of information. In combination with improved communications and trade, the printing press led to the spread of knowledge across social and political boundaries and put books in the hands of the masses. When the general education level of the population increased, the intellectuals of the society could focus their studies on more advanced subjects.

Information dissemination permitted increased specialization—leading to the emergence of a great diversity of trades and professions. Specialization, triggered by the printing press, again permitted the species to accumulate significantly more knowledge and deal with greater complexity.[1]

In each case, an innovation enhanced our ability to remember information and work with ideas expressed as symbols (words, numbers, and images). In each case, quantitative improvements in our methods and tools led to a qualitative increase in our ability to deal with complexity.

The reason for this is found in the nature of intelligence. One definition of intelligence is the ability of a person to meet and deal with various situations, based on experience and knowledge. We predict results based on our past experience, and we use that knowledge to determine a course of action. Each step in this process requires thinking.

Thinking can be described as a process of gathering information, distilling and relating it, and creatively viewing it to induce or deduce new ideas. Human thinking is limited in two ways. The bounds of our long-term memory constrain how much information we can accumulate without the help of aids such as writing. In addition, our short-term memory is limited. We have a mental "scratch pad" that can hold only a limited number (some say 7 to 12) of thoughts at a time. The constraints of memory limit our ability to distill, relate, and view ideas. As we improve our ability to manipulate symbols (such as language) outside our heads, we expand our ability to think.

The computer may enable the next big leap in the evolution of human intellect. Consider what the computer offers. It gives us direct, focused access to millions of publications from around the world. It allows us to, with almost unlimited capacity, store everything we know, and access it at will. It allows us to communicate with local, organization-wide, and global networks of colleagues with whom we might otherwise never communicate. It allows us to quickly sketch ideas in a variety of forms and freely manipulate those words, numbers, and images. With the advent of expert systems, the computer can even interact with us as a colleague would, pushing us to be more creative and thoughtful.

In summary, computers dramatically extend the memory of our species and our ability to work with ideas. These two skills are the basis of the thinking process. It is this interactive, dynamic nature of computing and communications tools that makes them so exciting.

Computers are supplements of the mind.

A Brief History of Computers

In the late 1940s, computers were designed as extensions to human intellect. They were initially used for scientific calculations, such as those to plot missile trajectories. These computers were used by a very few, whose work involved a great deal of information and complex analyses.

However, in the 1950s, computing took a different turn as it was applied to commercial tasks. These applications were in bookkeeping, where the computer was used to improve the efficiency of clerical work. The goal was to replace people rather than to extend people's thinking powers. This administrative focus continued through the 1960s, when many of the operational transactions that are necessary to run a business were automated.

As an example of the common view of the role of computers at that time, consider this description of computers from the 1960 *World Book Encyclopedia*: "A computer is an electronic or mechanical device that solves mathematical problems and performs clerical tasks. . . . One of these machines can do the work of thousands of accountants, book-keepers, and file clerks."[2]

Though traditional data processing allowed corporations to grow in size and complexity, it did little to enhance human intellect.

In the late 1960s and early 1970s, as technology progressed, the data resulting from operational transactions was captured in corporate databases. These database systems were called management information systems, but—as far as most managers and executives were concerned—the impact of the databases on thinking was minimal. Typewritten reports were replaced with computer printouts, but thinking went on as it had for centuries.

The 1970s saw the spread of word processors. Unfortunately, they were neither designed for nor used by people who write. Rather, they were used by secretaries to improve typing efficiency. In some companies, the thinking ability of the organization was actually damaged as secretaries were forced into typing pools (to make better use of machines, not people's minds), and managers found themselves without the paraprofessional support that freed them for their intellectual work.

The 1980s saw the rapid spread of personal computers throughout corporate offices. Did this indicate the beginning of a new era? Sadly, for the most part, no. PCs were, by and large, used as little more than expensive calculators and file cabinets. The networks that connected them carried operational data and administrative messages. The true potential of the computer as an intellectual supplement remained largely dormant.

The Parallel History of Tools for Thinking

Throughout this same period of time, a small group of information systems professionals pursued a different course. As early as 1962—when the attention of the computer industry was squarely focused on routine transactions processing—Dr. Douglas C. Engelbart, at the Stanford Research Institute, formed a research laboratory called the Augmenting Human Intellect Research Center.

Engelbart's lab began to develop tools that were *not* designed to capture more keystrokes or process data into reports, but rather to help people think. His research led to the invention of many of the devices and tools now considered on the leading edge of computing, including the mouse, windows, hypertext, and electronic publishing.

Engelbart's work in the 1960s set the stage for the revolution in end-user computing that followed approximately 20 years later. However, despite the fact that he is admired greatly by the computing community for his inventions and ground-breaking work, Engelbart's vision of enhancing human intellect through computer-based tools is only beginning to be understood.

In the 1970s, the idea of enhancing human intellect through computers wasn't a popular notion. People still saw the computing world through administrative glasses. This view has changed somewhat, but not dramatically enough. Much of the business world still connects personal or end-user computing with office administration or users who write computer programs. Nonetheless, those who do understand the potential of tools for thinking are doing business in dramatically different ways. These pioneers are proving that quantitative improvements in our ability to work with information can lead to qualitative leaps in our intellectual abilities.

Beyond Individual Intellect:
The Organization's Nervous System

To this point, we have discussed the use of computers to augment individuals and small groups. Executives can also use computers at the organization level, not just as a tool for leaders, but also as a medium for leadership.

Organizations may be viewed as organisms—dynamic systems that have instincts for survival, growth, and learning, with components that operate in concert with one another. To date, organizations have used computers to move operational information—like the hands and feet of the organism. Pioneers, however, are using information systems as the "nervous system" of the organism.

The concept of computers as an organization's nervous system is not new, but neither is it widely applied. Its potential was explored by Stafford Beer, who applied cybernetics to organizations. He views organizations as analogous to living systems, with the executive committee serving as the "brain" of the firm. In meetings and individually, executives provide the control and coordination mechanism for the complex system.[3]

The brain of the firm is connected by communications channels to the immense variety of the firm's operations. Such channels naturally exist, with or without information systems. Beer distinguishes channels coming into the brain of the firm from those going out of the brain of the firm. That is, the brain gives and receives feedback.

There is a mismatch between the quantity (variety, in cybernetic terms) of details in the organization and that which executives can handle. No executive, no matter how hard he works or how well equipped with computers he or she is, can direct in detail every activity in an organization. Thus, executives must filter incoming information to a volume that they are able to handle. In addition, they need "amplifiers" to extend their strategic messages to the day-to-day activities of everyone in the firm.

Filters and amplifiers exist to balance the variety of information flowing in either direction. For example, one filter on information coming into the brain of the firm is a secretary who screens calls for an executive. An example of an amplifier on information leaving the brain might be policy or strategy statements that allow top executives to influence many more decisions than they can personally make.

In addition to filters and amplifiers, a key factor in this nervous system is the variety-handling abilities of the brain of the firm—that is, the intellectual horsepower of the executives.

Information systems can help fine tune the nervous system of the organization in a variety of ways. They can:

- Create new channels of information into the executive suite
- Help executives adjust the filters on incoming information, making them either more or less permeable
- Expand the ability of the brain of the firm to manage complexity

■ Build new channels outward to improve amplification of executives' messages

Use of computers to ask what-if questions during an executive committee meeting is one way to expand the thinking ability of the brain of the firm. Computers can also help with individual activities— for example, a word processor can help an executive to express thoughts more clearly.

Though activities within the brain (the executive committee) itself are highly important, it is equally important to consider the underlying concept regarding an organization's nervous system: *connectivity*. The channels inward and outward affect the performance of the entire organization, not just that of the people at the top.

If, for example, executives want to create a new channel of information inside the company, they might start an internal computer conference with a select group of people. If they want to adjust filters on external information, they might design their own search criteria for an external database search. A videoconference to all employees that explains and illustrates a policy exemplifies an amplifier.

Note that not all the nerves in a body connect to the conscious brain. Autonomic systems, those that control the heart and breathing, for example, run without conscious intervention. Similarly, when information is reported to line managers, they take more complete control of their pieces of the business.

Some of the cases in this book describe executives who are using computers explicitly to fine tune their organization's nervous systems. Appendix 3 outlines these examples. Both now and in the future, I envision organizations with the potential to operate as pulsating, vibrant, healthy organisms—making full use of the power that computers have to improve individual and collective performance.

The Evolution of Executive Computing

I have made the case that computers extend human intellect and improve the functioning of the organizational nervous system. If all this is true, then why has executive computer use evolved so slowly?

There are good reasons for this lack of use. After four decades of administrative applications, it is no wonder that most executives believe that the computer is for their secretaries and analysts but not for them. Indeed, learning to use a computer takes time, and understanding how to apply it to mission-critical problems requires both effort and creativity. The costs of executive computer use are obvious; the benefits have been less readily apparent. For this reason, executives are naturally slow to explore what may be one of their most important resources.

The information systems profession has fallen into the same trap. Four decades of experience in producing operational transactions-processing systems has created a mindset that equates computers with tracking business operations. Many in the profession toss off tools for thinking as secretarial in nature, labeling these applications as office support. Some people assume that executives simply want faster access to the financial and operational reports that they have been getting on paper for years.

A prejudice against "small" systems or the personal use of computers has also blinded computer professionals. This attitude pits the executive working on a stand-alone personal computer against the executive who is connected, through a network or large computers to others in the organization.

These prejudices have melded into an "industry standard" definition of the term "executive information system" (EIS). The common view of an EIS is a user-friendly front-end, with analytic and graphics capabilities, connected in a customized fashion with centralized company performance and reporting databases.[4] When they hear the term "EIS," many information systems professionals think of easy to use menues that access on the screen operational reports that heretofore were delivered on paper.

While operational information is clearly important, it is not the only tool executives use. (One of the leading software packages designed specifically for executives contains status reports, interactive data query, a reminder system, electronic mail, and access to external data bases.*) The fact is, executives need both individual and networked computer applications. My definition of an EIS encompasses a wide variety of information tools.

The important point is to avoid bias in favor of any one type of system. Technological bias is anathema to any computing application.

---

*"Commander," by Comshare, Inc., Ann Arbor, Michigan.

If the person helping an executive to think through business challenges is biased in favor of a particular technology, the result is a solution in search of a problem.

As Chapter 20 will show, the key to success is applying the appropriate tool to the appropriate problem. I view organization-wide reporting systems as one tool among many in the executive tool kit.

By giving the term executive information system (EIS) a broader definition, we can help avoid bias by emphasizing the problem rather than the technical solution. My definition differs substantially from the common view. I define an executive information system as any application of a computer or communication tool in which the executive directly participates in the selection of the problem and the selection, design, or use of the tool (see Figure 1).

Despite technological bias from many in the information systems profession and an administrative mindset on the part of most people, a few leading executives *are* personally and regularly using a variety

---

FIGURE 1

A BROAD DEFINITION OF EXECUTIVE INFORMATION SYSTEMS

Executive information systems:

- Directly address the specific, selected goals of an executive
- Consist of one or more tools selected or designed by the executive, with the assistance of others
- Are used by

    The executive alone (For example, consider a word processor which clarifies thinking and writing.)

      or

    The executive and others (For example, consider a shared financial reporting system that creates P&L responsibility or an electronic mail system that builds teamwork.)

      or

    Others (For example, consider an expert system that captures the executive's ideas and vision and communicates them to operating management.)

of information tools. It is unlikely that they do so to save their administrative staff some time. What, then, motivates these leaders to invest their time to adopt computer-based information tools? There must be something—some powerful benefit of relevance to top executives—that drives them to break new ground. Could it be that they have discovered how to use computers to "grow" their minds?

The Search for Pioneers in Executive Computing

I set out to study these questions five years ago. While reviewing the literature about executive computer use I noticed, roughly speaking, that most articles in the popular and business press before 1987 and 1988 were pessimistic about executive use of computers. These articles cited steep learning curves and "unfriendly" systems as primary reasons why executives refused to use computers. After 1987, more positive articles appeared, touting the virtues of new, easy-to-use systems that solved all previous problems. The impression given was that scores of executives were flocking to now user-friendly computers.

A few articles both before and after 1987 got to the heart of the matter. In these articles, executives told reporters that computers had nothing to do with their jobs. Executives' perceptions about the *value* of computers were truly the central issue.

In 1987, I started calling a large number of executives who had been cited as users of EIS or personal computers. I found that, though a good number of CEOs professed to using computers, most of them, when pressed, indicated that they used them only occasionally, and many admitted that they simply had computers in their offices to set a good example.

Now I was more curious than ever about those few executives who were using computers. What secret had they stumbled onto? Did they, like me, believe the computer was an intellectual tool? As I discovered computer-using executives, I screened them carefully before asking for an interview. I suspected that, unless they regularly used a computer, they would not be able to articulate the relationship between mind and machine.

Therefore, the executives I focused on represent a small group of pioneers who use computers to extend their minds and their leadership capabilities. Other executives may be using computers to pull up on the screen what they once received on paper, but those executives, by modern standards, are not truly tapping the power of their computers.

In speaking with executives who use computing and communication tools hands-on, I learned that the types of applications they valued went beyond simply automating existing processes. The executives made it clear that computers and information tools are powerful leadership tools, and the bottom-line results are well worth knowing about.*

The Discoveries of On-line Executives

This book is designed for people who think for a living. It should prove valuable both to executives who already use computers and to those who don't use computers at all. It sets forth new ways for executives to think about computers in relation to their personal leadership challenges.

The time for enhanced leadership is right. Many corporations are huge and growing larger, and even small businesses are growing ever more complex. Many medium-sized companies are now multinationals. Business now involves intricate technologies and methods in areas such as engineering, finance, and manufacturing. Economies are more volatile, and competitive pressures more intense and fast acting. On top of this burgeoning complexity, executives' spans of control are increasing. These fundamental trends are stretching the leadership abilities of top executives to the limit. The growth—perhaps the survival—of many organizations may depend on a massive increase in executives' intellectual abilities.

I hope that the insights of the executives I talked with will stimulate creative use of powerful information tools by others who are feeling the pressures of leadership in an economically, socially, and politically complex world.

---

*I include in my definition of information tools both computing and telecommunications. You will see examples of uses of voice mail, teleconferencing, and videotape, as well as many types of computing applications. Sometimes I have used the term computing interchangeably with information tools to avoid being repetitious. For a listing of a range of information tools, see Appendix 1.

NOTES

1. Based on a speech by Dr. Douglas C. Engelbart.
2. *World Book Encyclopedia* (Chicago: Field Enterprises Educational Corp., 1960), p. 741.
3. Stafford Beer, *Platform for Change* (Chichester, UK: Wiley, 1975).
4. This definition was provided by Dr. Tom Lodahl in personal correspondence.

II

THE

LEADER

AS

COMMANDER

Accessibility and
Personal Involvement

Part II

The traditional view of a leader is that of a person who commands or directs. This type of leader maintains a hands-on approach to orchestrating the activities of a firm. The commander takes the helm and has a powerful influence over both the direction of the vessel and the details of how it will operate.

With all the talk today about participative management, this leadership style has taken on some pejorative connotations in some quarters. This is unfortunate. There are times when the leader must take charge—for example, to create a new company or to recover from crises. In some cases strong, centralized leadership is not only auspicious, but necessary to the survival of the firm.

Instead of making an assessment of the appropriate leadership style for a particular situation, many assume that "hands-off" is a more modern approach. But it is a mistake to dismiss the highly involved leader. Leadership style must adapt to the circumstances. Burnell Roberts (Mead) agrees that it is not always good to "put every issue up for vote." He related an example:

> There was a time in 1982 when we were not doing well as a company. . . . I had to set very strong direction. I decided what we were going to do, what we were going to sell, and what we were going to get out of. It was interesting because we had a very, very clear roadmap. There was no gathering at the water fountain to discuss the pros and cons. Everybody just got out and did their jobs. It was beautifully handled: We got things done smoothly and did far better then I ever expected.
>
> There are times when people need to know exactly where they're expected to go. They don't want fuzziness. They want direction.

Leaders who have a legitimate need to maintain centralized control must find ways of influencing and participating in decisions without becoming a bottleneck. Their input is often greatly needed and appreciated, but there are two ways in which they find themselves constraining the freeflow of activities in the firm: by their inability to make themselves fully accessible and by their limited capacity (in terms of time and attention) to stay personally involved.

If a leader is to have direct input into the detailed operation of the firm, he or she must be accessible to people throughout the company. Such accessibility is made difficult by the sheer size of organizations, hectic travel schedules, and competing demands on the executive's time. The first two profiles in Part II describe executives whose leadership strategy depends on their widespread accessibility to people.

In the first profile, Richard Pogue (Jones Day Reavis & Pogue) explains why he must stay closely involved in the activities of his large, international law firm. The concept of a strong managing partner (the professional equivalent of a corporate CEO) has a long history at Jones Day Reavis & Pogue. In his profile, Pogue describes the advantages that a centralized approach affords and the pressures it puts on him to maintain the respect of his employees and provide strong leadership. Pogue uses information tools to make himself accessible to those who need him, without being a bottleneck in the decision-making process.

In the second profile, Senator Gordon Humphrey (R-NH) lists accessibility as a primary leadership goal. He must put his personal touch on all key communications, since his mission as a political leader is to provide clear positions on issues. Humphrey uses information tools personally to ensure efficiency and responsive decisionmaking in his Senate office. By making himself accessible through information tools, he finds that both he and his staff are able to get more accomplished.

The second constraint on executive involvement is the limit on personal time and effort. Leaders who are called upon to give more direction must find ways of staying involved without straining their own personal capacity to handle complexity and without overcontrolling the people who work for them. The last three profiles in Part II discuss the need for expanding one's capacity to manage complexity.

Though Mark Edmiston, chairman of *The Cable Guide*, is a heavy delegator, he reveals in the third profile why it is important for him to be personally involved in such activities as planning and sales. In a young firm such as Edmiston's, his creativity and persuasiveness are key to growth. Information tools allow him to maintain the proper level of personal involvement without interfering with the activities of his employees.

Ellen Gordon, president of Tootsie Roll Industries, is a detail-oriented person. She likes to understand the mechanics of essential processes such as procurement, and she has a feel for the details of the firm's financial operations. Her use of information tools allows her to stay personally involved with many aspects of the company, helping her to be a strong operational manager.

Sandy Sigoloff, the famous "Corporate Doctor," played a pivotal role in directing Wickes Companies' emergence from bankruptcy. At the time, this situation represented the largest nonrailroad bankruptcy in U.S. history. Heavy management involvement was required to sort out the numerous complexities of this quagmire. Sigoloff used information systems to help him personally sort out the issues associated with such a sizable turnaround.

These profiles show ways in which information tools have strengthened hands-on executives by increasing their levels of personal involvement and accessibility, thereby helping them stay in touch with the complex activities of their operations.

CHAPTER 2

The Global
Law Firm

Richard Pogue

Managing Partner, Jones Day Reavis & Pogue

I have a lousy background in geography. So, when I made my first-ever visit to Cleveland, Ohio, to interview Richard Pogue, I had to ask the taxi driver, "What lake is that?"

"Lake Erie," he said disdainfully, shooting me a quick glance in his rear-view mirror.

When I recounted this story to Pogue, I got a raised eyebrow and a long dissertation on the merits of his fair city. "This is the best time in the history of Cleveland to be here. I mean, things are just taking off. It's unbelievable!" He went on enthusiastically about new hotels, new athletic stadiums, science museums, aquariums, and The Rock-and-Roll Hall of Fame.

As much as Pogue may love Cleveland, his business outlook is by no means parochial. Jones Day Reavis & Pogue is one of the largest law firms in the world, with over 1,200 attorneys located in 11 offices across the United States and 9 offices overseas in Tokyo, Geneva, Hong Kong, London, Paris, Riyadh, Brussels, Taipei, and Frankfurt. Richard Pogue is a man whose goal is to build what was once a regional law firm into a global giant.

The Challenge: Growing an Integrated, Global Firm

Pogue worked with his predecessor, Allen Holmes, to expand the regional law firm into a nationwide practice. When he took over the managing partner position in 1984, Pogue decided to capitalize on the strength of the firm's geographic dispersion and the momentum built by Holmes. Anticipating the growth of global economic and political activity, he had a vision of a worldwide law practice. "One of the first things I did when I took over was to say, 'We're going to be an international firm.' We thought that the commerce of the future was going to involve more and more an international aspect. The world is shrinking, and economic developments are becoming more and more intertwined among various countries. We wanted to be part of the process."

When Pogue made the decision to expand internationally, two underlying business strategies furthered his goal of creating an integrated, global law firm:

- Carefully assimilated acquisitions
- An integrated, functional organizational structure

His leadership strategy entailed a strong managing partner concept. Pogue directly participated in the decisions about how the firm would use information systems in support of these two strategies. He designed and used these information tools to work in concert with his approach to leadership.

Business Strategy: Carefully Assimilated Acquisitions

Pogue knew that a prerequisite for becoming an international firm meant having a New York location. Jones Day Reavis & Pogue serendipitously found a firm, Surrey and Morris, that was not only located in New York, but also had offices in London, Paris, Riyadh, and Washington, D.C. The merger—which occurred January 1, 1986— allowed Jones Day to go worldwide. Other acquisitions followed. Within the past six years, Jones Day Reavis & Pogue has made three major acquisitions.

Pogue's policy on acquisitions is quite clear and in keeping with his "one firm" philosophy. When he uses the word *acquisition,* he means acquisition—not merger. "We make it very clear to the people in the other firm before we agree to merge that if they join us, they're joining *us.* Their old ways have got to be put on the shelf. If they don't like it, that's fine; then there won't be a merger . . . because we've got a direction we're going in, and we don't want to be distracted."

His insistence on a complete blending of two companies is not without a basis:

> There have been a number of mergers in the legal profession that didn't work. In my judgment, it's usually because there's not an understanding going into the merger about who's going to call the shots and what the rules are going to be.
>
> A classic example was a wonderful old firm in Chicago founded by Todd Lincoln, Abraham Lincoln's son. It was a very conservative firm, and it merged about three years ago with a young, aggressive, bunch of litigators . . . totally different. They thought it would be good because they had complementary skills and practices. But they didn't agree going in about who was going to make decisions. The day they merged, they started arguing and hassling. Gradually they began to lose partners, and eventually they just dissolved. The thing just blew up in smoke. And it was really basically because they didn't agree before the merger on how decisions were going to be made.

Pogue's policy on acquisitions sets a clear direction for how firms will be brought into the fold. Once the agreement is made and the firm is acquired, the acculturation process must begin immediately. But it takes more than a simple agreement to make one company part of another.

In order for the policy of blending to work, Pogue must see to it that new offices feel a part of the Jones Day Reavis & Pogue family. Disenchanted or psychologically removed offices could jeopardize the culture and direction of the firm. Communication is the most critical aspect of merging organizational cultures, particularly when the entities are geographically separated. Without quick and easy access to one another, newly merged firms tend to operate autonomously, retaining their own separate cultures, which often are pervaded by a sense of "us versus them."

To fold an acquisition into the Jones Day Reavis & Pogue culture, Pogue relies heavily on information systems. One of the first steps taken after a Jones Day acquisition is to connect the new firm to the Jones Day global electronic network. For example, immediately after acquiring Hansell & Post of Atlanta, a very costly systems switchover was implemented to get Hansell & Post onto the Jones Day network. Pogue sees this as a critical aspect of merging new firms into the Jones Day culture.

The network puts the newly merged entities in touch with each other via electronic mail and shared databases. According to Pogue, this accelerates the assimilation process.

> Given the type of acquisitions we do, we want to have the new lawyers integrated into our overall firm as rapidly as possible. When they have their own systems, procedures, and their own means of communicating that are different from ours, it keeps them out of the mainstream. They aren't able to communicate as effectively or efficiently or rapidly with the other lawyers in the firm as we would like. We think there's a lot of value to getting them integrated quickly, and that means putting them on the same system.

Business Strategy: Functional Organizational Structure

The second strategy underlying the goal of a unified, global firm involves a functional organizational structure. Pogue knows this is a departure from normal practice in his profession. "In your typical multioffice law firm, each office is kind of an autonomous unit; they know the local territory, and they make most of their own rules. We don't do that at all. Our firm is organized functionally rather than geographically." Though the decision to operate functionally preceded Pogue, it blended nicely with his desire to expand the firm internationally. "Our [functional rather than geographic] organizational structure really enables us to have a one firm concept, where everybody is singing off of the same song sheet."

Jones Day Reavis & Pogue has five practice groups (functions): corporate, government regulation, litigation, real estate/construction, and tax. Such a structure allows the firm to provide a client with the best possible resources to get the job done, regardless of location.

> It doesn't make any difference whether a lawyer is in Paris, Los Angeles, or Cleveland; the primary relationship is to that practice group. So if the client comes with an environmental problem, the lawyer in Paris might call Steve Jones in Los Angeles. We try to find the person who's got the most expertise for that particular problem, and we don't worry about where they are. If we've done our job right, a client who walks into our Paris office will get the same quality of service that they would get if they walked into this [Cleveland] office.

Though the geography-independent functional structure is supportive of Pogue's desire to create one international firm, it also presents some practical challenges.

Clients must be convinced that they are receiving top-notch, cost-effective service, even though many of their attorneys are far removed from their client's location. And the right resources must be accessible to every remote office. In other words, the synergies provided by a functional organizational structure have to be achieved in spite of international dispersion. Each of the attorneys in a particular function must feel well connected to the other people in that function, even if they are located thousands of miles apart. Therefore, the challenges presented by the functional structure are two-fold: cost-effectiveness and connectivity.

Jones Day Reavis & Pogue achieves the cost-effectiveness goal through prudent use of electronic document exchange, computerized research, computerized dockets, and desktop publishing.[1] And, in fact, cost-effectiveness issues have been overshadowed by the value-added benefits of having access to top world experts on various legal topics.

> We've been doing this for about 10 years, and initially the clients were concerned about costs. But once they work with it, they realize that the benefit of getting the best expertise we have available on their problem far outweighs the cost. . . . [Our information systems] enable us to deliver better service to the client so much faster. The clients think of us as a firm that's on the ball and that can get things done promptly, efficiently, and effectively. We [even] have about 100 clients that we've put on line with us to do document exchange.

In terms of connectivity, Pogue says the worldwide Jones Day Reavis & Pogue network is essential to the continued effectiveness of a functional approach in the face of international expansion. "This is where the computers really do come in. Because all of the offices are linked, [the network] allows us to just ignore geography."

Leadership Strategy:
A Strong Managing Partner

A functional organizational structure that is dispersed across continents calls for a unifying force. In addition to the technical assistance information systems provide, the management structure of Jones Day

Reavis & Pogue also lends itself well to the functional approach. Since 1913, the firm has operated under the concept of a strong managing partner whose role is similar to that of a corporate CEO. There have been only five managing partners in the history of the firm. "The managing partner is, almost by definition, a unifying element," says Pogue. "Traditionally, law firms have been partnerships, not only in the legal sense but also in an operational sense."

Partnerships are run by committee. Jones Day Reavis & Pogue is run by Richard Pogue. "I get lots of input, and I encourage comments and suggestions. But at the end of the day, the managing partner makes the decision," he explains. "It's the managing partner's responsibility to make sure that the firm is successful, and he's got to have the authority to do that." The slowed decision-making process associated with a committee approach to management can put serious obstacles in the way of rapid, organized growth of law firms, according to Pogue.

Actions are quicker and more decisive under the managing partner structure. "Our ability to grow has been largely due to the managing-partner concept," says Pogue. "For example, my predecessor made the decision to create a national law firm. In those days, there weren't any national law firms. But when he said, 'We're going to open an office in Los Angeles,' we opened an office in Los Angeles. We didn't sit around and debate it for three years. We just did it."

But what do top-notch lawyers think of this central direction? The managing partner approach is unusual in law firms made up of high-powered, independent attorneys. Though the concept of a strong managing partner is a unifying force for pulling the firm together, it also creates a tough leadership challenge: Pogue must retain his top talent and discourage them from leaving for partnership positions in competing firms, where they might have more control over how the firm operates.

Pogue has to create a sense among over a thousand attorneys that he is worth following as a leader. To retain the best possible lawyers, he must demonstrate to them that he is worthy of their respect. Pogue meets this challenge with a three-part leadership approach:

- Inspire confidence through listening.
- Avoid becoming a bottleneck for decisionmaking.
- Construct an equitable means of compensation.

Pogue personally uses computer systems in taking this approach to leading his firm.

Inspire Confidence Through Listening

By listening, Pogue creates a sense of confidence in his leadership. Even though he has the power to make final decisions, Pogue makes a point of soliciting the thoughts of others. He consults two primary committees at Jones Day Reavis & Pogue, and he says he relies greatly on their judgment. A 10-member partnership committee and a 30-member advisory committee give him input on admission of new partners, compensation, and general administration issues.

Since the managing partner serves as a point of convergence for the entire firm, Pogue feels it's important for that managing partner to stay connected to everyone in it. In addition to taking advice from important committees, Pogue makes himself accessible to people throughout the firm. "We have a rule in our firm that the managing partner is accessible to any partner or lawyer. They can come to me at any time and discuss any subject they want to. They don't have to worry about the organization chart, or going through channels, or all of that. The associates don't use it as much, but the partners do; and they know I'll treat things in confidence."

It's fine to have an open-door policy, but what happens if there's no one behind the desk when you enter that door? Again, the global nature of the firm makes this a tough challenge. For this leadership strategy to work, Pogue needs to keep in touch with people despite hectic travel schedules, and the chance that the partner who wants to reach him may be in Taipei. Pogue must find ways of working that are not constrained by time and place.

Pogue uses electronic mail to extend his open-door policy to people at all levels of the firm, worldwide.

> The e-mail really encourages communication. There's a lot of stuff that people shoot to me on e-mail that I don't think they'd probably bother with otherwise. It creates a more collegial atmosphere.
>
> All 20 offices are on the system, and we have *constant* messages going back and forth. I probably get 35 or 40 messages a day, and I immediately shoot back my response. If I'm traveling and I'm in our Chicago office, I can plug right into the thing and get my own messages,

even though I'm not in my own office. I can respond right there on the spot.

Paralegals and secretaries will occasionally send him a message, and Pogue is pleased by the fact that he has contact with a broader range of people in the firm. "Normally, I don't think they'd ever do that. I mean, a secretary probably wouldn't just drop in here. They wouldn't ever call me up. But they feel comfortable sending me a message. They feel they have a link to me. Some have never met me, but they have a feeling that they're linked to the managing partner; and that would not happen without e-mail." Of course, Pogue answers every message he receives.

Paper memoranda don't seem to create the same sense of immediacy, according to Pogue.

> There is a more personal character to a message that comes through electronic mail than one that comes on a piece of paper. It's a more interactive medium. When I'm typing out a message to somebody on the system, I feel more directly in contact with them than I do when I dictate a letter or a memorandum and my secretary takes it away for half an hour. It just feels more personal and direct.
>
> I'm also more inclined to answer a message when it's sent through electronic mail. I carry memoranda around in my briefcase all the time, some of which I probably don't get around to answering, or my answers are delayed. There's just a psychology of wanting to wipe that screen clean and respond to all of the electronic messages. I can't tell you exactly why it's different, but it certainly is.

Avoid Becoming a Bottleneck for Decision Making

As a strong central leader, Pogue cannot afford to be a bottleneck for decision making. "In the modern world of business, decisions are made at an ever-increasing pace. If we want to cope with all the issues that are coming at us with intensity and speed, we have to be able to respond quickly. We don't have the leisure of a few years ago. We can't be effective if we don't communicate almost immediately."

Electronic mail helps Pogue avoid slowing down the decision-making process due to his lack of availability. Because electronic mail allows him to work independently of time zones, his input to decisions can be made quickly.

For an international business, this is extremely valuable. Pogue pointed to his computer screen:

> There's a message on here now from London. It's 8:30 at night there, and I know [the sender's] left the office. But I'll punch a message in here this afternoon, and when he gets to the office tomorrow morning, he'll have my answer right away.
>
> If I tried to use the telephone to do this, I only have a narrow band of time in which I can call people in other time zones. Then we start missing each other because we are in meetings. Ultimately, decisions are delayed. With e-mail, I can send a message any time of the day or night, and I can relay substantive information.

As the organization grows even larger in scope and more wide-spread, Pogue recognizes that electronic mail will continue to help him to stay in touch with all his offices. People at all levels of the firm around the world know he is listening to them, and that they have access to Pogue, wherever he may be.

Construct an Equitable Means of Compensation

In many law firms, the issue of compensation becomes a real bone of contention. With a dispersed firm, this problem could be exacerbated. Rumors grow in size and number the farther they travel. In addressing this problem, Jones Day Reavis & Pogue has an unusual solution.

The managing partner sets the compensation for all the partners in the firm:

> Compensation is absolutely confidential here, so none of our partners know what any other partner is making. It takes the focus off the haggling—"I should get $5,000 more than that guy." People are not worried about looking at what the next guy is making. That makes a tremendous difference in the way we operate. Our people like it very much. Of course, they have to have confidence that the managing partner knows what he's doing and that he's fair.

Figuring compensation for over 400 partners is quite a complicated task. "We budget how much net income we're expecting in the next year. Once we determine that number, I divide it up among the partners. I have a lot of information coming in to me about each partner—what they've done, and how they're performing—and an outstanding committee of 10 partners to advise me. Based on that information and advice, I make adjustments."

Given the sensitivity of such information, Pogue has never delegated the task. In the past, he labored over it by hand. But as the firm grew, the process became more and more time consuming. Pogue now uses a spreadsheet to help him sort out the complexities. "When it is time to set compensation, [my personal use of] the spreadsheet is really extremely helpful. . . . The computer has probably sped up the process by a factor of 10."

Future Expansion

In the future, Jones Day Reavis & Pogue will rely increasingly for its growth on Pogue's international strategy. "We're now looking to the international part of our practice to be the lead part of the practice. It's just booming," says Pogue.

Pogue feels particularly well positioned for the increased unification of the European economy in 1992. "The way we look at 1992 is that the conditions are going to lead to many, many corporate mergers, acquisitions, joint ventures, and so forth. The pace of that activity is already accelerating, and that means more legal business. As an American firm, we have a lot of experience with those types of transactions, and we already have a presence [in Europe]."

As the firm grows, information systems will continue to help Pogue achieve his business goals and objectives. "We're spread out all over the world. Our network of computers really enables us to pull the whole thing together."

EXECUTIVE SUMMARY

Because the position of managing partner is so central to the operation of the firm, Pogue recognized the need to be accessible to others around the world.

From the outset of his plans to pull together an international law firm as a single entity, Pogue was convinced that computers were vital to his strategy. By design, the electronic network evolved simultaneously with the development of the international locations and the "one firm" approach.

Pogue's primary goal of a functional organization had to be attained despite an increase in the number of employees and international geographic dispersal. Without his access to the Jones Day Reavis & Pogue network, it would be difficult or impossible for Pogue to maintain the same levels of contact with attorneys around the world.

Without the network, it would also be difficult or impossible for the firm to continue to operate functionally and provide clients with the same level of service. Because of his personal involvement with the computer, Pogue is in a better position to lead his organization in the application of tools that tie people together.

Information systems are clearly critical to Pogue's ability to personally stay in touch with the people responsible for the activities of this rapidly growing firm. In making the decision to use computers himself and to use them in the design of his organization, Pogue has impacted both his own ability to lead the firm, as well as the ability of the firm to deliver high-quality legal services to a global clientele.

NOTE

1. Peter Spacek, "How to Cut Your Legal Costs," *Fortune,* 23 April 1990, p. 185.

CHAPTER 3

The Political

Executive

Senator Gordon Humphrey (R-NH)

In an April 1987 statement to the Associated Press, Senator Gordon Humphrey (R-N.H.) had this to say about the situation in Afghanistan: "I am greatly impressed with the morale and spirit of the mujahideen. I would prefer to take a Kalashnikov (a Soviet-made rifle) and fight the atheists rather than go back to my office, but I will use my desk and my office as my rifle."

This was no idle threat. Though some people may disagree with Humphrey's political ideologies, everyone finds it hard to argue with the high marks Humphrey's office receives for efficiency. "I often get comments from the press that we're the most responsive office in the Senate," says Bill Anthony, press secretary to the senator.

Speed, Order, and Precision

It's most accurate to describe Humphrey's office in the plural. While his staff is housed in the Hart Senate Office Building, Humphrey prefers to work from a hideaway office in the Capitol building. Humphrey is not the only senator with such an office. Seventy-nine other senators have been assigned such hideaways to provide them with a place for reflection, tucked away from the countless demands of their work. And "tucked away" is the phrase for it. I felt like a mountain climber as Humphrey's press secretary led me to the office. There are rounded sets of stairs that reminded me of steep Venetian bridges—

three sets of them! I was nearly out of breath by the time we reached the office.

In many ways, the hideaway office where Humphrey spends most of his time could be compared to a cockpit. Because the tiny spot is cloistered up underneath the dome of the Capitol, it has a curved shape similar to that of an airplane. The similarities don't stop there. The wall facing Humphrey's desk holds two computer screens and a television monitor. To the right of his desk, a laser printer is housed.

It's appropriate that Humphrey's office resembles a cockpit, since he is a former airline pilot. Professing to love "speed, order, and precision," Humphrey finds his management style reflects his background. "I believe in management by objectives. We set formal objectives. We have goal memos for each area of interest—specific goals. My staff makes a progress report every week on what they did and what they propose to do next week. It's a very orderly system that enables you to see who's performing and who isn't. I try to figure out where the problems are, what causes the problems, and how to remedy them."

Humphrey believes his use of the computer facilitates his management approach. "It helps me communicate with the staff, and it helps me manage by objectives. I can track people's objectives better, see where the problems are sooner, and hold people accountable."

Time, the Scarcest Resource

"There's never enough time to do this job right," said Humphrey. "Time is the scarcest resource." The location of Humphrey's hideaway is of critical importance to saving time during his day:

> Every time a senator wants to cast a vote, if they're located in a Senate office building they have to take the elevator to the basement, ride the subway—and usually they have to wait for the subway—go upstairs, vote, and then repeat the whole process to get back to their offices. It takes between 20 minutes and half an hour to do the round trip. Typically we have four or five votes a day around here. So that's at least 80 minutes out of a day. An hour and 20 minutes. That's a lot of time.

Because Humphrey is linked by electronic mail to the "main" office, he feels comfortable spending most of his time in the alternative office. Humphrey insists that electronic mail keeps him in closer touch with his staff than many other senators who physically share office space with their staffs. "It's not my place to be critical, but I know that in most other offices, it takes days to get a response from a senator to a memo. I respond to most [electronic mail] memos within one hour. Obviously, if I'm in a committee meeting, that's not the case. But in general, staff get decisions around here fast, and they like that. It keeps the work moving, and uses your staff resources well. They're not sitting around waiting for an answer."

There's also an issue of physical wear and tear. "It is a stressful job, in both a physical and emotional sense. There's no heavy lifting, but that's about the only thing they left out," says Humphrey, laughing. "The hours are long and irregular, and you get caught up in these battles where you care about the outcome." Humphrey's answer to the high level of stress is to work his way through the workload as efficiently as possible. "The computer makes my life easier, and that's really important under such circumstances. You have only so many hours in the day, and besides that, you have only so much energy. The more efficiently you can work—in both respects—the better."

The Home Front

Of course, like all other senators, Humprey has an office in his home state. The staff in New Hampshire is connected to his Capitol hideaway by computer. The senator feels that, because he and his home office staff are so well connected through electronic mail, his working relationship with the New Hampshire staff is very similar to his relationship with the Washington staff.

When Humphrey is in New Hampshire, he can use a computer in the office or his home to stay in touch with the Washington staff. "The computer keeps me in touch even when I'm up in the wilds of New Hampshire," says Humphrey, smiling. "During a recess, I can stay in touch with the staff so things don't get backlogged and pile up, inundating me when I return. When I get back to Washington, I'm up-to-date except for the three or four hours I'm enroute."

The asynchronous nature of communicating via the computer is of particular value to both Humphrey and his staff. "I don't like being interrupted. With the computer, I can deal with my memos when I have a chance. The staff is in the same position: They don't get interrupted as much. They deal with their memos when they have a moment, when it's convenient to them and fits the flow of work. Of course, when a message is marked 'Urgent,' it receives faster attention."

An anecdote demonstrates just how urgent a message can be. Just days after I completed my interview with him, Humphrey had the following exchange on electronic mail:

> From: Hardy, Laura
> Date: May 09,90 1:26 PM
> Senator, your neighbor Darryl has called the Fire Department because there is smoke coming from your house which is getting into his house. The Fire Department is on their way over to your home now to check it out.

> From: Humphrey, Senator
> Date: May 09,90 1:27 PM
> I'LL GO RIGHT OVER.

"Even *I'm* amazed that my staff didn't use the telephone in that case," says Humphrey, laughing. "But they did mark the computer message 'URGENT!'"

The Senator as Communicator

"The essence of being a senator is to communicate—to your colleagues, to your staff, and to your constituents. We do a lot of communicating in this office, both directly and through the news media," explains Humphrey. Humphrey may depend on electronic mail to keep in touch with his staff, but outside his organization, communications must take another form. Senators depend on staff to write much of the voluminous communication that is issued from their offices. But every piece must reflect the senator's views.

Humphrey personally stays on top of this huge publishing operation. "Because communications is such an important part of this job, I edit most of the stuff that goes out of this office: press releases, speeches, and statements. I also edit the constituent letters that go out in quantity—when we're sending out a lot of letters on one subject."

Humphrey enjoys writing, and feels it is an integral part of his role as a communicator. "It's important in this business to express yourself accurately, and I'm a good writer. I like things to be the way I would say them myself. The best staff in the world can't anticipate quite how I want to phrase things."

Humphrey uses a computer to extend his writing abilities. "I either write my own speeches [on the word processor] from the outset, or I heavily edit speech material that is given to me. . . . Senators do a lot of speaking, and that's not something you can delegate. In order to do the job of communications correctly, you have to involve the senator directly."

In fact, Humphrey believes the quality of his floor speeches has improved as a result of his use of the word processor. "The most important difference is that I can change things at the last minute. I often follow the debate on the floor with my television monitor. Depending upon what has been said in the foregoing debate, I can quickly make some changes if necessary, or add some new points of rebuttal or whatever, print it out, and then 20 seconds after I push the button, I'm on my way down to the floor with hard copy."

Scribbling notes on a previous version of the speech is not an acceptable alternative, according to Humphrey. "It's important, when you're speaking, to be comfortable. Not to be tilting your notes around to try to read stuff you wrote in the margins. It's also important to *appear* comfortable. The easier it is for your eye to follow your printed material, the more comfortable you are and the better speaker you are."

The word processor isn't the only information tool Humphrey uses to write. To stay up-to-date on late-breaking news, Humphrey asks his staff to research wire stories on line, and then pass them to him via electronic mail. In addition to keeping him informed on a general level, this helps him to be prepared for calls from reporters. "It really allows you to stay up-to-date. If you just rely on newspapers, you can be 12 or 24 hours out-of-date."

Efficiency in Government Begins at Home

Humphrey is well known for his efforts at making government more efficient. He has supported legislation to balance the budget and was a leading voice in opposing congressional pay raises. He has won many awards from Congressional watchdog groups—the Sound Dollar Award for example—and awards from the National Taxpayers Union.

Humphrey believes this focus on efficiency begins in his own office. Consistent with his political beliefs about organization and efficiency, Humphrey applies every possible tool to fine-tune his own organization. "Computers save me time, make me more effective, and give me a quieter, more orderly office." Bill Anthony, press secretary to Humphrey, confirmed that Humphrey's personal use of computers embodies the senator's philosophy of efficiency. "Often I'll come in here early in the morning, and he'll have left me [an electronic] message at 1:00 A.M. I'll tell you, taxpayers get their money's worth out of him."

EXECUTIVE SUMMARY

Senator Humphrey feels that he has the best of two worlds. His isolation from the frenetic activity of the typical Senate office allows him to accomplish a great deal more work than if he were faced with a maelstrom of interruptions. At the same time, he is located closer to the heart of activity for the Senate—the Capitol. His use of electronic mail facilitates this arrangement.

With his critical role in communications and policy making, Humphrey must find time for clear thinking and still remain in close touch with a variety of people in different places. Information tools allow him the luxury of uninterrupted working time while making him completely accessible to the people who rely on his decisions and input to accomplish their jobs.

CHAPTER 4

500 Magazines

Every Month

Mark Edmiston

Chairman and CEO, *The Cable Guide*

It was a steel-gray, bitterly cold, late afternoon in the center of New York City. When the weather is bad in New York, you not only see it and feel it, you hear *the response. Cab horns honk longer, people yell at each other louder, and even the sirens seem more ominous.*

The street noise drifted into the distance as I stepped into a quiet lobby. I took an elevator to the 12th floor and stepped out into a silent hallway filled with look-alike doors. The noise of New York seemed far behind. I realized how thick the doors were when I opened the one labeled "The Cable Guide." Sound tumbled out into the silent hallway. The office was in a state of perpetual motion, the air filled with energy and activity. I envisioned a night picture of New York, where automobiles appear as streams of silver and gold light—that was the way people seemed to move through this office. Everything was in entrepreneurial high gear.

All this activity has its rewards. Within the space of 10 years, The Cable Guide *has grown to become the nation's sixth largest magazine, with a rate base of 9.5 million and a circulation of over 11.6 million. That's ahead of* People, Time, *and* Playboy.

Mark Edmiston, chairman and CEO of The Cable Guide, *exudes the same energetic aura as the office. He is warm and engaging, but he talks and moves quickly. The pace of his conversation is exactly what you'd expect of a highly successful entrepreneur.*

Poised for Growth

The magazine was founded in 1980 on the basis of an interesting idea: community-specific guides for the cable-television viewer. Each cable system receives a guide that specifically lists programming for its local area. The publication started out as a simple 16-page listing of HBO, Showtime, and other pay services. The company originally sold the listing only to cable operators, who then either gave or resold it to cable subscribers.

When Edmiston, his partners, and a group of investors bought the company in 1987, they purchased a well-run company poised for growth. "[The previous management] had done everything right, up to a point. They just didn't have the inclination to take it the next step and turn it into a consumer magazine," Edmiston explained. He and his partners had a clear goal in mind: "We were seeking to become *the* supplier to the industry."

As the former president of *Newsweek,* Edmiston certainly had the publishing experience necessary to lead this company to its next stage of growth. But when he first came to *The Cable Guide,* Edmiston had a steep learning curve. Though no stranger to publishing, he didn't know much about the cable business. He spent time on the road, talking with cable operators and attending cable conventions. "I tried to read and understand as much as I could about the cable industry. Then I basically drew, in my own mind, a picture as to where we'd fit into the future."

This picture developed into a four-part business strategy:

1. Expand production.
2. Improve editorial content.
3. Attract advertising revenues.
4. Expand to other formats.

Business Strategy: Expand Production

The goal of being the industry leader was the basis for the business decision to enlarge production. "There were three competitors in the business, and we felt there was going to be consolidation. We had to be capable of taking on any additional production volumes that came along, because, if we didn't, someone else would take them. In fact, we have already taken over our largest competitor, so our decision to enlarge production was a good one."

Expanding production capacity turned out to be a complex challenge. Edmiston couldn't simply add staff. "Human beings can only do so much. You can keep adding people, but, aside from the costs, there is an absolute limit to the amount of processing that can be done by individuals."

It is easy to understand Edmiston's concern for people's ability to process information when you know the complexities of putting together *The Cable Guide*. To produce the publication today, information is collected from 700 different programming services across 500 different cable systems. Edmiston elaborates, "Each magazine really is unique. Other magazines do regional editions, where they have the basic magazine and then insert pages. We actually lay out the magazine from front to back in 500 different ways. We turn out 500 magazines a month. I don't think there's any other publisher that can even come close to turning out 500 different magazines a month!"

This task presents mammoth production challenges. With everyone sharing information yet producing such different publications, at some point adding staff adds to the confusion and complexity, rather than alleviating it. Edmiston turned to automation as the enabler of growth. "My own use of a computer gave me the idea that we could automate this entire process. Because I was using my own computer, I kept up with the computer trade press and the developments happening in the industry. I knew [that, with automation,] we could put out a much higher-quality magazine within the cost constraints of this entrepreneurial venture."

Some steps to automate the process had already been taken, but Edmiston went further. He immediately authorized the purchase of $2 million worth of electronic typesetting equipment and an additional $150,000 for a desktop publishing system. Almost every aspect of production at *The Cable Guide* is now automated—including the artwork. "We have done the editorial entirely with computers. It's all desktop publishing. Our art department doesn't have any drawing boards. Everything is done on the machine. We have artists who do illustrations for us on their machines and then send us a disk. I would say that we are the most automated publisher in the country right now."

The payoff comes not only in terms of size, but also in profitability. Edmiston notes: "When we bought the magazine, we had about

150 employees and $30 million in revenue. Two years later, we have 175 employees (17 percent growth) and $50 million in revenue (67 percent growth)." Edmiston expects even greater payoff in the future. "I see this trend continuing. We will continue to grow quickly in terms of revenue and slowly in terms of numbers of people."

The key to growth in production at the company, says Edmiston, is information systems. "The thing that has made it work is the computers, very honestly . . . both the personal computers as well as the large computers we use for the massive production."

Business Strategy: Improve Editorial Content

The second of Edmiston's strategic objectives was to dramatically improve the editorial content. As Edmiston put it, "We wanted improved editorial so that we could compete with *Us* and *People* in terms of star quality. [Improved editorial would help us] attract advertising from major national advertisers such as General Motors and Proctor & Gamble."

First, he hired a top-notch editor and a staff of professional journalists. "And that changed the character of the magazine. Before, we had interviews with B or C stars, or never-would-be stars. Our editorial quality has improved so much that we're now able to get interviews with stars like Cher, Arsenio Hall, Michael Douglas, and Clint Eastwood."

Because the editorial process is automated, Edmiston is able from his personal computer, to browse through upcoming stories. "[Reviewing the editorial] keeps me in touch with what's happening there. It gives me a feel. Our product is re-created every month and will soon be re-created every week. It's important to have a feel of what's going on." He notes that this involvement keeps him informed. "I'm a magazine publisher and a CEO, but I'm not a great television watcher. I'm so bad that I'll go to a movie and I won't remember that Meryl Streep played one of the characters," says Edmiston, laughing. "So it's good for me to kind of drift though the stuff to figure out who's hot and who's not."

Having advance notice of upcoming stories also helps Edmiston in the advertising sales process. By knowing in advance when a particular article is going to appear, Edmiston can advise key advertisers regarding optimal timing of their ad campaigns.

Business Strategy: Attract Advertising Revenues

Improved editorial content led directly to Edmiston's third objective: building an advertising base. "The quality of the story became more what we need in order to attract the advertising."

Original *Cable Guide* customers were the cable operators. But with the improved editorial, Edmiston wanted to reach through the cable operators and get directly to readers, adding a second distribution channel. Once the magazine reached readers and circulation began soaring, the advertisers were more interested. At that point, the company had to learn how to sell to the advertising industry:

> We had to build an advertising sales operation from scratch. The magazine had been in business since 1980, but it was basically unknown in the advertising community. We [once] had a bunch of advertising media people in a focus group and, when asked about advertising in cable publications, one woman said, "I'd love to. It's a great medium. But there must be 500 different publications. It's too much work to find out who publishes them all."
>
> Well, at that moment we represented about 50 percent of the entire market! We could have delivered 5.5 million of those people right away. There was a lot of education that had to be done to the advertising community, and it's still being done.

The Cable Guide differentiates itself to advertisers primarily by its flexibility. Advertisers increasingly want to reach more highly targeted markets. Because of its flexibility in production, the publication is ideally designed for that purpose:

> Advertisers are using computers more and more to identify exactly who is buying their product. The scanners in supermarkets are providing companies with much more highly specialized information. So, for example, they now know exactly who is buying smooth peanut butter versus crunchy peanut butter. A great deal of that information varies by geography. So they begin "versioning" their ad campaigns. They say, "OK, we know crunchy peanut butter is now big in the Northwest, four Southern states, and the Chicago area. Let's not bother advertising crunchy peanut butter in the Northeast, where no one buys it."
>
> They are also trying to get more value for their dollars. [For example,] The Ford Thunderbird runs in stock-car races. Ford can run a color ad nationally in *The Cable Guide* that shows a beautiful picture of a Ford

Thunderbird. They can then say in the ad, "Don't miss this particular NASCAR race and watch the Thunderbirds win." At the same time, they can list the precise dealers where the customer can buy a Thunderbird. This can be much more precise than simply listing the "Boston-area" or "New York-area" dealers. We can be more precise because we are producing system-specific guides. We can say, "Here's the dealer in Southern Westchester County," or "Here's the dealer in Uptown Manhattan."

This flexibility is different from the regional editions offered by other publications. "Newspapers often run a page of ads and then a page of dealers, because that's the smallest unit that can be delivered by that medium. Of course, television is even worse because they just send the same signal everywhere. But we're so specific that, if your car is broken down, you can *walk* to the dealer we list," says Edmiston, laughing.

He explains his customers' point of view: "It's like a Lego set. It's basically anything you want to build, from an advertising standpoint. They can customize their ad pitch much more precisely than they can in any other medium, literally."

The tremendous flexibility allowed by *The Cable Guide*'s computerized production process allows advertisers to do things they haven't done in the past. Because of this, the sales process is educational and conceptual in nature. And selling advertising isn't limited to calling on advertising agencies:

> This flexibility literally makes us a new medium. It's brand-new in the advertising world. So, generally speaking, it's necessary to make the sale with the client company rather than the advertising agency. The advertising agency tends to homogenize media, and we don't fit into any of their slots. It's hard to explain these concepts to a lower-level person in an agency with whom we may do business, but it's easy to explain to the marketing director at a major company. It's very much to our advantage to reach the client and talk directly about what our magazine can do. That tends to be a higher-level sales call.

For this reason, Edmiston is personally involved with selling to key accounts. "I have to keep up with these key contacts, who they are, and what our relationship is with them. For any given sale, you easily have four or five people on the agency side and two or three or more people on the client side. So you can have seven or eight people who influence the decision, even if ultimately, only one person makes the final decision. You've got to bring them all aboard before you make the sale."

To keep up with a complex web of contacts for a variety of accounts, Edmiston uses a personal database:

> I need to know who's making the decisions today, because this changes as people move around. I track whether they are an ongoing advertiser, a former advertiser, or a potential advertiser. I also keep some information in [my database] about their particular problems or challenges. I get my information from experience and from talking to the salespeople, and then I keep references to that information in my personal contacts database. Knowing who is where and what they're doing is where the database comes in.

Another aspect of building an advertising base involves tracking overall advertising performance. As CEO, Edmiston must develop a clear picture of the advertising operations to do effective strategic planning. To help him stay on top of this part of the business, Edmiston develops personal spreadsheets of key indicators of performance. "Through my experience at *Newsweek,* I developed key indicator reports on advertising and circulation. These are report formats on the computer, [and I created them] myself. They are summaries of other reports, and they indicate the key things I should be worried about."

In addition to telling him what he should be worried about in the near term, these reports help Edmiston spot trends and do better planning. "You have to look at those kinds of things over a period of time. [For example,] advertising is ordered on a fluctuating basis. It's hard to tell when an order will come in. Most magazines keep records of bookings. They say, 'At this point in the year, I have 20 percent of my bookings.' But then it's hard to project out to year end."

By building up a history of spreadsheets, Edmiston has learned an important lesson. "I have discovered that when an ad is *run* is more important than when it's booked. In one report format, I have a history I've developed as to what percentage of the total year January represents. Of course, within one month the dial tends to swing over a fairly wide range. But as each month is added on, that dial tends to stabilize, and by July or so I know within a couple hundred thousand dollars where I'm going to end up for the year."

It is important to Edmiston that he compile his own projections. "Too many CEOs lose touch," he says. "One of the reasons why I do my own projections is for that very reason. When you do the numbers yourself, it really helps you get a feel for the business. You begin to develop instincts for where things are, what's important, and what's not important. The computer makes it possible for you to get down into the organization."

Another reason Edmiston uses the computer himself is to get a more objective, unfiltered view of the business. "You're trying to understand true information, but it is being filtered by another person. Let's say that the person is making a monumental effort to be completely honest and straightforward. Nevertheless, they're filtering it. We're sitting across from each other, and they're trying to figure out what I expect and how I'm going to react; at the same time they're trying to convey information."

Edmiston makes an analogy to filtering information in the editorial process:

> People used to ask me if *Newsweek* was objective. I always tried to be careful in answering, but the answer is, "No, of course not." Right from the minute you say how many stories are going into the magazine, you're making a judgment.
>
> Every time a person processes information, they make judgments as to what is and what is not important. [If someone else compiles all the numbers, they are] making those judgments. . . . It's clearly impossible for a CEO to have all the raw information and try to compile it himself; that can't be done. But I find it better to have data that is *assembled* rather than *processed*. Then my computer allows me to do some of my own processing.

Not only does he appreciate the ability to adjust filters on the information he receives, but he also likes the dynamic quality of working with information on a computer as opposed to paper. "I can interact with a computer, but I can't interact with paper. I can put the data in the machine and then take different looks at it and see what happens. I can ask what if's. If you get a paper report that sits on your desk, that's finished—you can't work with it in an interactive way."

But what does all this work accomplish?

> What the [key indicator] reports show me are the relationships. The raw numbers I could get on paper, but what I'm looking for are the relationships. I need to see what's happening from a more macro view than what the data tell me. We put out the normal reports that any other business puts out, but what I'm looking for is what is happening within those numbers. You can give me the business financials, but what are

the implications for next year? What's happening in the various categories of the business?

Edmiston's hands-on approach to advertising sales and planning has paid off. Advertising at *The Cable Guide* grew 140 percent over a three-year period. For two years in a row, it placed in the top three on *AdWeek's* annual list of the nation's hottest magazines in which to advertise. The Publisher's Information Bureau (PIB), an organization that compiles information comparing advertising performance in the publishing business, ranked *The Cable Guide* first among all PIB-measured magazines in terms of advertising page growth.

Business Strategy: Expand to Other Formats

The fourth step Edmiston wanted to take was the expansion of the product into other formats—including a weekly magazine. "I wanted to raise the sights of the people here . . . to let them know that we are not just magazine publishers, but suppliers of information to the television industry."

First, he developed an idea for the direction of product-line expansion. "We had a segmentation strategy to try and reach different types of television watchers. We had a monthly [publication] and a daily video guide [that airs on the screen]. The weekly was the next logical step towards a segmentation strategy."

Once he had the idea for the weekly, Edmiston wanted to test its validity:

> I sat down at the computer and said to myself, "Let's assume I'm right. What does it mean for the business?" The first plan for the weekly came out of that. I did the entire thing on my computer in one weekend. I just sat down and did it in about 20 hours. It really wasn't that hard because I know how to do a magazine business plan, and I had enough data points to apply to the situation. So I created it from scratch.
>
> I built a couple of plans for circulation, and I built an advertising and manufacturing plan. If I hadn't had a computer, it would've taken at least two weeks just to do it. But the question is, could I have gotten it done? I probably would've been interrupted so much during the course of two weeks that it never would have gotten done.

The process was one that Edmiston feels he could not have delegated:

It would have been very hard to explain to someone. Once I worked with it on the computer and got it out on paper, it was easier to understand. People could then look at it themselves. We put the model I created on a mainframe and did it more precisely. The numbers shifted around a little, but not significantly.

By forcing myself through that process on the computer, I was able to identify the weak points and the strengths. The real strength was that we didn't have to add a lot of people. I discovered that while building the plan on the computer.

Once again, the payoff is clear. "Computers have really improved my ability to think things through and speed up decisions. There probably wouldn't be a weekly now if I hadn't sat at home that weekend and worked it out on the computer. I don't know when we would've been able to get that off the ground."

A Heavy Delegator

I don't mean to create an image of Edmiston running *The Cable Guide* single-handedly. Though Edmiston is hands-on in terms of staying involved in the business, he is hands-off when it comes to letting people do their jobs. His approach to providing leadership involves a great deal of delegation. I am a very heavy delegator. I think I probably have what you would call informal contracts with my managers. We sort of agree that 'Here's what we're going to do,' and 'Here's where we're going to go,' and 'Here's your responsibilities within that, and I'll leave you alone as long as you're doing it. If you stop doing it, or have a problem with it, then I'll help.' I tend to stay back and let these people do their jobs.

To feel comfortable allowing others to make their own operating decisions, Edmiston needs to stay abreast of how various parts of the company are performing. He faces the common paradox of managing without meddling. To get around this paradox, Edmiston pulls company financial data into spreadsheets that he creates. By accessing the data directly, Edmiston can avoid excessive intervention in what others are doing. "I'm looking at the business through the computer. What I'm not trying to do is micromanage the people who are carrying out the plan. If I didn't have the [data], I might have to keep going to these individuals and saying, 'Well, how are you doing? What's happening?'" He offers an example:

> The circulation guy is out doing his thing. I am monitoring his performance independently of him. He's not telling me how he's doing. I'm seeing how he's doing when I look at those key indicators. How he does it is his business. What I try to look at are the key business factors. I'm not worried about how many expense account lunches the guy has to have in order to accomplish that. I look at expenses in relation to sales.

By looking at the specific information that he is interested in and putting it in the format in which he wants to see it, he is better able to coach others and contribute to their success:

> By showing me trends, the computer helps me to anticipate things that are going to happen. Then I can sit down and discuss something that seems to be happening rather than coming in after the fact and saying, "What happened?" You can get a terrific explanation to the question, "What happened?" but by the time you get it, it's too late. [Access to performance information] helps me to get out in front of problems and discuss them with the people who can take action on them.

Edmiston feels that the computer helps him not only with the content of these coaching sessions, but also with his style. "The computer allows me to have much less confrontational and much more substantive discussions with the people who work with me. I can guide the agenda." Here too, he offers an example:

> When I know that the performance in the Chicago office is not as good as it should be, I can talk to them about the real issues. We get past all the arguments about excuses, and we get right down to the heart of the matter. I come to them with a problem we share, and I have them answer clear, direct questions. This works much better than going to them and saying, "How is everything going?" and having them tell me in the order they want, the way they want, as much as they want.

Edmiston uses his information system as a tool of decentralization. It makes him comfortable with a higher degree of delegation and improves his abilities to coach, rather than control, people.

A Bicycle for the Mind

Edmiston has broken down his business strategy into personal objectives. And for each, he uses the computer to augment his effectiveness.

The benefits, Edmiston said, are manifested in the very ability of the firm to grow.

Edmiston summed up his feelings about his personal use of computers with a story told to him by his friend, Steve Jobs, cofounder of Apple Computer:

> Steve told me this story, and I'm sure he's used it many times, but it impressed me. He read a *Scientific American* article back in the '70s that did a thorough analysis of various animal species and how they use energy. In a list of about 67 animals, ranging from cheetahs to tortoises, humans came in somewhere in the middle. Not too impressive. But then they put the human on a bicycle and humans moved to the top of the list. Steve told me he thinks of the computer as a bicycle for the mind, and that's essentially the way I think about it. If you don't know where you're going or why, the computer's not going to make things better. But if you know you're going to the corner store and you need to get there quickly, the bike is going to make a big difference.

EXECUTIVE SUMMARY

Edmiston's years of publishing experience and seasoning are ideally suited to the job of helping a young company mature and grow. To contribute the most, he must stay involved in a variety of detailed, growth-oriented activities.

Information systems afford Edmiston the ability to lend his years of experience and knowledge to crucial activities such as planning and selling, while concurrently leaving people the space in which to make their own decisions. In addition, his personal vision for what information tools can accomplish has greatly impacted the entire organization's ability to expand quickly and profitably.

CHAPTER 5

"How About Some
Pop Raspberry?"

Ellen Gordon

COO and President, Tootsie Roll Industries

As I stepped out of the taxi, my feet landed firmly on the ground in Chicago, but my mind reeled back in time two decades to my childhood in South Carolina. What sent me back was a deep whiff of a very familiar scent: a Tootsie Roll.

A Goal of Long-Lasting Quality

Tootsie Roll Industries is housed in what was once the original plant for the Tucker automobile. It's ironic because Tucker went out of business—and nothing could be further from the truth for Tootsie Roll. The company has consistently grown each year in net sales and net earnings. In 1989, sales reached a record high of $179 million, and profits after tax were $20 million. In 1990, sales were over $190 million.

Tootsie Roll has a long history. The company has been in business since 1896, when Leo Hirschfield, an Austrian immigrant, introduced a recipe for a chocolate penny candy. Tootsie Roll began international expansion in the 1960s. In addition to the Chicago headquarters, the company now has operations in Tennessee, New York, Mexico, Canada, and the Philippines. Tootsie Roll is beginning to explore other international markets.

Acquisitions have played a role in Tootsie Roll's growth. The company purchased the Mason Division of Candy Corporation of

America (makers of Dots) in 1972. In 1985, the company gobbled up Cella's Confections, Incorporated, a chocolate-covered cherry manufacturer. The most recent acquisition, in 1988, was the Charms Company.

Selected as one of *Forbes* best 200 small companies, Tootsie Roll is run by a husband-and-wife management team. Ellen Gordon is president and Melvin Gordon is CEO of the company Ellen's father purchased in 1948. Since that time the company has remained in the family, and the Gordons own 50 percent of the stock.

Ellen Gordon says they're looking forward to the next 94 years at Tootsie Roll. "We are very conscious of what we are about. We're candymakers, and we feel it's very important to put out a quality product that people will still want to eat a long time from now. We have very long-range plans."

Reinvestment is a fundamental part of the Tootsie Roll strategy, according to Gordon. "We put a lot of money back into our company. Our production process is highly automated and computerized. We're producing much more candy than ever before, with fewer people."

This focus on quality and production costs has important results for customers: After almost 100 years, you can still buy a Tootsie Roll for a penny.

Personal Involvement

To maintain high quality standards, Gordon believes in being personally involved with the company. She likes to stay in close touch with two critical success factors:

- Company operations
- The Tootsie Roll family

Keeping track of an international business at a detailed level is difficult, particularly when the executives who run the company are likely to be found in any of a number of places. In addition to the requisite executive travel schedule, the Gordons shuttle back and forth between homes, spending the week in Chicago and weekends in New England.

Melvin Gordon says they depend on the computer to accommodate their mobile lifestyle. "We might be in any one of our homes or a number of offices. We have computers in all of those locations . . .

whether East Coast, West Coast, or here. We can get our mail, our marketing information, everything. You know how the company is doing no matter where you are."

I explored the mobile Ellen Gordon's critical success factors and then discussed how her use of information systems relates to them.

Critical Success Factor: Company Operations

"Purchasing is a very important part of a commodity business," explains Ellen Gordon. "Tootsie Rolls are made of sugar, corn syrup, milk, cocoa, and other commodity products. We're also dependent on commodity purchases for packaging—paper products and packaging materials. How we purchase is extremely critical to the bottom line." Purchasing is, in fact, so critical that top management is directly involved in purchasing decisions. "As we've gotten more complex through the addition of different factory sites— you know, acquisitions and the like—top management needs to know more about what's going on with purchasing on a current basis."

In making purchasing decisions, Gordon finds the ability to model scenarios to be extremely valuable:

> On the computer, I can ask what if. What if corn prices go up? What if milk prices go up? What if sugar prices go down? What happens if we order different volumes? I can do those what if's very quickly, and I can include numerous variables.
>
> Having that kind of information helps me make decisions. The better your information, the better you can act. Perhaps we need to change our product mix. By looking closely at orders and having exceptions highlighted for me, it's possible to spot situations more quickly. This might allow us to get things shipped more quickly. The sooner things are shipped, the sooner we are paid.
>
> Sometimes I will even approve a few requisitions, just to keep my hand in. [Requisitions are] the basis of our purchasing and payables system. I don't want to lose touch with how that works. I have to be familiar with the requisitions process so that I can draw up more meaningful reports.

She was eager to illustrate her point by turning to her computer. "Here, I'll show you. Let's do some Pop Raspberry, OK?" As I watched, I realized that her hands-on leadership style would not be able to accommodate the size, complexity, and speed of the business today without the use of computers.

Gordon also keeps a close eye on marketing and sales operations. Here too, she uses the computer to directly access information. "I can bring up any customer that I want, and trace their orders to date. I might want to see how Tootsie Rolls are doing in a certain area of the country, or maybe I want only to find out how one broker is doing. I can bring up all this information in seconds . . . in any way I want to see it. Then I can start thinking about strategy."

As a strong operational leader, Gordon also likes to have detailed information about the company financials:

> I believe it's important to have a thorough understanding of the company's financials, so that I can get a better feel for setting strategy and direction.
>
> Sometimes when you get a financial report, it shows you variances or problems, or it highlights something that's different. But it's not enough just to see that it's different. You have to see what happened. What made up the numbers? Why? By getting into the databases, I'm able to see how things come together. It's very important to me to have that deeper understanding.

Tootsie Roll is continuing to develop additional operational databases for use by Gordon. She says, "I'm so excited about what this access to information provides. We're just on the forefront of some of the most exciting possibilities—controlling inventory, managing sales, seeing targets and priorities on a daily basis, budget forecasting . . . being able to better control our financial resources."

Better access to information supports Ellen Gordon's management style. "We're so much of a hands-on company, an entrepreneurship. In meetings, the management team wants to look at the numbers behind the issues. We used to have to send that kind of request to the accounting department, and they'd tell us it would be ready in x number of hours. Now, we just pull it up in the meeting ourselves. It allows us to correct situations right away, and time is money."

Ellen Gordon's sharp eye on the money means we all still find Tootsie Rolls a real bargain.

Critical Success Factor: The Tootsie Roll Family

Similar to other entrepreneurships, Tootsie Roll has a strong sense of family. Gordon values this highly and strives to retain this feeling.

To give me a better feel for what the Tootsie Roll family is like, Gordon offers to take me on a tour of the production facilities. We look like fast-food restaurant managers as we don the protective paper hats that are mandatory for entry into the production area. She opens a heavy door, and I am immediately enveloped by the seductive scent of chocolate hanging heavy in the air.

It is the fulfillment of a childhood dream: candy in every corner. The manufacturing area is so large that employees use bicycles and electric carts to get around. I am most fascinated by the Tootsie Roll Pops. A snake of hard cherry candy filled with a Tootsie Roll center slithers toward a large piece of equipment, and then POW! out pops a Tootsie Pop, complete with stick. Gordon carefully fishes in the river of fresh candy, pulls a still-warm Tootsie Pop out by its stick, and hands it to me.

Armed with my fresh Tootsie Pop, I follow Gordon into the production area. Gordon's philosophy about people becomes readily evident. "We encourage our managers to participate. We want ideas to come up from all over. We have a family atmosphere here. When we think about a family atmosphere, we think about ease of communication, both between individuals and departments. It's also important for me to understand people, their strengths and weaknesses, and what makes them tick."

Participation and her personal understanding of people are enhanced through Gordon's face-to-face contact with employees. As we move through the production area in our electric cart, she stops to chat with manufacturing workers, calling them by name and telling me personal facts about them as we drive away. She asks one employee, "How are you feeling?" and later explains that the woman has recently had minor surgery.

But even in a small firm, it's impossible to touch base with everyone personally each day. Gordon believes in extending her ability to communicate with employees to continue to maintain a family-oriented culture. For this reason, she uses electronic mail. Gordon believes that electronic mail is a boon to her participative philosophy. "People who may have been shy about gaining access to the chairman or president now have an easy way to do it. They are probably more apt to do it. Anybody can write me a message. The other day I found "Happy Birthday" on my screen from somebody I don't talk to very often. Once in a while I see her and we say 'Good morning.' But she took the initiative to send that message."

Gordon appreciates the new perspective on people that electronic mail gives her. "I remember once reading a spy story. The secret agent knew that someone was faking the messages because there was a different touch on the Morse code machine. And that struck me. Maybe too, there's a different touch, a different feel, a different angle that you get on a person when you communicate with them through e-mail."

Extending Executive Brainpower

As a strong operational leader, Gordon is interested in every aspect of the firm's business. She is enthusiastic about how the computer extends her mental abilities to handle detail and complexity. "Because the computer has so much capacity to manipulate information, your capacity as an executive increases because you can do much more. The information doesn't have to all be in your head for you to have ready access to it."

It's not just a matter of more data, however. Gordon also uses the computer to think about her firm's operations and stay in touch with her people. "And as you get more and more sophisticated on the machine, that's when it's exciting. You start creating. I can do things now that I never dreamed I'd be able to do. It provides a whole new way for us to manage our business."

EXECUTIVE SUMMARY

"Milking a cash cow" can be more challenging a task than it sometimes appears. To do this in the face of rising commodity prices and increased energy costs requires meticulous attention to detail. Ellen Gordon's use of information systems has allowed her to stay personally involved at a level of detail that produces effective planning and efficient operations for the company. Her efforts at staying on top of financial details have contributed mightily to the company's ability to produce a quality product at a reasonable cost while increasing profits.

CHAPTER 6

What Happened

When the Wizard

Went to Wickes

Sandy Sigoloff

CEO, LJ Hooker Corporation, and Former Chairman,
CEO, and President, Wickes Companies

Ming the Merciless. Hatchet Man. Sandy the Ax. Hired Gun. These were the words I had read in endless articles about the man across the table from me . . . the same man who was now saying in a concerned voice: "Don't you want some of these Danishes? I had Louise bring them in for you because she told me you had a long drive this morning. You must have gotten up early. You should eat something." I have to admit, I was surprised. Sigoloff struck me as sincere, thoughtful, and conscientious.

However, there's no question that Sandy Sigoloff makes hard decisions—decisions that hurt people. But the same decisions that hurt the few often rescue the many. And rescue is Sigoloff's specialty.

The Corporate Doctor

In 1982, Sandy Sigoloff already had a good track record for mending broken companies. He had put Republic Corporation, a West Coast conglomerate, back on its feet. And, in less than a three-year period,

56

he had rescued Daylin Incorporated, a $600-million retailer based in Los Angeles.

After Daylin, Sigoloff went to a "normal" healthy company, Kaufman and Broad, a homebuilding and financial services firm. But normality didn't sit well with Sigoloff. He needed to fix something. And a company called Wickes needed fixing.

When the Corporate Doctor knocked on the door, the patient was almost too weak to answer. Wickes, a $4-billion building-supply retailer, was $2 billion in debt to 250,000 creditors. This was the patient that would make the Corporate Doctor famous.

The Ming Dynasty

Sigoloff says that, when he came to Wickes, the odds were 1,000 to 1 against the company making it. "It meant doing severe things, but humane things. It meant doing everything with the intent to win. We only knew three words: *We will win.*"

It's not easy to hold a team together when you're going about the business of eliminating 14,000 jobs. Under such conditions, it's easy to understand where disparaging nicknames and unflattering adjectives come from. Though many of the nicknames and adjectives given to Sigoloff came from others, Ming the Merciless was self-ordained. Sigoloff came up with the name as a means of comic relief during incredibly pressurized times.

Ming was the villain in the old Flash Gordon serials. He ruled the planet Mongo (the bankruptcy) and the one thing he wanted most was Princess Aura (reorganization). All Sigoloff's close associates also had nicknames: Captain America, Zephyr, and Earth Commander.

When the Ming Team arrived, Wickes was clearly fighting for survival. "Wickes was not just one Chapter 11. Wickes was composed of four major Chapter 11s, each one having about seven or eight bankruptcies under it. So there were about three dozen filings going on simultaneously, all of which were significant. At the time, the whole thing together was the largest nonrailroad reorganization in the history of American business," explains Sigoloff.

How do you go about managing a problem that big? "It's important to recognize the difference between being benevolent and being tough," says Sigoloff. "When you're fighting for your survival as a corporation, you are tough."

Sigoloff says the critical components of corporate resurrection can be thought of as three *C*'s: cash, complexity, and communication. "To get cash, you have to track it. If you want to deal with a crisis, you have to analyze all the variables that caused the crisis and figure out what it will take to repair it. And you have to be able to communicate the good and the bad of what you're doing under crisis, or nobody will believe it's ever going to get better."

The First *C*: Cash

When a company bleeds, it bleeds green. "It all comes down to one thing: cash," explains Sigoloff. "In the beginning, we needed to know where every penny was, every single day. Where do you generate the cash for interest payments? Do you have the cash for merchandise and capital equipment?"

"I wanted to know beginning and ending cash every day," he continues. "I wanted to know where it was. Which bank is it in? How can we transfer it around? What's our relative rate of divestiture when cash is coming in? When can it be deposited? I wanted a treasury system that didn't exist. I wanted it immediately, and I wanted everyone to be able to use it."

It was not always as simple as making a phone call and asking about the cash situation. "We worked 20-hour days. We traveled extensively. I could call Joe and ask, 'How's cash?' But Joe could be in New York and I could be in Charlotte, North Carolina. He might not be there when I wanted to know it. What if I needed it when I was on a critical telephone call with someone asking me how sales were last week?"

At the time Sigoloff arrived, the computer systems simply weren't designed to give him what he wanted. Therefore, information systems were adapted and and new capabilities constructed by internal staff according to Sigoloff's explicit instructions. In their offices all the members of the management team had terminals that were connected to the mainframe. They also had portable computers with modems to access the mainframe when they were traveling. The system gave Sigoloff the ability to trace the company's lifeblood and test assumptions:

> We used the computer to track cash—to monitor the health barometer of the company. We had store sales [results] daily, so we knew cash

within a few percent. We knew where we were in the bank accounts on a daily basis. We knew essentially where the big payments were, because they were all forecasted both weekly and monthly. So it was possible to be accurate about where your cash was within 10 to 15 percent of audited numbers every single day.

Knowing where the cash is today is a start. Knowing where it will be tomorrow is the next step. Sigoloff had to plan ahead to be able to take management actions that would improve the cash flow situation. His planning challenge was complex. "We also had to develop the capacity to do planning for diverse businesses that had sales in excess of $4 billion. Many of those were retail, and many were suffering from depressed areas or regional problems and competition. What's happening with sales? What's happening with the gross margin? Can we run the store with less labor? We had to make assumptions and test them."

Sigoloff and his team used a computer-based financial model to make planning assumptions. Management of the multiple divisions of such a diverse business would have been impossible without direct access to the computer, according to Sigoloff. "You could not have dealt with inventory. You couldn't have kept up with sales. You couldn't have dealt with anything relating to cash."

The Second *C*: Complexity

The second critical factor that concerned Sigoloff was the complexity of managing an organization in crisis. "When you've been in a prolonged crisis, the number of things that need to be repaired quickly is beyond belief."

Complexity taxes the capacity of a leader to track events. "You have to keep up with so many things. [For example,] I wanted to know everything about our obligations under Chapter 11. I wanted the entire Chapter 11 on the computer. Claims, filings, proofs, etcetera. Sigoloff not only had to view a broad scope of events, but he had to see them with clarity. "There's the problem of being able to recognize fact from fiction. You probably don't know what the true problems are because people will view them their way, which might or might not agree with your view. And the good people have already left."

The magnitude of the tracking problem made paper solutions infeasible. Sigoloff explains: "We were tracking 800 to 2,000 simultaneous events that were time-related and time-phased."

To track the many complexities of the situation at Wickes on a daily basis, Sigoloff participated in the construction of what he called a master calendar. The master calendar ran on the mainframe and could be downloaded or accessed by personal computers. "We could call it up by time, by person, by code, or by priority against major objectives that were linked to each other in different ways."

Keeping an eye on events is only a foundation for determining what to do about them. Sigoloff had to orchestrate hundreds of simultaneous activities, making decisions on priorities for each. The master calendar was a decision support system for Sigoloff:

> Each person had to load his events, then I assigned priorities to those events. You could then ask [the master calendar] questions by path and priority, and you could rearrange it. It gave you a benchmark for your ability to estimate time and effort. You knew what your manpower loading was, and you also knew fact or fiction about reaching certain goals. You could sit down with 12 people, and in 10 minutes you could tell whether or not you were on target and on time."

It was not just a matter of priority setting and scheduling. The myriad events were interconnected, and sequencing was critical:

> Items on the master calendar had a start date and an end date. The calendar also showed, by priority, which events had to come before others. It displayed order and time. It was a PERT [program evaluation review technique] chart—one that, instead of just going in one direction, moved up and down and sideways so that a single event, which had a start and stop date, might have been connected to 20 or 30 things that had to go through other phases to get to a conclusion.

Sigoloff designed the system to meet his unique needs. "I have this obsession with viewing interactive simultaneous events. Conventional PERT chart packages display multiple events. This is just another form of that type of package. It was our own adaptation of the concept of a PERT chart."

Use of the master calendar system that Sigoloff designed was not limited to the executive suite. The system extended everyone's ability to handle this complex situation, and it kept his team focused on key events. With the calendar the team was coordinated and committed to follow-through. "By creating what I wanted, we had in fact created a management vehicle for use by the entire corporation." Sigoloff found that the master calendar helped him galvanize a group of people into a tightly coordinated team. "It gave us a common language of communication. Everybody who had a staff responsibility had to put it into a common vehicle—the master calendar."

In addition to providing a meeting point for coordination of activities, the master calendar gave the management team a shared view of the situation at Wickes. "It gave all of us a visual image of progress on a week-to-week basis. Assignments were on the master calendar, so dependencies were immediately obvious. [Everyone] understood the repercussions on others if they failed to deliver or missed their deadlines."

In Sigoloff's opinion, the complexity of managing such a huge crisis made the master calendar an absolute essential. "We could not have managed something as complicated as this if we had not ordered the computer capacity of the company to do what we wanted it to do. We simply could not have done it."

The Third *C*: Communicate

Though tracking cash and managing the details of the crisis were important, perhaps the most integral aspect to Sigoloff's successfully reviving Wickes was communication.

> Communicate, communicate, communicate—the good news, the bad news, what you know, what you don't know. We had to keep a constant flow of information regarding every event that was important to the company—from meetings with the creditor's committee to an asset sale. Communication was important because it indicated action and responsibility. It also pulled the team together and gave us a common vocabulary.

Sigoloff had four primary audiences with whom he had to keep close contact:

- Courts and creditors
- Board of Directors
- Management team
- Employees

Communicating with Courts and Creditors

Clear communication with the courts and creditors is a critical component of successful emergence from bankruptcy. "We had to make information available to creditors and to the judge. We had to work with all the people who wanted to know more details about the company. When you're in Chapter 11, all of the [accounting] data essentially belongs to the bankruptcy court. It is very important to control [information], very important to keep copies of it, and equally important to know that it is technically correct."

Through his personal use of the computer, Sigoloff became very familiar with the internal financial data. His proficiency allowed him to construct the information for the courts and creditor committees in such a way that they felt extremely well informed. This put Sigoloff in a more proactive, rather than reactive, position. "It became a communication tool to take the pressure off of the question-and-answer style that many creditors have."

Communicating with the Board of Directors

Similarly, maintaining clear communication with the Board of Directors was essential. Sigoloff decided to add to the usual meetings another channel of communication with the board: He gave board members direct access to the information system. "We thought there was no sense spending a lot of time trying to communicate financial information to the board when we could give them computers and let them read it themselves. So we gave every director a computer at home, and we sent them to school."

Five of the eight directors were active users of the system, and Sigoloff says that the impacts were quite positive. "It was my desire to keep the directors informed. And it took the pressure off of me to make the calls [to explain events]."

Sigoloff says that the computer provided the board with much more dynamic and valuable information than the typical digested director's book:

> Some of the directors didn't use the machine, but those who did could come to a meeting with a knowledge base, rather than my having to inform them once they got there. We could go straight for the jugular on the tough problems. The ones who really used [the machines] would

come to the board meetings saying things like, "OK, I'm not happy with the cash model and forecast that you gave us. Let's go over that today."

At first the board was simply linked to the financial databases. Later, the directors were linked to the rest of the company through electronic mail as well. Information tools brought the board closer to the company's activities, making it a more effective partner in solving problems.

Communicating with the Management Team

Perhaps the most active communications channels were between Sigoloff and his management team. Here, contact was constant— every day, every hour, around the world. "Time was the enemy. You did everything possible to keep everybody knowledgeable and informed, wherever they were in the world. Basically, it was a 24-hour work watch."

Electronic mail proved valuable for keeping the management team connected. "[Electronic mail] was a way to keep communications open. It was a communication base. For example, I might send a message to a member of my core team saying, 'Bill, I looked at line 16 of such-and-such a company. What do you think has gone wrong?' E-mail provides a means of communicating constantly, in a personal way. The person always has a [mail]box, and they can respond to it."

Electronic mail extended the hours of contact for Sigoloff. "It was always possible to send back a bunch of messages that you thought about on the plane. And you could send them that night, and it was on the desks of the individuals in the morning. And then, by the time you got to the office an hour or two later, they had given you the answer. Speedy Gonzalez."

With all the time Sigoloff spent traveling, the need for electronic mail was clear. "It was much more effective than the telephone. By the time I arrived in a different city, I could have half a dozen messages waiting for me, without regard to time zones. E-mail also allowed us to communicate with more than one person at a time. We were able to send messages to four or five people simultaneously and get responses back." The ability to send electronic mail to more than one person helped Sigoloff encourage people to talk about the same problems, thus keeping them focused on the most important ones.

Electronic mail and shared access to databases built a common on-line environment. The systems became a basis for teamwork. "By looking at the same information in the same format (internal databases and the master calendar) and by sending the same message to entire groups of people simultaneously (electronic mail), we were able to develop a common language and a common focus on what needed to get done. It was basically a matter of keeping people informed with the same knowledge base so that we could discuss a subject."

Communicating with Employees

Maintaining morale in the face of massive layoffs was a formidable task. But it was absolutely necessary. The stores had to go on serving customers well to remain in business. Sigoloff knew he had to be personally involved in communicating with employees at all levels of the firm. Logistically, this was the most difficult audience for Sigoloff. There were over 100 home-improvement stores alone. Including manufacturing facilities, warehouses, showrooms, retail outlets, and distribution centers, Wickes had employees in over 400 locations.

Much of his contact with employees was face-to-face. "We did a lot of communicating in meetings, and we went to the field to be physically seen. The whole philosophy behind that was that we were going to learn more about the company from the people who ran it than we would by analyzing it. For instance, I never missed an annual dinner, because it was important to be there. Everybody knew you were busy, and it was the willingness to make the effort to get there that was important."

Before presenting new ideas in face-to-face meetings with any of his four primary audiences, Sigoloff liked to prepare himself by thinking through ideas he wanted to present. "I needed quiet time to prepare a new idea before I launched it on people. It was important to take the time to get to know what you're doing, particularly when you're dealing with financial statements and new projects."

In putting together a salable pitch to communicate a new idea, Sigoloff sorted through information on his computer and put it together in his own unique way. "I wanted, because of the magnitude of our problems, the ability to analyze these things [on my own]—not necessarily in the format in which somebody would give it to me."

He was not talking about just accessing data. Sigoloff wanted to play with the numbers and ideas, looking at different ways of communicating his message, until he found just the right approach to suit his audience and his style. "I used spreadsheets and other financial tools, as well as a word processor. I might think through an idea using the spreadsheet, or by accessing the company financials. Then I made long lists. The word processor allowed me to keep the lists active and to sort the information by different businesses and different people."

Sigoloff actively worked with financial data, sharing it and analyzing it by using models. He talked with others via electronic mail and organized his communications and directives with word processing. All these tools helped Sigoloff communicate better with the people who would save Wickes.

Fact-Based Thinking

Permeating each of Sigoloff's three *C*'s was an underlying concept: fact-based thinking. Sigoloff's mind moves quickly, but he had to feed his creative and decisive intellect with the facts to make well-structured, well-founded decisions.

As step 1, Sigoloff had to get access to the facts. In a crisis, fact-finding is time-critical. The normal reporting cycles of a large business were far from adequate. He offers an example:

> The one-year business plan was reviewed quarterly by the board and monthly by the staff. A hard [final accounting] closing might come two or three weeks after the month was over. If you are basing the operating of your business on that, you're out of phase the three or four weeks it takes to close a month [and analyze results]. We couldn't, in our judgment, run the company effectively with all the things we were doing—very heavy investment in capital equipment, strategic redirections of the business—by looking at closing information so infrequently.

Sigoloff needed a means of spotting problems much sooner. "That meant we needed two kinds of closings: a flash closing and a hard closing. [To do that] we had to get the information directly from the field. So we used electronic mail to communicate. [E-mail] became our source for getting the preliminary program data very quickly. Then we integrated it into the [executive system]."

Sigoloff also needed a means of insuring the accuracy of the facts he received. "Someone might say to me, 'Oh, that's probably not a problem. Just an abort on sales because of rain, or something like that.' " To see past the easy explanations, Sigoloff directly accessed raw operational data. "It's always nice to know that, in those circumstances, you can look at both ordered information and raw data. I would work with the numbers myself [on the computer] and say, 'Umhum! The overhead in the G&A smells.' When I saw something like that, I sent an electronic-mail message asking for clarification of line item number 26 or 27. Then I would have discussions with others."

Did raw data bring information overload? Just the opposite, Sigoloff explains. "It was so easy to stay informed that you really didn't feel [overly] dependent on anybody, and I think that's very important. Not that you don't trust everybody that works for you, but it was there for you to evaluate yourself if you wanted it."

By staying on top of the facts, Sigoloff cultivated a sense of what he wanted people to pay attention to. Over time he got better data, and more problems were handled at a lower level:

> Many times you want to check the conclusion with the raw data . . . not to embarrass [people], but to train them to do a better job. The real test is to create a manager—to develop people. That's what this is all about. The question is, has this manager really been effectively trained to produce usable information?
>
> I wanted to train the managers to ask all of the questions before the information gets into the system. I want them to think through the contingencies like What happens if energy prices go up? What happens if we have a flood or tornado? What happens if I have a water shortage? I wanted to train the manager to do all of this stuff before I got to it. [Access to information is] a coaching tool because what you're really trying to do is make people better managers without [discouraging them].

With facts in hand, Sigoloff had to consider many alternatives and their implications for the future. He wanted to see the situation from as many points of view as possible. Listening was the means to this end. "The flip side [of communicating] is listen, listen, listen. You have to understand what people are telling you in order to sort the truth from fiction."

Listening involves encouraging healthy dissent, according to Sigoloff. If people do not feel comfortable disagreeing, then a leader is not listening properly; the leader will not get different perspectives on a problem. Here, too, Sigoloff saw the information system as a component of his leadership strategy. By equipping his people with the means of disagreeing with him, the computer improved his own deci-sion-making capabilities. "[Providing others with access to internal information] gives the person you interact with the knowledge base to disagree with you, and the more disagreement you can have to evaluate a problem, the more likely you are to get a successful answer."

With access to facts, in the form of clear and timely data, and people's opinions, Sigoloff was well positioned to make decisions. He elaborates on why he felt it was important to do much of his thinking and decision making on line: "Many times, a decision is one where [a CEO] wants the privacy of reflection on things—even though he's been advised. My computer system was extremely important in reviewing the progress of the company."

The Value of Computers to the Ming Team

Sigoloff's hands-on, action-oriented style fit the needs of the Wickes crisis perfectly. "It wasn't a situation where, if it didn't get done today, you could do it tomorrow. If it wasn't done today, you might not be here tomorrow."

The complexity was daunting. "You cannot keep up with it, no matter how much you travel, no matter how many 20-hour days you put in, unless you have the capacity to assemble, digest, and distribute the necessary information."

One magazine described Sigoloff's strength as "his ability to consume information and make decisions on a dime." Sigoloff credits the computer for helping him gain that reputation for speed and respon-siveness. "I don't know how a CEO of a large corporation can stay in touch with his business unless he has the capacity to evaluate informa-tion rapidly. The computer helps me do that." Sigoloff says that, without computers, he and his team might still be trying to sort out a gameplan to exit Chapter 11:

> We wouldn't have had the common base of communication for follow-ing commitments. We simply wouldn't have had the capacity as a management group to do all the things we needed to do under enormous pressure. I've said it a hundred times. A lot of the credit for the speed with which we got out of bankruptcy goes to the programmers who were driven crazy to create the formats to allow [the executives] to work directly with this data. At the time, there were no programs for this stuff.

Clearly, his access to timely, relevant information and communications helped pull things back together at Wickes. "Without the computer systems [I designed and used] at Wickes, we wouldn't have known where the cash was; we wouldn't have known how to predict, track, and project; and we clearly would not have been able to evaluate historical and projected data about the businesses we kept or sold."

Sigoloff's leadership strategy and his information systems were so closely tied that they seemed a single force. "You just never thought about it being there because it was constructed to be inconspicuous, friendly, and critical to the ability to do the job."

"[The computer] was as normal to corporate life as coffee," concludes Sigoloff.

EXECUTIVE SUMMARY

When an organization cannot heal itself, a "doctor" must step in and fix it. Crisis calls for hands-on, centralized leadership. Without a strong leader at the helm, an organization might not be able to respond quickly and coherently to a crisis. It is clear that Sigoloff had to be closely involved in pulling things back together in an extremely complex and precarious situation at Wickes. His use of information systems allowed him to sort through the intricacies of the situation and develop a strategy for successfully weathering the crisis.

PART SUMMARY

In Part II, we have seen several different types of situations that called for the "commander" style of leadership: global coordination, growing entrepreneurships, cost-containment/efficiency, and crisis management. In all of these diverse environments, the leaders relied on information tools to help them remain accessible and personally involved with the diverse activities of their organizations. By expanding their effective "reach," the computer made their hands-on leadership style feasible in large, dispersed, complex organizations.

THE
LEADER
AS
COMMUNICATOR

Credibility, Clarity,
and Coordination

Part III

Most leaders consider communication to be their primary function. Leaders who place great emphasis on their role as communicators feel a need to constantly improve their personal communication skills.

There are many avenues that lead to the improvement of communication in an organization. Leaders can consciously establish more effective channels of communication and encourage feedback from all levels of the organization. They can also set an example by improving the clarity and consistency of the messages that they construct and deliver.

The executives in Part III discuss ways in which their use of information tools allows them to do a better job of communicating with people both inside and outside the organization.

Communication channels often extend beyond an organization's boundaries. An increasingly global business environment calls for the establishment of new relationships with customers and peers in foreign countries. Burnell Roberts, chairman and CEO of Mead Corporation, discusses how he uses a computer to keep track of a shared network of personal, high-level contacts that extends across companies and across continents. Additionally, Roberts's use of electronic mail has allowed him to improve communication with overseas employees and with people at various levels of the organizational structure.

When it comes to communication, clarity is uppermost in the mind of Ken McCready, CEO of TransAlta Utilities. He believes that the clarity of his personal communication inside and outside the organization is vital to his success as a leader. In the second profile, he describes how he uses information tools to create more precise means of sharing information and ideas with others.

The two other profiles in Part III are concerned with communication during and after times of crises. Prolonged crisis situations often result in unfavorable employee attitudes. In these situations, leaders must restore morale and rebuild eroded trust. Both Thomas Plaskett of Pan Am and Thomas Stephens of Manville Corporation have had to reestablish management credibility in the midst and the aftermath of crises.

One way that leaders can reestablish trust is through communication. The manner in which they deliver and respond to messages sends

70

powerful signals to crisis-ridden organizations. At Pan Am, Plaskett involves himself closely in the development and delivery of communications to employees. He uses information tools to help him construct clear and consistent messages. Through communication, he has been able to restore some of the trust and support he needs to continue Pan Am's uphill struggle for survival.

Thomas Stephens faced a crisis of similar proportions when he took over Manville Corporation. The company was thrust into bankruptcy when it was overwhelmed with asbestos claims. Stephens had some difficult communications assignments: restore the morale of dejected employees, pacify angry representatives of claimants, and build a working partnership with a brand new Board of Directors. His ability to communicate effectively with these important constituencies was greatly enhanced by his personal use of information tools. Because of his clear and convincing presentation of critical information and because of his ability to listen and respond effectively to employee input, Stephens established the trust necessary to lead the company out of the crisis.

The common theme of Part III is the enhancement of the personal communication capabilities of leaders. Each of the four profiles, presents a unique, tailored approach to applying information tools in service of this critical leadership goal.

CHAPTER 7

Realities of

Global Competition

Burnell Roberts

Chairman and CEO, Mead Corporation

I have a checklist that I go through before every interview. Is my tape recorder charged and ready to go? Is my solar microphone in my case? Do I have my background materials with me? Do I have a pad of lined notepaper? And before I went to my interview with Burnell Roberts, CEO and chairman of Mead Corporation, I added something to that checklist: Is that pad of paper an Ampad brand?

It wasn't too difficult to find an Ampad-brand pad of paper in my office—you probably have them in your office, too. Ampad is a recent acquisition of the Mead Corporation, a 140-year-old company that is one of the world's largest manufacturers of paper—producing more than 1.2 million tons annually. (I knew I wouldn't have to hear any nonsense about the "paperless office" in *this* interview.) Mead Corporation also owns Mead Data Central, an electronic retrieval service that provides information to the legal, governmental, medical, and business communities.

Mead's size, financial health, and product mix position the corporation well for global competition, and Roberts believes that a slowdown in the U.S. economy will cause companies to increasingly focus on global markets. "If a company is going to continue to grow, it probably can't satisfy its demands strictly domestically," he says.

In the past, less emphasis was placed on international markets. "It used to be that we would ship over there when business here was bad. Then, when business was good here, we would bring it back . . . like an accordian. No longer are people doing that. We're saying that the growth over there is so dramatic, you must make a commitment to that market, in both good and bad times."

Roberts points out that the global market for U.S. forest products is excellent. "We have a tremendous growing season in the U.S. There are more trees here [than there are in most other countries], and they're more easily accessible. We just fit very naturally into the international market."

Mead has had overseas operations since the 1950s, but Roberts doesn't underestimate the challenges posed by globalization. "American business is still learning how to deal with the realities of global competition."

Roberts is very personable, and he likes to do business in a personal way. For his company to compete globally, Roberts believes he and his management team must do an excellent job of establishing high-level, personal contacts internationally. Opening up new markets for products and taking advantage of new business synergies and opportunities requires knowledge of people. To begin doing business in new areas around the world, client relationships and peer relationships must be established in new locations.

Roberts must also encourage global team building. As the company grows and moves into new locations, it is easy for employees to lose a sense of being part of the Mead team. Staying in touch with people at all levels and locations becomes more critical as the company spreads out. It also becomes more challenging to determine whether or not the right people have been assigned to the right positions. In other words, it gets harder to maintain a high-performance team.

These three challenges—knowing people worldwide, encouraging teamwork, and selecting the right people for the job—compose an important part of Roberts's leadership strategy.

Establishing a Global Network of Contacts

Development of a network of worldwide contacts is essential for survival in global markets. Unless influential people in foreign companies know your company and the people in it, they are unlikely to open doors to business opportunities. "Every company wants to be known and recognized," says Roberts. "If you have access to people, you have a tendency to keep visiting them. That builds up a relationship over the years. They know your company, and they are more likely to tell others about your company. You have your own network, which you keep active, and you hope they are taking advantage of their Mead network of contacts as well."

Establishing the corporation's network of contacts is not something that Roberts does alone. The process is greatly accelerated when the whole management team collectively builds the company's network. By combining and exchanging contacts, each individual extends his or her own list, and the overall knowledge base grows.

But Mead is a large corporation, and the pooling of knowledge is not easily accomplished:

> We all know a lot of people. But how do you ever *use* that information? We have people who go to Europe a lot. For example, someone may need to make a trip to Germany. Now, how does that person find out that someone else knows [a valuable contact] in Germany? In a company where you've got 130 locations, we all know a lot of people. But how do you get to them? How do you know them? You have to have a central source.

The top executives at Mead have developed a shared database of international contacts, which they constantly update. When they go overseas and meet new people, they enter information into the database. The entries in the database include potential customers, potential business partners, local officials, or people who might be instrumental in introducing Mead's top managers to potential clients. "We put into the database who they are, what they do, what their businesses are, and so forth . . . as a reference for the next people going over. It's a network."

The database provides access to contacts that the Mead top management might not otherwise have:

> It saves a great deal of time and effort. If another Mead person has a lot of contacts in a particular country, you might not know that. You might spend a tremendous amount of time building a network that already exists. It's also clear that there are people whom some of us wouldn't meet or know without the database. Networking is built on pieces of information. You might be able to tap a network of 10 people very quickly with the database.

Roberts consults the database before he makes trips overseas. "If I'm going to do any international travel, I pull up out of the computer the people that we know in various countries: their names, their positions, and who knows them in our company." Roberts offers a common example of how the database is used:

> I go to Europe on occasion and talk with a lot of security analysts and investment banks. I give a number of speeches. I use [the database] to invite certain people to attend the speeches. I may not know them, but if somebody from Mead knows them, I can get their address and invite them. "So-and-so from Mead knows you, and I'm coming to give a speech in your area. We'd like to invite you to come have lunch with us at the presentation." And they quite frequently accept. [Without the database] I would never know everyone we should invite.

Encouraging Global Team Building

In addition to establishing an international network of contacts, Roberts's second objective is to encourage a strong sense of teamwork across all the Mead locations. "We are putting a major effort into team building . . . not just domestically, but on an international basis. We need to get people involved, throughout the world, in the success of the business."

Roberts believes that listening is critical to teamwork. The only way people feel part of the same team is when they can share their ideas and have those contributions acknowledged. "[Teamwork] really only works when managers and supervisors, no matter what country they're in, really want to listen to each other."

Listening not only builds teamwork, but brings innovation. "We really are very big on listening to people's ideas. It's a very open-door company. And you have to be willing to take risks with ideas. By listening and by taking some risks, people will continue to bring ideas to you. The worst thing I worry about is that people might say, 'Well, they're not listening, so I'm not going to take them my idea.' That would be the kiss of death." Listening is an issue that Roberts believes will be long-lived. "The importance of listening will certainly increase as we continue to grow. As we expand across countries and cultures, we will have to make extra efforts to understand each other. Listening well and being open to new ideas is key."

To reinforce this culture of openness at Mead, Roberts wants to make himself accessible to people at all levels and locations of the organization:

> In most organizations, the people closest to top management have a big effect on how we define and understand reality. Each of those people has his or her own way of looking at things. I admire those people [at the senior management level] very much, but I do want a variety of perspectives on our problems and challenges in order to balance my own view. And people in different locations at different levels have fresh perspectives on situations.
>
> I think there are some organizations where the CEO hears only from a certain layer of people. But this is certainly not true in my case.

One way Roberts gets around the problem of being isolated from other levels and locations is through the use of electronic mail. "Electronic mail is a marvelous facilitator of communication. I get wonderful messages from people. I got two within the last couple of weeks with suggestions as to things that we should do in the company. 'Why don't you do this? Why haven't you considered that?' I just think that's neat. These were people down in the organization who I didn't know." One of the messages Roberts received was from a college student whom Mead had hired for the summer. Roberts responded to him, thanking him for calling a situation to his attention. "I don't think that he would have called or come to see me otherwise. I think electronic mail ties in very closely with our open-door policy."

Receiving messages from other levels of the organization is important, but it's equally important to answer those messages. "Silence isn't golden when you're trying to build an organization and focus people's energies on helping the company compete. When they're willing to share their ideas, you have to listen and respond. The message goes out whether you did or didn't respond." Here, too, the computer helps. "Electronic mail makes responding easier, more convenient, and, as a result, more likely."

Roberts faces a communications challenge not only across organizational boundaries, but also across geographic boundaries. In particular, his accessibility to overseas personnel is necessary for global team building. "When you're trying to work with someone in Switzerland, it can be very frustrating to deal with time zones. Electronic mail has helped. We can now send a message at night or whenever we want to, and when we get back in the next morning, there's an answer waiting."

What's most important to Roberts is not so much the speed, but rather the ease and intimacy of electronic mail. He uses the computer as another channel of communication to make people feel more a part of the global team:

> Sometimes it can be very lonely sitting in a foreign country, away from headquarters, wondering what's going on. . . . [Electronic mail] provides a vehicle for people in our foreign operations. They feel they have faster access to us and are more a part of the total corporate unit. There's a greater tendency to communicate via electronic mail than there is to make a phone call when you're dealing with the complications of time zones. Electronic mail is just so much more convenient.

To gain the advantage of immediacy and the feeling of being connected, Roberts feels he must use the system himself. "If you suddenly have an insight or idea that you want to share with someone, you might lose that thought or forget to send it later if you can't get through to them immediately on a phone call. E-mail provides another informal channel of communication that's always available. It's there if you're traveling or if you're in the office." Another reason Roberts uses electronic mail personally is to enhance his thinking and writing. "My writing is much more fluid and much more personalized when I do it myself, as opposed to dictation. My personality comes through much differently on electronic mail than in a memo, because electronic mail is more like informal communication."

Roberts summarizes how he uses the computer to build global teamwork by saying: "The speed, clarity, convenience, and access that electronic mail provides enables us to support our overseas operations much more effectively."

Picking the Right Team Members

As the company expands globally, Roberts feels it is more important than ever to have the right people in the right positions. He believes in playing an active role in picking and promoting people in his organization:

> If we've got somebody who leaves a key position, I might want to do my own run on who might fill it. I may narrow it down to five or six people, and then I want to look at the relative strengths of each one. I look at compensation information: somebody's grade point, what their

options were last time, what their salaries are. I also might notice details as to whether they have learned a foreign language or have foreign travel or living experience.

He feels his personal involvement in personnel decisions is critical because it allows him to add his own experience and creativity to the process. His personal use of the computer facilitates his direct involvement:

> The value of the [on-line human resource] system over paper files is that, with the paper files, you are already getting someone else's filter on the information. They have gone through it and passed judgment on it. They've done some sorting. I really like the raw material for several reasons.
>
> [First,] it's sometimes hard to enunciate precisely what you're looking for. Every job is difficult to describe in its entirety. If you can go through the raw data, you can be sure you've covered everything to your own satisfaction.
>
> [Second,] I also think it's true that top management is often more willing to take a chance on certain people than others might want to. People need to be stretched. I might take a chance on someone stretching themselves to fill a position, whereas someone below might not want to take a risk on that person's ability. I think risk orientation gets higher the farther up you go in the organization. People at lower levels want to be sure they're doing the right thing, and that may temper some risk taking on their part.
>
> [Third,] there are things in the system that trigger my imagination when I'm looking at the raw data. Those same things might not trigger other people's imaginations. As you think about jobs and what kinds of people are needed to fill them, your ideas change. The system allows you to take different cuts at how you're looking at information. I can fumble around in there, and I may come up with names that others would never have come up with.

Computing as a Necessity

Use of the computer has become a habit for Roberts, as well as the rest of his company. "I'm really not sure that we could get along without it now," he says. "It would be very difficult. I mean this in both the personal and the general sense. I'm convinced that the company would have a tremendous problem operating without it. And personally, for me, it would be extremely difficult to go back to working without a computer."

Why are the information tools so important to Roberts? "Without my direct access to information, I'd have to have a lot of [paper] reports coming in to me that I now don't need . . . everything from following the stock market, to plans, to the human resource files. I believe I would end up feeling much more isolated from the business if I didn't have my computer, and I don't think I would be as effective without it."

EXECUTIVE SUMMARY

Building a global company such as Mead requires a great deal of international teamwork. Good teamwork depends on good communications—the ability to reach, listen, and respond to people. Knowing and communicating with people was critical to Roberts's ability to positively influence the global expansion of Mead.

Through his use of the computer, Roberts has connected himself more closely to his company and to the world. He knows more people because of the on-line database of international contacts. He encourages global team building through electronic mail. And his use of the personnel database allows him to field the best possible team.

His creative use of information tools has enabled Roberts to find new ways of improving his communication with people both inside and outside the corporation. Thus, the computer is an extension of his leadership strategy.

CHAPTER 8

An Atypical Utility

Ken McCready

CEO and President, TransAlta Utilities

It just so happened that my interview with Ken McCready, president and CEO of TransAlta Utilities, was scheduled during Stampede Week in Calgary. If you've never heard of Stampede Week, let me assure you, it is a very big deal. It's a week of rodeos, parades, competitions, and live entertainment nonpareil. And, in the first week of July, it starts the moment you set foot in Calgary.

As I made my way toward the airport exit, two sliding doors opened to reveal scores of Calgarians in Western dress with big smiles and warm greetings for travelers just arriving to their fair city for the big event. One particularly handsome "cowboy" looked me in the eye, held up a long piece of metal, and solemnly asked, "Ma'am, have you been branded yet?"

"Ah," I thought. "So this is Calgary—not your typical city."

If Calgary is not your typical city, TransAlta certainly follows suit by not being a typical utility. Founded in 1911, TransAlta is the largest investor-owned electric utility in Canada. Given its long history in a relatively stable industry, you might expect a staid, rule-bound organization. Not so. But there was a long road to the unique environment now at TransAlta.

A Customer-Satisfaction Survey

Ken McCready came to TransAlta in the early 1960s, and he has witnessed many changes over that nearly 30-year period. "Before my time, TransAlta's culture was more like that of a classic utility company: The departments were more like watertight compartments. But my predecessor was the architect of changing that."

Following the path set by his predecessor, McCready was determined to build a culture of openness and responsiveness to customers:

> We had gone through a period where we had very high rate increases—at least as far as our customers were concerned. The greatest pressures from our customers during that time concerned cost control and productivity gains. In other words: "Keep the bill down." That was the main way customers evaluated our performance. Then we came to a period where we had very modest to no rate increases, and I felt that the customers' way of evaluating the company's performance was shifting from cost or price to service.

To get an idea of how well the company was performing on its customer-service objectives, an extensive survey was conducted. The survey confirmed McCready's suspicions about a shift from a focus on price to a focus on service:

> We did some soul-searching after conducting the customer survey. Their idea of service was a much broader one than we had anticipated. Our idea of service was physical in nature. We thought they were only concerned with whether or not the lights were on when you turned them on. But the survey results indicated a distinction between physical service and the ways in which service is delivered.
>
> We got very high marks on how polite and friendly our people are, we scored high marks on reliability of power, and we got high marks on fast response to problems. But we didn't get high marks on flexibility. Up to that point in time, we prided ourselves on being "fair" to all customers; to be "fair," we tried to treat everyone the same. But we weren't taking into account the fact that the customers had individual problems. This hampered our ability to be flexible. I like to characterize it like this: "They listen patiently to everything I say as a customer, and then they go away and do what they would've done in the first place!"
>
> In the past, we used the excuse of being highly regulated to explain why we couldn't be more flexible with customers, but we were foreseeing a more deregulated environment. We decided we needed to change to a culture where satisfying customers was important. So we changed the mission statement from "*providing* customers with safe, reliable electric service at the lowest possible cost," to "*satisfying* customers with safe, reliable electric service at the lowest possible cost." Before, we were providing service, but we weren't satisfying individuals.

McCready knows that positive change comes about only when those on the front line in direct contact with customers are capable of making things happen in every function of the business. Based on the survey results, McCready was more convinced than ever that a culture shift toward flexibility and customer satisfaction was necessary:

> The strategy I decided to employ to effect this culture shift was one of getting people at all levels involved in a process of designing the solutions. I couldn't tell people how to change the culture. I had to set up an environment where they themselves changed the culture.
>
> Any change a leader makes in an organization requires dealing with embedded assumptions and practices, particularly in a big organization. In an industry that is as heavily regulated as we are, you end up with a lot of rule-bound procedures. It's not very flexible. So, when we discovered that, indeed, customers were interested in better service and that their idea of service had to do with the flexibility of people in dealing with their individual situations, we were faced with changing a very major assumption about how to deal with customers. This was the shift from treating all customers "fairly" to satisfying individual problems in a flexible way.

To respond to the customer survey by "setting up an environment" for a culture shift, McCready focused on the following areas:

- A massive quality-of-service initiative
- Strategic alignment of goals and objectives
- People development
- Key relationships with ranking government officials

In each of these four areas, information tools helped him lead the way to a new, customer-focused way of doing business.

Quality-of-Service

To create the proper environment for a shift to a customer-focused culture, McCready instituted a quality-of-service program. This extensive, ongoing effort involves a whole series of initiatives designed to change rules, policies, practices, and procedures throughout Trans-Alta—to make the company more customer-friendly. The project started with the VPs, moved to the department heads, and now permeates all levels of management.

"To kick off this project, we had a meeting of all the vice presidents and department heads. I didn't know what I was going to do in terms of assigning people to this thing. I called for volunteers on each one of these initiatives during the meeting. Then I made a note of who had functional responsibility, and then I chose a captain and an adviser."

Sixteen individual problem-solving teams were formed. "They're all headed up by people in the organization who *don't* have normal line responsibility for that area. The teams cut across the organization." In other words, a person from operations might head up the quality effort in the marketing area:

> This allowed people to look at problems from a completely fresh viewpoint. They got truly involved in the process of designing organizational change by being taken out of their comfortable niches and put into problem-solving teams outside their realm. They had to reason through problems intellectually and do a lot of communicating with others to define problems and suggest solutions.
>
> The problem-solving teams outlined areas for change. Once it was time to implement a solution, the team passed the baton back to those who had operating responsibility for the area. The problem-solving team didn't usurp the department's authority to carry out the changes, but they gave people a new look at the kinds of things that were going on.

The key to success was matching the right people to the right problems, regardless of any departmental ties. The challenge that McCready faced when he started the project was to find the appropriate mix in terms of combining projects and picking people. "I was looking for combinations of these projects. We started with 27 projects and crunched it down to 16."

With numerous people assigned to 27 different projects, McCready had a difficult task before him. "Crunching" the projects down to 16 and ensuring that the right people were assigned to each project was a complex task. To accomplish it, McCready employed a spreadsheet:

> When I do any work that involves a table, I start with a spreadsheet, because it's matrixed, and I often don't know where it's going to end up until I'm done. The spreadsheet allows me to move things back and forth easily while I'm thinking through it.
>
> I needed the spreadsheet in order to think about how I wanted to set up the structure for the program and its project management aspects.

Now it is our shared framework. The project manager for the program is now maintaining the spreadsheet, following my format, and bringing the information to me.

Training was another cornerstone to the quality program. The company put 1,200 people through extensive training sessions, which included a great deal of feedback from line employees who deal directly with customers. "We selected people from the organization to be trainers, and then we trained the trainers. I started off that train-the-trainers session with a review of what we're doing, why we're doing it, what we hope to achieve, and what their role is in it. The train-the-trainer approach was immensely valuable, because you never learn something so well as when you have to teach it."

After personally appearing at the first session, McCready made a videotape that was shown during subsequent training sessions for 1,200 employees. "The videotape of my speech was shown at every one of the 67 training sessions that were held—including the one in which I participated."

McCready feels his most important role in the quality-of-service program is as a communicator.

Most of what I do is communicate. I don't do much else. I communicate ideas and concepts and directions. Often, the ideas and thoughts I have to communicate are of tremendous complexity.

The quality program is a massive thing. It has policy-level implications; it has strategic elements to it; and it has many, many tactical pieces in terms of implementation projects. Keeping track of that kind of complexity is, in many ways, daunting.

My role is to see that people who are working on projects have a context for what they are trying to accomplish. For example, I created five major groupings for the 16 quality-of-service project initiatives. Then the 16 projects are broken down into sublevels and subprojects and task groups.

As an aid for handling complexity, McCready finds an outline editor to be of great value:

If you can't separate things out in order of importance, your communication becomes convoluted and muddled. The outline editor is set up in a hierarchical fashion. Therefore, it allows me to easily relate less important things to more important things. I use it primarily to keep my communication clear and put things in context for people. It's a way of managing.

When I first designed the quality-of-service program, the outline editor allowed me to see what the groupings and sublevels should look like. It also allowed me to track project descriptions and objectives to test how well they fit into their categories. It helped me see that the efforts were placed correctly and defined properly.

As the project matured, McCready found he needed to further clarify his thoughts and communicate them to others:

All of the team captains meet quarterly on this project. I find that the outline editor helps me chair this quarterly meeting with a rather large group of people—usually 40 or 50. In my role of providing context for what is happening, I can encourage people to assess their progress and help them see how their efforts fit or do not fit into the overall hierarchy of ideas. So often people have ideas that are, in themselves, good ideas. But the ideas may not fit into the overall context.

Thus, the outline editor helps McCready clarify and communicate his thoughts about alignment of objectives in the organization:

[The outline editor doesn't provide] a hierarchy of control; it provides a hierarchy of ideas and needs. The final test on everyone's ideas is "What value does this add to the customer?" In days past, we were more concerned with what value an idea added to the company or how an idea fit within the objectives of a person at a higher level of the organization. So, you used to have more emphasis on people satisfying their bosses. Now there is more emphasis on satisfying customers. It's not a typical corporate hierarchy.

It is much easier to redirect people from a poor direction to a good direction if I've done a good job of communicating to them the context of their efforts. The outline editor helps me construct and communicate that context.

Priorities and Commitments

The customer survey indicated that people at TransAlta needed to be more flexible in handling specific problems. Therefore, McCready had to guide the culture toward more diversification and flexibility on the front line, while maintaining a well-aligned corporate strategy. Unless people are pulling in the same direction, it is difficult to accomplish anything. Executive priorities and commitments must match the strategy of the organization as a whole. McCready wanted to build shared vision about the direction of the company and then ensure that individual actions matched that strategy.

In accordance with his objective of strategic alignment, McCready designed an exercise in which everyone on his executive team had to agree on a list of priorities for the company as a whole. "It allowed us to get to a better sharing of a common strategy, with everybody buying in. Everybody had to agree that all of the statements were important enough to include on the list."

Once McCready created the list of priorities, he and the other members of the executive team individually ranked the priorities in order of their importance to them as individuals:

> Each statement was typed on cards and then sorted by each member of the executive team. I then used a spreadsheet to do the arithmetic necessary to seeing patterns of agreement and conflicts in priorities. We all looked at the results of the spreadsheet in a meeting, and we had a great discussion about it. It resulted in significant agreement on goals and team building.
>
> Someone else could have done the arithmetic, but I wanted a good, direct feel for the agreements and conflicts. Sometimes I want to know what's behind information, rather than simply seeing a summary of information. That lets me know how significant or important an issue is. I probably made different judgments as a result of being directly involved in that process than I would have if someone else had done it for me.
>
> Because I had a better feel and understanding for people's ideas and opinions, I was able to help clarify where we had different judgments on priorities. It made it easier for me to lead a discussion that resolved those differences. Then we had the whole senior management team pulling in one direction, and all of us were confident that we were pulling together in the right direction.

Employee Performance Tracking

You can't satisfy customers unless you have motivated, well-developed employees. The next step in shifting the TransAlta culture was to pay even closer attention to the people resources within the company.

McCready believes in the importance of being directly involved in selecting key people and rewarding performance at all levels of management:

This is my most important job. The future of the organization is going to depend on how we develop people. Human Resources contributes to that, but I can see so much more than they can alone. I've had experience in other areas of the company, and I know and appreciate the problems people have in all of those diverse areas. I'm very keen to be personally involved in not just watching, but also contributing to the development of our future managers.

I keep a list of all the managers and my assessment of their performance, along with some input from other senior people. I'm looking at their promotability. I really don't believe in succession planning in a mechanical sense. I'm very strong on moving people around. I got here through a series of horizontal promotions, not many directly vertical. [With this horizontal approach,] you get people who are experienced in more aspects of the organization. Mostly, we have a lot of people who appreciate the problems that other people have.

A spreadsheet model helps him track the complexities of this listing. "It's sort of like a depth chart for a football team. I track the person, the department they're currently in, the rank they have now, how soon they're promotable, and what their possibilities are for the future. There aren't any calculations going on, but it allows me to compare and contrast, and it helps me think through the individuals relative to one another."

Relations with the Provincial Government

Satisfying customers is not simply a matter of making things work internally. As the president of a provincial utility, one of McCready's important roles involves working with high-ranking provincial-government officials with whom he regularly discusses matters of vital importance to TransAlta. Often, external regulations and legislation impact TransAlta's ability to respond to customers and provide quality service. Therefore, the development and management of relationships with government officials is a key part of McCready's leadership role.

McCready describes the importance of these relationships with an example:

I was once dealing with a cabinet member for the provincial government on a matter that was of critical importance to the future of the organization. I was having a difficult time explaining a particularly complex problem. So I had to shape the presentation in the direction of my audience.

I had to make a major contribution myself to the process because only I knew how the minister was struggling with the problem. It wasn't good enough for me to get it from somebody else. I find that analysts, even really smart analysts, get their own idea of a problem. Then they decide to present things in certain ways. What you end up seeing as a problem or a potential solution is very much at the mercy of what someone decides to show you.

McCready decided to describe the problem to the minister by using a spreadsheet. "This wasn't just a spreadsheet of numbers. It was a model that demonstrated relationships between concepts," he explained. "The graphs we developed with it were very important to explaining complex concepts. I ended up doing a lot of work on the [spreadsheet] model myself. I'd work on it at night, bring it in on a disk in the morning, and give it to the manager of the rate section and ask for input and validation."

McCready explains that his hands-on work with the spreadsheet was vital. "Appreciating and presenting the problem and solution required working with it directly. I could change it and make it mine. Supporting data and relationships were what I had the analyst fill in for me. But the model itself then became the communication medium for the analysts and me, and for the cabinet member and me."

McCready says that the model was more than a personal thinking tool; it became a medium for communicating to his staff members what he wanted from them. "I don't just give people orders and have them go off and do things for me. We work on problems together. It is more a process of sharing knowledge and skills. With the spreadsheet model, we are able to incorporate different perspectives about problems. It's really a new medium for communication."

McCready notes the benefits to both parties. "It gave me a lot of leverage because my appreciation for the problem was much greater; I was not in a superficial position on it. And it gave the analysts much more in the way of stimulus to create new ideas and gather new kinds of data."

The payoff was evident. "On the problem involving the cabinet minister, the analysts and I went through several cycles of working with the model until we got a series of presentations that I knew were bulletproof. By doing that, I managed to get a very complex point across to the cabinet minister, who was interested in understanding it but who didn't have much time to understand it."

Sharing a problem and developing a valuable solution goes beyond simply persuading someone of your own point of view, says McCready:

> This was not just a situation where I was trying to simply persuade the cabinet minister of my position. In fact, I ended up being much more useful to him because of my level of understanding of the problem. We turned up ways of looking at the problem that no one else would have. In the spirit of really searching for a solution as opposed to simply selling a position, if you share a conceptual computer model, you can go through the data in a different way.

The value of the computer model in solving the problem was readily apparent to McCready. "In this situation I used the computer to accomplish something that just otherwise wouldn't have happened at all. It's not a matter of whether it would have happened faster or more efficiently; it simply would not have happened. As a result, we got the [regulatory] situation changed from awful, insufferable, and impossible, to just plain terrible," said McCready, laughing.

The New TransAlta

In response to the customer survey and an increasingly deregulated environment, McCready developed a leadership strategy for making TransAlta more customer-focused and flexible. To accomplish these goals, McCready set out to create a culture of "openness and truth seeking" at TransAlta.

"We really encourage everybody to give up any notion of pride of ownership of ideas," says McCready. "We're very vigorous in putting forth and attacking ideas. We get people together with different points of view, different abilities, from different disciplines and different ways of thinking. As a result of this culture, we're able to move very fast. We take diagonal slices through the company to put together problem solving teams. We try to make the hierarchy disappear when it comes to problem solving."

TransAlta doesn't sound like a typical utility, and it's not. By taking dramatic steps to respond to customers both inside and outside the company, McCready has helped to shape an organization that is highly responsive.

McCready's use of computers has increased his ability to accomplish his goals. "The way the computer helps me is with problem solving and communications. It allows me to think and communicate in an iterative fashion. I can keep rearranging information and ideas until they are clear and concise. . . . I'm better positioned to contribute. These thinking tools lever my creativity and my ability to make the organization more innovative. They're part of the tools for my job."

EXECUTIVE SUMMARY

McCready's use of information tools helps him to clarify his own thoughts. Thus, he can better communicate a context for his ideas to others and establish shared perspectives on problems. He sees his role as that of a communicator, and he believes that information tools are critical to his ability to successfully fulfill that role.

McCready chose a communication-oriented leadership style to drive a cultural transformation.

CHAPTER 9

Piloting Pan Am

Thomas Plaskett

Chairman, CEO, and President, Pan Am

Sometimes things go from bad to worse. As if it weren't enough to already be in a precarious financial situation, in December of 1988, Pan Am took another hit—the bombing of Pan Am Flight 103. In addition to the tremendous emotional impact this tragedy had on the families and friends of the victims and the employees of Pan Am, it was financially disastrous for the corporation.

Thomas Plaskett—chairman, CEO, and president of Pan Am—believes that the bombing was largely responsible for the $243-million year-over-year increase in Pan Am's operating losses in fiscal year 1989. It significantly set back programs that had been put in place to stabilize the airline's operations and financial position. "The horrific nature of that tragedy I don't think can be fully appreciated unless you've lived through it and seen its devastating impact. Not just the incalculable human loss, but the impact on the company in 1989 was devastating."

Nonetheless, Plaskett continued with his stabilization strategy, and in late 1989 and early 1990, results began to show encouraging signs. "There have been dramatic improvements in the product and in our customers' perception of the product. We were first in on-time performance in the first quarter of 1990. It was a tremendous boost for our employees, because they began to see things happening."

Positive trends in passenger traffic and revenues began to emerge. But then, in mid-1990, the company took another hit—the Iraqi invasion of Kuwait:

> The rapid escalation in fuel costs, due to that conflict, has given us another setback. Because of the higher costs, we have, out of necessity,

had to raise fares in an uncertain economic environment. It's like climbing out of a foxhole, and every time you get your head above ground level, somebody kicks you back in. Every time we try to climb out, the enemy shows up as some external event, out of our control.

The company is not out of the woods yet, and Plaskett is frank about this:

Who knows how the Kuwait situation will play out? What we plan to do is stay the course in terms of our strategic direction. We're going to keep working to improve service, and we're looking for every dollar of cost savings we can get without compromising service quality. We're just going to manage our way through it. I think we can weather the storm, but it sure has strained our flexibility.

An Inherited Situation

Pan Am's problems have a history. "The company was a pioneer in the airline industry," explains Plaskett. "It blazed the trails to connect the United States with other parts of the world." Early successes led to complacence:

I would describe it as an attitude that Pan Am was the chosen instrument for implementing U.S. foreign policy through the development of air transportation. It was a dynasty. . . . People didn't believe it would ever be exposed to competition. What really developed inside the organization was the belief that, no matter what happened, Pan Am would always be here.

This belief was, of course, misplaced. "Over the past 15 years, the company has been faced with one problem after another," notes Plaskett. "In analyzing how Pan Am got in the shape it's in, I'd have to say there's plenty of blame to spread around."

Though the government protected and promoted the growth of Pan Am during the first 30 years of its existence, it later caused the company grave problems. According to Plaskett, the primary blow came when it allowed domestic airlines the right to fly internationally but refused to allow Pan Am to fly domestically.

Management was also a culprit:

Management simply lost touch with the marketplace, and they couldn't see far enough ahead. They failed to make some timely decisions, and frankly made wrong decisions on many occasions—for example, the acquisition of National Airlines in 1980. . . . There was a bidding war between Lorenzo, Pan Am, and TWA. The price of National Airlines got bid way up, and the acquisition cost was too high. Also, Pan Am management felt that the acquisition of National was the only way to get a domestic system. However, there were already clear indications that deregulation was going to provide other options.

Plaskett says unions also must share in the blame. "Recalcitrant union leaders were unwilling to recognize that the world around them was changing. They pushed the company to uneconomic labor agreements—the highest costs in the industry, at one time—and they weren't willing to accommodate or make changes until the company was on the verge of bankruptcy."

Plaskett wasn't forced into the position of taking on this huge turnaround challenge. In 1986, while he was at American Airlines, Plaskett was ranked by *Fortune* magazine as one of America's top ten most-wanted managers. Qualifying characteristics for the honor included "steady progress through the operating ranks, some background in international business, excellent communications skills, self-confidence, the ability to take risks, and high integrity."[1]

With those kinds of credentials, Plaskett clearly wouldn't have had any problem finding a job. So why did he want to enter into the fracas at Pan Am?

As I looked at it, I said to myself, "Yes, there are a lot of problems. But Pan Am still has some tremendous intrinsic strengths and value." In the first place it is a widely recognized brand name throughout the world. Secondly, there wasn't any doubt in my mind that [the people of Pan Am] knew how to run an airline. They simply had been lacking the right plan; they were lacking leadership. The third thing of real value was the international route system.

Cynic Recycling

When Plaskett came to Pan Am in January of 1988, he found employee morale dismally low. "There was a confrontational environment between the management and the employees. And this is a service business. When you've got people who are delivering a service who are unhappy about their situation—themselves, their management, their company—they're not going to do a very good job."

Compounding the situation was the fact that Plaskett had to ask these same employees to take a pay cut. "You're asking people to serve customers, be friendly, and feel good about it, when they've just taken a 30 percent pay cut. The challenge of keeping your service levels up, let alone restoring them to a higher level, might at first glance seem impossible."

Ironically, another problem was arrogance—a remnant from the company's early industry-leading days. "I think our people thought they were a lot better than they really were. They thought the reason we got complaints and bad marketplace reactions was because of management. In many cases, there was an unwillingness to recognize that their personal interactions with the customer were sometimes creating problems as well. There wasn't a recognition that the customer signs the paycheck."

Plaskett wanted to reverse employee attitudes, but he had to rebuild trust in management in order to do so. Plaskett's primary leadership strategy for turning morale around and rebuilding trust involved a comprehensive communications program. "It had to be a communications program based on the credibility of the person delivering the message. I had to get out and spend time with employees, sit in cockpits and talk to crews, talk to flight attendants . . . talk to them in a straightforward, candid, honest way, or all the communications activities would be wasted."

His initial approach to building personal trust was personal meetings. "We structured a series of meetings with employees around the system—voluntary meetings. We probably only got about 5,000 of the 25,000 to attend, so we didn't reach everyone we would have liked to have reached." But the information gradually got out to employees through informal channels. Plaskett began to develop a positive reputation as a new style of corporate leader.

Clarity and Consistency

Face-to-face communication was vital, but there were other critical aspects to Plaskett's role as a communicator: written communications. Such messages consisted of letters, internal and external speeches, and newsletters.

In building his personal credibility with employees, Plaskett knew that he had to deliver clear, consistent messages that he himself directly participated in formulating. "In my view, an executive who is not directly involved in the communications process internally with employees is out of touch. I don't think you can delegate that. You're the one who's providing the leadership. Therefore, it ought to be *your* thoughts, expressed in *your* words. And only by doing it that way will you establish the kind of credibility that I think you need to be an effective communicator."

Building personal trust through direct communications with people created a tremendous work load. "I've never counted the number of letters exactly, but we must get between 200 and 300 letters a day in this office. Complaints, suggestions, I get *epistles* from people . . . you know, term papers! Customers, stockholders, and employees write." Plaskett lifts a thick manila folder from his desk. "That's my urgent file," he says, laughing.

To personally shape messages, Plaskett needed either to dictate them or to write them himself. Over the years, Plaskett had used a variety of dictation devices, with little success. "I was never very successful at dictation. I guess it's the way my mind works. I would lose my train of thought, and I couldn't visualize enough of what I had already said." For his personal messages, he chose to use a word processor, which enabled him to express his ideas better. The computer screen served as a medium for clarifying his thoughts and providing more consistency in his messages. "The word processor helps me to visually formulate and structure paragraphs, and sentences, and thoughts."

With the aid of the word processor, he's also able to get more done by working with the words on the screen rather than editing successive printed drafts. "It's so much more productive in terms of the volume of communication I can put out. I don't have to do 25 drafts of something. I can produce more work, and it's of higher quality because of the way I interact with the computer."

When it comes to correspondence, Plaskett does get help from his assistant. But his use of a word processor allows him to achieve his goal of being more personally involved.

If he had only conventional means of responding and had not personally answered many of the letters he received, Plaskett believes that morale would have been adversely impacted. "People would have said, 'Nobody ever pays any attention to me' or 'I'm not even sure he reads his letters' or 'Nobody cares about my ideas.' Ultimately, many of them would have given up. The attitudes were fairly negative when

I arrived, so we were trying to do things to improve them. My answering so many employee letters was one of the things that helped."

Consistency across his many messages was also important in restoring credibility with employees who had access to a very active grapevine. "In a business [such as ours], where the informal communications channels are so strong and so fast, you run the risk of shooting yourself in the foot if you've got inconsistent or unclear messages." By keeping both internal and external messages on his computer, Plaskett is able to thread pieces of different messages together, checking them for consistency. Therefore, if he gives an outside speech or makes a speech to the board, he can ensure that the messages are consistent with those he sends to employees. "I can tie communications messages together. They're all sitting there on the [computer] disk. I can take parts of one letter or speech or report, and bring in something else, and knit it all together so that the pattern and the flow are consistent."

Whenever possible, Plaskett also strives to include a personal touch to his communications. His personal database contains information about his friends, business associates, industry colleagues, and other people he communicates with directly. "I know [his] wife's name, I know how many kids they have, and their names. I pick that stuff up from Christmas cards. I constantly add information to the database. Then when I write to them, I can add a note about Susan who's a Junior at Georgetown this semester."

By using the word processor and the database, Plaskett believes he has improved both the quality and quantity of his communications with others.

The Climb to Recovery

Unfortunately, the recession declared in the U.S. and the uncertainties associated with war in the Persian Gulf forced the Pan Am management team to file for reorganization in early 1991. However, Plaskett says that because this is strictly a "financial restructuring," the company will continue to operate "as usual." He remains confident in the strategy his management team has pursued thus far, pointing to the fact that sound constructive relationships are in place with employees and that Pan Am has effective labor agreements with all of its unions.

The maintenance of employee trust and loyalty remain vital to restoring Pan Am's health. "This business is extremely dependent upon individual and collective performance of human beings in producing our product. We must have a common understanding of what our product is, how it is to be delivered, what is expected, why things are or are not working."

This, in turn, should translate into good corporate-wide relationships with customers. "Our customers have to see a consistency in the level of service they receive. If we aren't effective at communicating to our employees what we're trying to achieve and what we expect of them, we're not going to get that level of quality."

Plaskett's strategy is straightforward. He works to build trust in his leadership abilities. The way he goes about this is through clear, consistent communication—and lots of it.

In spite of new setbacks, he anticipates progress. "We're obviously not where we want to be. We've got a lot more we need to do, and there are many uncertainties associated with the [economy and the] situation in Kuwait, but I think we finally are beginning to see the payoff. We're on the climb out."

Plaskett insists he needs his computer to continue the climb. "Without it, the amount of my work product would diminish substantially. I mean, I already spend enough hours, given the difficulty of our situation, in trying to manage this place. And to [not have] something that increases my productivity would be, I believe, tragic for the corporation. We just wouldn't get as much done. We wouldn't make as much progress."

EXECUTIVE SUMMARY

By communicating with a great many people in consistent and clear ways, Plaskett has improved his credibility with employees. His use of information tools is critical to both his productivity and to his effectiveness as a communicator. The word processor increases the amount of work he is able to get done, and as a result he is able to be more involved in answering letters, constructing speeches, and creating personalized messages.

NOTE

1. Roy Rowan, "America's Most Wanted Managers," *Fortune,* 113, No. 3, 3 February 1986, pp. 18–25.

CHAPTER 10

The Aftermath

of Asbestos

Thomas Stephens

Chairman, CEO, and President, Manville Corporation

Thomas Stephens does not have a neat desk. In fact, it looks sort of like mine—management by piles. There's plenty of paper, and a couple of computers thrown in for good measure. But if Stephens's desk seems chaotic, the man himself presents a totally different picture. There is an aura of composure about him—the kind of calm born of experience and perspective, of surviving difficult times.

Negotiating an End to Bankruptcy

In 1982, things at Manville Corporation looked pretty bleak. The company filed Chapter 11, and it was facing staggering financial liabilities primarily due to the obligations it had to compensate victims of asbestos. The backlog of asbestos cases had grown to 17,000, and a much too conservative estimate of future claims totaled 50,000. The insurance carriers stopped paying, and the litigation began.

In 1985, Stephens left operations to become CFO. The following year, Josh Hulce resigned as president of Manville and Stephens was appointed president. Stephens later took on the CEO's job when John McKinney retired.

Immediately after his arrival at Denver headquarters in 1985, even before he became CEO, Stephens was embroiled in the intricate bankruptcy proceedings facing Manville. The negotiations were at a standstill after three years of discussions. The often acrimonious ses-

sions involved eight constituencies: present claimants, future claimants, commercial creditors, trade creditors, property claimants, co-
defendants, the government, and the insurance companies. "It turned
out to be an eight-party negotiation fighting over what surely is the
most complex legal, economic, social, and emotional problem yet
faced by an American company," said Stephens in a 1988 article he
wrote for *Financier* magazine.

He described the negotiating process to me in detail. "In most
bankruptcies, you have the management of the company on one side
of the table, and you've got the people that the company owes money
to on the other side of the table. Both are typically trained to be fairly
sophisticated, financially." But Manville's bankruptcy proceeding presented some important differences:

> In the case of this bankruptcy, there were eight parties at the table, not
> two. And a lot of the people at the table were not sophisticated from a
> financial perspective. To get them to vote for the plan, you had to
> convince them that the reorganized Manville Corporation—projected
> out into the future—was a better bet. They had to be convinced that
> they were better off trying to create a strong, healthy company than they
> were to liquidate it immediately.

In addition to financial naïveté, Stephens had to face the over-
whelming emotional climate of the negotiating process. "You're talking about people who represent people who are ill and dying, or have
died. There's a tremendous amount of emotion. It's a fairly challenging
sales job to say, 'Don't focus on punishing; let's focus on how to create
value over time so that claims can be paid.'"

Effective communication was the key to Stephens's strategy. "The
real challenge in communication was to talk to a wide variety of groups
and convince them that the plan that had been proposed was in
everyone's best interests. Visuals and crisp presentations were a very
important part of that."

Stephens was working on very complex problems that needed to
be recast in simple, clear formats. "One of the real keys to presentation
is organization, so that you get your ideas across. Just pulling together
bullet charts is real useful. You walk in there, and you've got all your
key points laid out in a crisp, logical presentation."

In preparation for the negotiating sessions, Stephens worked on
spreadsheets and created his own charts and slides by using his personal

computer. "I can sit over here [at the computer] and knock out a presentation in about five minutes."

Obviously, during these negotiations, Stephens was a very busy man. I asked him why he took the time to do this himself. He told me that this approach allows him to contribute his perspective in interpreting the numbers:

> Number one, it's intellectually stimulating to me to get involved hands-on and to create a presentation. That's something I've always enjoyed doing.
>
> Secondly, the quality of the presentation is a direct function of how much time and effort you spend in getting ready. Sweat equity. If I prepare it myself, I'm comfortable with it, and it's going to be of better quality than if I just run into a room with something somebody else prepared for me.
>
> I used to do these types of spreadsheets by hand, and it was tremendously tedious work. I couldn't examine nearly as many scenarios as I now can with the electronic spreadsheet. I can look at the information from so many more perspectives. It's become an extension of my brain. It relieves me of the drudgery of the work and simultaneously expands my ability to do the work better.

His personal investment in creating convincing presentations paid off. Armed with a tenacious negotiating style and clear, logical presentations, Stephens managed to get the eight warring factions to agree on a reorganization plan, which was approved by the bankruptcy court in December of 1986. It was the end of one of the major battles for the corporation, but it was not until October 3, 1988, that Stephens was able to celebrate the end of a long and difficult journey. On that date, the U.S. Supreme Court removed the final obstacle to the Manville reorganization.

Meanwhile, Stephens had a company to run.

Keeping the Ship Afloat

During the process of negotiating the reorganization, the company was on its knees, recalls Stephens. "We'd been in bankruptcy for a number of years. We had come through a number of recessions. We didn't have a clear business plan. We didn't know whether the company was going to be alive in the short term." To get this paralyzed company going again, Stephens had to develop and gain approval of a series of business initiatives.

But Stephens couldn't act alone. He had his Board of Directors to consider. After the company went into bankruptcy, the Board of Directors had undergone an overhaul. "We literally started all over again. Nine new board members were brought in, and we cranked up a brand-new board with only a few carryovers from the old board."

For Stephens, building a relationship with this new Board of Directors was fundamental. "I wanted the board to have confidence in me and confidence in the fact that I knew what I was talking about. The most important thing between a CEO and his board is confidence. If they ever lose confidence in you, you're in trouble."

In terms of confidence, Stephens was starting over. "We had a lot of catching up to do," says Stephens. "We spent a lot of time communicating, talking about our businesses and our competitive position." Again, presentations were critical to Stephens as he brought the new board up-to-date. He felt his use of spreadsheets and graphics for board presentations was particularly critical when he first entered his job.

I again asked him why he needed to do this himself. "If you really want to know what's behind the data, you have to have the discipline to dig it out, put it together, organize it, and present it. As a new CEO, I thought [credibility] was extremely important. I knew I had to find out what I was talking about quickly. Doing the operating reports and putting together the analysis [on the computer] for every board meeting made me do my homework."

He used spreadsheets to model complex problems and think through financial considerations. "I work with spreadsheets myself because they give me a better feel for problems and opportunities. I can examine things the way I want to, and I can look at it from many different angles."

New to his job, Stephens faced a tremendous learning curve. The intricacies of the bankruptcy, on top of the complexities that are attendent to any new job, made it vital that he be able to absorb and reflect on large amounts of information. The accessibility and ease that the information tools brought to Stephens's learning helped him sort out the complexities of the situation and present his conclusions clearly.

Though it was important for Stephens to think through the company's financial problems personally, it was equally important to work through issues in meetings with his executive committee. Both then and now, Stephens uses spreadsheets for these types of meetings, with models projected onto a large screen. "[The models] allow us collectively to use more of our energy being creative, rather than simply wondering what the answer is. We can just literally let our minds wander, and we can ask dumb questions. Sometimes dumb questions will open up a crack. 'Gosh, I never thought about doing it that way.' It lets you become more creative and observant, rather than more analytical and precise."

Participative Planning

Stephens worked with the board on strategy; he worked with his staff on the details of the business plan. He told his people, "Forget the bankruptcy. Whether it works or not, if we don't know what we're going to do with our businesses, we sure don't know what the company is going to be capable of accomplishing. Let's understand who we are, where we are, where the opportunities are, which businesses we should stay in, and which businesses we should exit."

The business plan was not a moldy document consigned to a dusty shelf. Its purpose was to rally the organization around a fresh vision, and remotivate a dejected work force. For the plan to be a living document, Stephens was determined to get as many people as possible involved in the planning process. "We told everybody in the company: This is your company. You not only have an opportunity to speak up; we want you to. Get involved!"

But gaining participation from jaded and skeptical employees was not easy. Simply asking for involvement was by no means going to guarantee it. "There's always a trust problem when you're trying to manage your way out of a difficult situation. People need to be sure that you really mean what you say. The only way you can gain their trust is by involving them in fixing the problems and by communicating."

Part of the strategy of gaining participation and communicating with employees involved what Stephens called "Come to Jesus" meetings. He went out into the field for breakfast meetings. "It was just plain talk . . . getting the issues on the table." Another way Stephens encouraged communication was with a quarterly letter from him, mailed to employees' homes, soliciting their advice and opinions. In these quarterly letters, Stephens asked employees to write to him with their thoughts and concerns. He guaranteed them a personal reply within 10 days.

The mail started pouring in. To handle it, he set up a system using his word processor:

> I said, every Sunday I'm going to take two hours and I'm going to answer employees' letters. We set it all up on the computer, with the help of two of my assistants. That way I could personally answer every letter. I didn't have to type them all out; I could just change some key phrases and references to general subjects.
>
> I had promised to answer every one of those letters. Without the computer, I simply couldn't have done that. The computer was critical to my ability to build their trust."

His personal responses showed employees that he was listening. As a result, they participated more actively in providing suggestions and ideas for the planning process.

Using Other Channels of Communication

Another important channel of communication with employees was videotape. "[Videotape] is a great way to be in a lot of places at one time. Let me give you a great example. We were negotiating with the Trust on a share repurchase, and some very nasty things came out in the newspaper that were based on information taken out of context. It painted a very negative picture. It essentially said, 'Manville may go back into bankruptcy.'"

Stephens's first concern was for the salespeople:

> These are the people who represent us every day to our customers and others. They speak for us to the people that we work with. We've got to keep them informed.
>
> So, on the spur of the moment, we went to the [video studio]. We asked a group of people to come join us, and we said, "OK, now you represent sales and you represent West Monroe, and you represent Europe. Ask questions you think other people would want to hear." We had no scripts, no rehearsal; we just kind of threw it together and said, "This is where we are, and this is what's really going on." The tapes were in air express to every salesperson in the company within six hours.

I asked him if the video presentation worked. "Did it work?" Stephens says incredulously. "Let me tell you a story. About three weeks ago, I was doing a speech in Waterville, Ohio, and a salesman drove all the way from Detroit to Waterville to say to me, 'Tom, thank you for understanding our world. I can't tell you what it did for me to know the answers to these questions before I had to go see our clients.' So you see what a little piece of videotape can do."

In preparing the video, Stephens had recognized the contribution key people in the field make to the image of the firm. "Keeping the salespeople informed is extremely important. When you have informed salespeople, you have informed customers. By letting them know what was going on, we slowed down the rumors and put both the salespeople and the customers more at ease."

Video as a channel of communication works both ways. In some cases, employees are informing management by video:

> It's not easy to explain to a Board of Directors exactly what it is you need to do out at that plant in Bluffton, Indiana. There's nothing like seeing it. So when we have a new capital budget, when we want to build a new whippersnapper or fix a widget, we send a guy out with a $500 video camera, and we take a picture of it.
>
> We get an hourly employee at his machine, and let him tell the board about how we're going to invest $10 million to make this machine run faster. Now you're talking about *power*. Not only does that hourly employee say, "I get to tell the Board of Directors what the company's going to do! It's *my* machine!" (You've got one dedicated employee when you do that.) But also, the board hears it from the best expert in the world—the guy that runs that machine every day.

This application of videotape allowed the Board a channel of feedback they normally wouldn't have—the video cut through the layers of management between machine operator and board member. Such applications of video demonstrate an executive's conscious design of information channels to motivate people at all levels of the firm.

Communicating with Shareholders

With the support of the board and a business plan in hand, Stephens was ready to present the shareholders with a clear path to recovery. In the second quarter of 1989, Stephens held the first "annual" shareholders' meeting in seven years. CEOs generally enjoy share-holders meetings about as much as cats enjoy swimming. And the seven-year gap between meetings had given shareholders a long time to harbor questions and concerns about the Manville reorganization. The meeting promised to be a difficult event.

To be as prepared as possible for shareholders' questions, Stephens had others put together data and briefing books. But, using his word processor, Stephens wrote his own speech. "I guess I never sweated over words any more than that speech. We went through that thing 10 or 20 times. It was on a floppy disk, so I'd go home and change words and add phrases, and we'd come back and talk about it. . . . It was a great use of the word processor."

Stephens sometimes has others draft a speech for him, and he is quick to point out that he has an excellent speechwriter. "Sharon is a very gifted writer. She's creative, she knows how to make things sound good, and she knows me. We spend enough time together so that she can 'Stephenize' it." But after he receives a draft, he then likes to "fiddle with it" on the word processor. I asked him why he couldn't just mark up a paper copy of the speech. While reply-ing, he was shaking his head vigorously. "No! Again, the quality of the presentation is a function of how much sweat equity you put into it. By using the word processor, I can easily change things. I can easily see how something would look or sound if I worded it differ-ently. By editing on the screen, I can put more of myself into the speech."

Stephens didn't always work this way, of course. But he learned the value of his personal involvement the hard way. "When I've really fouled up, when I've really not done a good job of representing the company, is when I've just grabbed the folder with a speech that somebody else put together and I didn't spend the time to get comfort-able with it." The word processor makes it easy for him to mold the words to his style, while getting extremely comfortable with the con-tent. "There's something about taking that disk, putting it in the computer, going through it, and really getting comfortable with the words and feeling ownership. Then I can walk into that room, face 50 people or 500 people, and speak with the confidence that it takes to make an effective presentation."

Considering Acquisitions

In 1986, the company had a net loss of $45.2 million. In 1987, profits were $164 million. In 1988, there was a net loss due to the settlement, but operating profits were up. In November of 1988, Manville began paying off its debts. The company entered 1989 with $2.4 billion in assets and borrowing capacity of over $1 billion. With the company back on its feet financially, Stephens could begin to focus on growth.

Acquisitions are a part of Stephens's growth strategy, but they can be highly risky. He believes that, in general, American companies botch acquisitions because (1) They don't know how much to pay for the company, and (2) They get into businesses they don't know much about:

> Learning a business is something the computer can't do for you. But in terms of paying the right price, that's fairly analytical. I mean, you've got to look at it from a lot of different dimensions and play the what-if games. One of the things I did last night was to play around with different pricing [of an acquisition opportunity] . . . what impact this would have on earnings per share, cash flow, and so on. It allows you to focus more on "What kind of a deal can I offer so he wins and I win too?" rather than just throwing money at it.

In any negotiation, the greater the number of options, the better your chances are for having both parties satisfied. The spreadsheet allows Stephens to think through more scenarios and find a win-win approach. I asked him why his CFO can't do this for him:

> I do talk to John and ask him what he thinks. But again, it's that sweat equity. You've got to get emotionally involved in a complex problem, and the only way I know how to do it is to get my hands dirty.
>
> Don't get me wrong, I don't try to make all the decisions around here. I delegate. But the two most important things I do are investment decisions—where we spend our money—and picking people. And the computer is a very important tool in looking at complex investment decisions and making sure they work.

Bolstering BTUs

In this profile we get an idea of just how complicated leadership can be. There is a strong emphasis in Stephens's story on the computer as a tool to help manage complexity. Word processing, spreadsheets, presentation graphics, and videotapes helped him understand the daunting situation he inherited. In addition, they helped him communicate clearly and straightforwardly to courts, claimants, the board, shareholders, and his staff. Later, information tools helped Stephens think through complex deals and brainstorm approaches to acquisitions.

It's clear that the computer has helped Stephens analyze, communicate, and convince. But he seems most interested in the creative possibilities the computer offers. "You've got to see this as a way of expanding your mental ability. It literally takes the boundaries off of your ability to think and lets the brainpower focus more on creativity and less on discipline. You know, the mind has got just so much BTU power, and you can use it to discipline and organize, or you can let it flow and be creative."

Stephens believes he wouldn't be as successful without the computer. "It's like taking John Elway aside before a game and telling him, 'You can't throw any passes to the right side of the football field.' He may still win the game, but you've taken away a powerful part of his portfolio."

EXECUTIVE SUMMARY

Stephens uses a broad range of tools, and he believes they have all helped him be much more effective in accomplishing his primary goal of building trust through clear communication.

People sometimes think of computers as impersonal. But, in fact, with the example of the letters to employees, Stephens showed how the computer helped him to communicate in a more personal way. Without the word processor, he could not have promised employees that he would answer every letter himself.

PART SUMMARY

Communication is part of every leader's job, but may or may not play a central role in one's leadership strategy. When it is critical, a leader must strive to be clear, consistent, convincing, and far-reaching. Throughout Part III, we have seen how executives extend their communication abilities through their use of information tools such as electronic mail, word processing, shared databases, and voice messaging. We saw examples of how these tools helped them reach larger numbers of people, bolster their credibility, and construct more clear and consistent messages. In Part IV, we will examine the closely related role of the leader as coach.

IV

THE

LEADER

AS

COACH

Focus and Feedback

Part IV

A recently revived view of the executive's role casts the leader as coach. Articles concerning coaching as a management technique appeared as early as the 1950s. However, after that point in time, there was very little discussion of the executive as a coach until the early 1980s.*

A coach encourages others to take responsibility for their thoughts and actions by guiding rather than controlling. Implicit in the notion of coaching is the creation of a partnership in which hierarchical power distinctions are reduced in importance. A simple way of thinking about coaching is to consider it in terms of *context* as opposed to *content*. The leader in this role is concerned about creating circumstances that encourage success, rather than developing a step-by-step process for success and imparting that to others. Two important means of coaching involve focusing people and creating feedback loops.

Focusing helps people discern where they should place their most concerted efforts. Setting a personal example and asking people probing questions are part of the focusing process.

Setting a personal example and conscious questioning are coaching approaches used by Bill Gantz, president of Baxter International. In the first profile in Part IV, he tells about the early stages of a merger and the attendant business challenges. One of Gantz's key challenges was to create a spirit of cooperation and mutual respect. Part of the way in which he accomplished this was by staying personally well-informed and by keeping people focused on facts rather than emotional issues. He explains how information tools improved his ability to accomplish these aims.

The creation of feedback loops is another approach to coaching. Feedback loops are channels of communication in an organization. By letting people know on a number of different dimensions how they are performing (as individuals or groups) on an ongoing basis, leaders encourage them to improve their performance.

Such feedback loops can be much more pervasive than a typical performance appraisal. Feedback loops can motivate and inform. They can be a guiding force that is ubiquitous and ever present. Feedback

---

*Roger D. Evered and James C. Selman, "Coaching and the Art of Management," *Organizational Dynamics,* Autumn 1989.

loops have powerful systemic impacts that allow coaches to greatly leverage their efforts. In essence, feedback loops become extensions of the coach.

Coaching through feedback loops is a theme that runs through the remaining three profiles in Part IV. To broaden the perspective of people working in a newly formed company, Bill Esrey of United Telecom and US Sprint had specific external information added to the system so that people at Sprint could compare their performance to industry benchmarks. Esrey uses information systems to create an environment that emphasizes world-class excellence.

Richard Crandall is another firm believer in performance feedback loops as coaching tools. To focus employees on the critical success factors that will help Comshare retain market leadership, Crandall has instituted an executive information system that contains a variety of measures of performance. The measures are reviewed by the entire management team and people throughout the organization. Crandall describes how performance measures are evolved at Comshare and how the information system supports that evolution.

Debbi Fields of Mrs. Fields Cookies faces an enormous coaching job. With over 600 widely dispersed stores, she has to find ways to motivate and develop people at a distance. She has a two-part coaching strategy: presence and feedback loops. Like the other people profiled in Part IV, she uses information systems to give people performance feedback on a variety of measures. In addition, she manages, via an expert system, to make herself available as a coach on an ongoing basis to everyone in the Mrs. Fields "family."

Each of these profiles demonstrates different approaches to coaching. Part IV shows how information tools help encourage better performance by focusing people on priorities and by providing new channels of feedback on accomplishments. The profiled executives, each in his or her own way, have found that information tools can hone their coaching skills and greatly amplify the impacts and reach of their coaching activities.

CHAPTER 11

An Arranged

Marriage

Wilbur Gantz

President, Baxter International

The early '80s brought an abrupt close to a 15-year period of unbridled growth and prosperity in the healthcare industry. It was the end of an era. The government then released a whole herd of healthcare cost-containment measures, and Medicare reimbursements were hardest hit by the thundering stampede. At the time, I can remember my father, CEO of a public medical center, talking about the difficulties of managing in an increasingly regulated environment.

Hospitals weren't the only ones feeling the pain. In 1984 alone, Baxter Travenol's earnings dropped 87 percent. "We knew that to prosper in a new environment, we would have to make some drastic changes," explains Baxter's president, Bill Gantz. "We needed a broader base of products, more R&D programs for cost-effective products, and we pinpointed homecare as a definite growth area."

Though the drop in earnings set off an expected chain of cost-cutting events, what industry watchers were not prepared for was Baxter's boldest strategic move—the $3.7 billion acquisition of American Hospital Supply Company (AHSC) in 1985.

A Strategic Merger

To outsiders, the merger between AHSC and Baxter seemed questionable during such tight times. To the Baxter management team, it made perfect sense. "The merger could obviously help us meet the objective of broadening our product line; and second, we believed that AHSC's research and development would be particularly valuable to us in shifting our R&D priorities. There was also a small effort in home healthcare that American would contribute."

Not only would the merger meet the stated strategic objectives, but it also offered significant business synergies. Baxter could take advantage of American's superior nationwide distribution system, and American would benefit from Baxter's strong international presence.

But having bought AHSC, how could it be merged into the Baxter fold? Gantz says they were faced with just three alternatives:

> When you merge companies, you have to deal with employee groups that have operated successfully for a long time on their own. You can deal with that in several ways. You can take one of the companies and "cookie cutter" that culture, and use that as a model for operating. That's easy to describe, and you can ask people if they want to be part of that culture or not. It's easier, because at least you have half of the organization that already understands what you want to do. And the other half can say yes or no to it. The second way you can do it is to leave everyone operating autonomously as they are. That's relatively easy too.
>
> But the challenge that we set for ourselves at Baxter was to take this opportunity to create a new culture attuned to the business environment that we see developing for our industry and our company in the '90s.

Why did Gantz choose the most difficult approach? "We're now in a transition period," he says. "We're seeing some major changes in global markets that hadn't occurred before. Now we're facing [Europe's free trade environment of] 1992. We're in this unbelievable period where trade barriers are down, capital is moving freely, Eastern Europe is opening up. We have to reposition ourselves for global markets. We decided to work on building a new, combined culture that would meet those requirements."

In other words, the Baxter management team set out to follow the massive business merger with an extensive cultural merger. Gantz says: "We made a decision when we did this to truly bring the companies together. We were determined to integrate them and form them into one organization."

According to Gantz, it's not easy to pull an organization together across companies and across continents. Five years later, this ambitious task is still in process. "When you decide to put companies together, you really find out what indigestion is," says Gantz. "The merger was a very turbulent process. I think it's like getting married. You don't really know what it's going to be like until you're in it," he says, laughing.

To forge a new, responsive, shared culture, Gantz's management strategy included three key objectives:

- First, he wanted to establish the underpinnings of a new culture by creating a unified cultural theme for the company.
- Second, he wanted to establish an open, fact-based environment for decision making.
- Third, to be an effective leader, he wanted to gain a reputation for credibility and fairness with the new people.

The Foundation of Culture

Gantz felt that the cultural merger could be accelerated by focusing both companies on a common, unifying vision. "The central theme— what we want to build the culture around—is quality," explains Gantz. "By 'quality,' I mean concentrating on customer requirements and making sure you meet those requirements every time. This concept lays the groundwork, or creates a foundation, from which the new, combined culture will continue to emerge."

Baxter began its quality program in the same year as the AHSC acquisition. "It's something we embarked on in 1985, so it's been underway for quite some time. We have made a major investment in this." To demonstrate the importance of the quality program, the Baxter management team put their money where their mouths were. Budget resources, time, and effort were committed to the quality program— particularly in the area of training.

Though a concept may be sound and the training well planned, people are not always eager to jump on the bandwagon. "What you start out with are beliefs throughout the organization that you're doing a pretty good job today, and that the customer has always been happy in the past, so why do we really need to worry all that much? 'Everything's OK,' is the attitude that is often expressed. There's a complacency that exists."

Gantz's perception of complacency within his organization led him to consider the second leadership strategy, one in which computers play a significant role.

Creation of an Open, Fact-Based Environment

One way to facilitate cultural change is to get people to shift old thinking patterns. An attitude of "doing things the old way" is divisive when you are trying to merge groups. Each group has a different "old way," and group members tend to be attached to it.

Gantz encouraged people to take a new look at the way they worked by examining their opinions, actions, and decisions in a logical way. To bring about this shift, Gantz set out to focus people on the facts. "One of the most difficult aspects of going through a merger is to get people to do things based on facts rather than emotions. Even if you can't gain consensus, if you are operating on a factual basis you can get people to understand direction and strategy."

Budget and planning meetings were particularly susceptible to emotional volatility:

> In the early years of the merger, the budgeting and planning processes were extraordinarily painful. Because we were shifting priorities, not surprisingly, we ended up with enormous conflicts on how we should budget and how we should plan.
>
> You can't please everyone; often, you can't even get consensus. What you are aiming for is to have open discussions of the facts and the issues. You want to try to come up with a strategy and a budget which the organization understands and supports.

Because budget and planning meetings had a tendency to be more volatile than other types of meetings, Gantz wanted to keep these discussions focused on the facts. "There was considerable time and effort put into strategy and budget development. We had to put together the facts in order to develop a strategy."

In the spirit of setting an example, Gantz personally prepared for the meetings. The process proved so valuable, that he still does a great deal of his meeting preparation himself. "Before a meeting, I get in [to the internal operational databases] and look around. I smell things. I like to see pictures and graphs of the trends." By preparing ahead of time, he formulates questions that guide the discussion in the right direction. Gantz feels strongly that he has to do the meeting preparation work himself on the computer. "I could always get someone from our staff to do it for me. I used to do that. But that takes time, and it also changes the way I work with the information. If I hand something over to someone else to do, then I can't interact with the computer."

Why does he need to interact with the computer? "In terms of thinking creatively about a problem, I can't do that in a static way. When I use the computer myself, I can look at things using my own experience and knowledge. As the model unfolds, I see things I want to adjust and change, and this gives me insight into problems. Working with the information on the computer helps me think through things more clearly."

After experiencing the power and flexibility of thinking on-line, Gantz says it becomes second nature. "After you've worked with the computer for a while, it becomes part of your normal process of thinking about problems. I still use paper reports for the end of the month. But when I'm thinking about problems, I need the dynamic back and forth the computer gives me."

During meetings Gantz has live financial models displayed on a large screen. By drawing everyone's attention to the numbers, the group tends to stay more on course during discussions, instead of veering off into emotional exchanges. "[Augmented meetings are] really helpful for budgeting. People have to get together on various aspects of a problem. They have to agree on the assumptions. It's much easier to get an agreement when you're all sitting together watching the numbers roll out. You get a conversation going with people, and they get the issues straight in their minds."

The opportunity for input and interactive examination of what-if scenarios creates more shared understanding between meeting participants and more buy-in to the results. People feel a part of the planning and budgeting process when they have the opportunity to test their own assumptions in the group setting. "I found that the what-if models helped us communicate ideas and concerns much faster. It gave us a shared language."

Credibility

Ultimately, Gantz's challenge is to get everyone thinking about what's best for Baxter, not just for their division. A focus on the facts achieves part of that goal. What remains is to encourage people to analyze situations and make decisions with the greater good in mind.

Gantz takes this as a personal challenge. He sees his role as that of a coach, helping people learn new ways to think about key business decisions. "People have to know the facts and be able to discuss the issues. It sounds obvious. You'd think that people in business would operate this way all the time. But let me tell you, they don't. To help people become better managers and leaders involves coaching—you have to help them become fact-based and thoughtful about the decisions that they make."

This is not a simple task. People are less open to new ideas during periods of major change. "I find that in the uncertain period of a merger, people are less willing to engage in a real exchange. I don't think it's deliberate, but it's almost as though a denial occurs."

Gantz took responsibility for making himself into an effective coach. This required personal effort. "Coaching is a two-way street. You have to build credibility with people in order for them to be willing to listen to you and share ideas with you."

Building credibility was particularly important with the people from AHSC, who didn't know him. "Coaching is a lot more difficult when you're merging companies. When you've grown up with people and you've brought them along, there's a high level of receptivity to your thoughts and suggestions. [On the other hand,] a manager from the new company might say, 'I'm not going to listen to him; he doesn't know anything.'"

Gaining and maintaining credibility requires that he stay well-informed and avoid partiality. "The more informed you are, the better the understanding you have of where [the new people] are coming from," says Gantz. By being well-informed on both internal and external issues, Gantz is better equipped to help people think through problems by asking intelligent questions. "Before I go to a meeting, I'll take a look at some pertinent information and I'll print out three or four charts and take them with me to the meeting and ask, 'Why is this happening?' By consistently being well prepared to ask the right questions, it sets the expectations ahead of time. People know that they must think through issues thoroughly because they know I will have the information at hand to ask them questions."

But coaching involves more than having the facts at hand. The reality of the situation must be communicated in a nonthreatening way. Gantz finds the computer effective not only as a source of information, but also as a medium for communication. "The computer allows me to coach with a factual base. When you have bright, capable people, the computer is a great communications tool, because you don't have to tell them things. They can see it themselves, right on the screen."

He describes a typical coaching opportunity. "We'll sit around the screen and go through [internal] information and play with it, and do what if's. If I'm trending at a sales increase of 9 percent, and the manager comes in and says we're going to do 13 percent growth next year, I start asking questions. It's a powerful way to ask questions. I tell them, 'If you truly believe this, I'll support you; but here's my assessment.'"

Of course, not all the relevant facts are found within the company. Gantz would also like his people to base decisions on the realities of the external business environment and competitive marketplace. As with internal operating data, Gantz approaches the challenge of shifting people's attitudes and approaches by staying well-informed himself. "My job is to provide perspective . . . to help people think about larger implications of issues. I can only do that if I'm well-informed. It's impossible for people to keep up with everything that goes on in the outside world. I can help by following changes in the external environment." Gantz keeps up-to-date by accessing external databases:

> I just find that, from a competitive point of view, the amount of information on the computer is unbelievable. I can pull up information on anything. I can go into the system and pull up information on x company and see what they're doing, how they're growing, what the products are.
>
> I can even go in and get the reports of what the security analysts are writing. These are issues that tend to be very fast developing. Even when issues are covered in the newspapers, events change very quickly. I can scan through the headlines and decide if I want to see the full text of the article.

Gantz explains why immediate access to external data is so important to him. "It's a dynamic environment that we live in. We have expectations about how competitors and customers are going to behave. If I see on the database that a competitor is ending up with results that are a lot better than we had anticipated, or a lot worse, it leads me to ask a question of what it means for our analysis. It helps me to be a better coach."

Gantz provides an example. "If you're in a strategy review, someone might come in and say, 'Well, the market's terrible. We only have a 5 percent sales growth, but it's better than the market.' Well, I might have been looking at the [external databases] before the meeting.

So I will say, 'Wait a minute, J&J got 9 percent. Can you please explain that to me?'"

Most corporate leaders keep themselves informed by having their staff groups distill and analyze information for them. Though Gantz relies heavily on the reports that people prepare for him, he feels it is also useful to supplement this with information he gathers on his own. Gantz says hands-on access is more convenient, and hence, more likely to occur:

> It used to be that we'd have to wait. If you wanted an analysis of a company, you would go down and ask for it; three weeks later you'd get a report, and you'd forgotten what you asked. I'd probably be less inclined to do this kind of analysis if I had to wait around for someone else to do it for me.
>
> Now I can pick up that information instantaneously, which for me is very valuable. When I'm thinking about something in a competitive context, I can immediately integrate that information into how we're thinking. I'll go in, before a strategy review, and pull up a couple of competitors just to see what they're doing.

It's not just a matter of timeliness. Gantz likes to feel his way through the data. "Of course, I still have people do a lot of things for me. But my use of the external databases is different. I can't transplant my approach to problems or ideas into someone else's head."

Staying well-informed is just one aspect of building credibility. People must also be convinced that coaches and leaders are consistent and fair in the way they deliver messages. This is particularly important in controlling rumors and making people from diverse parts of the organization feel that they are being treated equally. Voice messaging and facsimile transmission help Gantz deliver the same message to several people at once. "I'll call and leave the same message for four people so they can all hear the same thing at the same time."

What's wrong with just giving people a telephone call?

> I could use the telephone instead of these tools, but I would lose the ability to send exactly the same message at the same time to a group of people. People appreciate receiving information simultaneously. It eliminates rumors and speculation. For example, if my people in Europe know about something at the same time that the staff knows in Chicago, they feel more part of the organization, and they don't have to rely on the rumor mill. The same thing is true for the people who came over from AHSC. They have the facts, and they know they're getting them

promptly. It helps improve the whole level of communication and trust in the organization.

A Commitment to Change

Gantz wants to encourage Baxter employees to be open to change in terms of melding two cultures and in the broader context of competing in a rapidly changing global economy. He took it upon himself to lead the way. Gantz's personal use of computers is a reflection of his openness to change. Gantz's willingness to embrace new ways of doing business is reflected in a story he told me:

> I'm just reading Harry Truman's book, *The Buck Stops Here,* in which he addresses the issues of leadership. Basically, he says that the difference between the really good presidents [of the United States] and the weak presidents is that the good presidents know that something needs to be done. They take a stand, they make a decision, and they execute it. If you make a wrong decision, you correct it. Those presidents do well. The presidents who are afraid to do anything, who don't take a leadership position, don't end up doing very well. There's a lot of truth to that.
>
> In business it's the same. I think you're a lot better off moving ahead, doing things, changing. You can't be fearful of moving into the unknown. An enthusiastic attitude toward change is going to be essential in running large, multicountry organizations. This is particularly important for global organizations where there are so many barriers to change. There are immense cultural and logistical barriers in a global environment. If you're very conservative, if you're reluctant to change, you'll be a dinosaur of the '90s.

EXECUTIVE SUMMARY

Gantz's use of information systems was more than a symbol of openness to change; the tools helped him to be a better coach. By keeping him well-informed, internal and external databases and financial modeling systems helped him to gain respect among, and set a good example for, the employees he needed to coach. Furthermore, his access to facts and use of financial models in augmented meetings helped him integrate the new, merged culture by basing discussion on common facts rather than past differences.

CHAPTER 12

The Birth and Growth of a Company

William Esrey

President and CEO, United Telecom, and
Chairman and CEO, US Sprint

Something interesting hangs on the wall of Bill Esrey's office at US Sprint. It's a crumpled scrap of paper that has been smoothed and framed. The message, addressed to the then United Telecom chairman, Paul Henson, was scribbled by Esrey while standing in a Colorado telephone booth:

> *PHH*
> *Rocky agreed!*
> *WTE*

Though its aesthetic appeal is questionable, there's little doubt that this scrap of paper represents what is in many ways a work of art: the moment when "Rocky" Johnson, chairman of GTE, verbally agreed (over the phone, of course) to let United Telecom have a controlling interest in US Sprint. This represents a milestone in a complex story that began some years earlier.

When Esrey came to United Telecom in 1980, plans were being made to move into the long-distance market, even though the breakup of

AT&T was not yet complete. Given the "David and Goliath" nature of United Telecom's position relative to AT&T, the management team knew it would need a distinct strategic advantage. In 1983, the board and management agreed that a fiber-optic network would be the mainstay of the company's competitive thrust.

"We started off in early 1984 with nothing," remembers Esrey. "We had only a handful of employees who were going to build this network, and fiber was in very short supply at the time. We had no rights-of-way. We didn't have the total financial wherewithall. So we committed to the board to find a financial partner because the risks were awfully large relative to the size of the company."

As the search for a partner proceeded, United Telecom continued to invest. The venture began to take longer than expected, and it was losing lots of money. Amazingly, the board stuck with the plan. "The downswing was deeper and more sustained than we had estimated," says Esrey. "Luckily, we really had good, open communications with an outstanding board."

Hanging onto a long-term vision isn't easy:

> An article in the *New York Times* said, "They have to be bluffing. They have no intention of doing that; they're just trying to keep others at bay."
>
> There was a lot of dissension within the company, particularly from the profitable [local telephone company] side of the business. They kept saying, "What are these people doing? We're making all the money, and they're losing it over there!"
>
> There was a lot of skepticism. But all those challenges were what made it exciting and what motivated people. You could come in here on a Saturday or Sunday afternoon, and you would find all kinds of people working feverishly. They were working hard, not because of deadlines, but because they all felt part of accomplishing something that nobody had ever tried to do.

Meanwhile, the search for a financial partner continued, and in 1986 a fifty-fifty partnership was put together between United Telecom and General Telephone & Electronics Corporation (GTE). "GTE had experience, market presence, and penetration. They had a much bigger business from the revenue point of view. What we had was the network strategy—the competitive advantage." Thus, US Sprint was born.

"You had an organization that was coming together from all over," Esrey explains. "GTE Sprint was headquartered in California; Telenet in Reston, Virginia; US Telecom in Kansas City; and GTE in Stamford,

Connecticut. It was such a fast-moving business, and communications were critical." Decisions had to be made quickly, and Esrey is not one to let distance slow him down. "[The need for] rapidly moving information and being able to get together in one way or another to make decisions really caused us to rely on [information technology]."

The executives used a combination of video teleconferencing and electronic mail to stay in touch and make timely decisions. "The telephone would have been adequate for accomplishing this, but I just don't think it would have been as effective as teleconferencing and electronic mail. Videoconferencing provided a different dimension. It helps build relationships better when you can see people. Electronic mail provided for the separation of time sensitivity."

As the company came together, there were still doubts about its viability. "All during this time, I kept asking myself if we were doing the right thing," admits Esrey. "What people saw from the outside at any given time was not a pretty picture. We didn't expect to go through times where we didn't earn our dividend. We didn't expect to actually lose money. But we rode it through."

In 1988, GTE decided it had had enough of a ride. It had taken extensive losses and write-offs in the long-distance business. Soon after the Colorado phone-booth negotiation between Esrey and GTE chairman "Rocky" Johnson, United Telecom took over an 80 percent interest in US Sprint.

At the time, people thought GTE had gotten out just under the wire. But the picture changed abruptly. US Sprint's turnaround in the last half of 1988 astonished onlookers, including Wall Street. The stock zoomed up over 100 percent. That same year, Esrey added to his CEO responsibilities at United Telecom by also taking on the same role at US Sprint.

The uncertain childhood of US Sprint was over, but now it was moving into a feisty adolescence. As Esrey took over the reins at Sprint, he found an abundance of energy and activity, but a clear need for focus.

Focusing a Young Company

As an avid athlete, Esrey is always aiming for the next big challenge. This attitude extends to his business career, as evidenced by his decision to take on the US Sprint presidency:

When I decided to go over as president of US Sprint, people said, "Why?" The Board asked me, "Why in the world would you want to do that? We've gone through two presidents over there. It's a rat's nest. We don't want you to get tangled up in all of that."

But from my point of view, that was where the potential was for the shareholders. And we're in business to make money for our shareholders. Ultimately, it was my responsibility.

To meet the challenges of another corporate helm, Esrey had to manage in two places at once. United Telecom and US Sprint had separate headquarters offices. "The logistics of trying to be in both places at once became very difficult . . . even though Sprint is only three or four miles away. Where's your secretary? Where are your phone messages? Where's your calendar? Where are your notes? I mean, you're not going to pick up boxes every time you go back and forth each day. Information tools really became essential at that time. They really began to help me personally."

In addition to heading up two locations, Esrey found himself taking on the management of a new type of corporate culture. He had to lead a young company into maturity. His position at the helm of US Sprint required distinctly different leadership skills from his position at United Telecom:

United is a fairly predictable, stable culture. They have procedures down pat; fewer decisions need to be made. It's a big, successful operation that has figured out how to do things, and that's the way they're done.

Sprint is sort of like a racehorse that's running around, changing rapidly. The growth is explosive. There are a lot of new people, many of whom we say we've given "battlefield promotions." They've got five decisions to make today, and they'd better make them today because there are five more tomorrow.

In such a fast-paced environment, people tend to lose direction. "We had a lot of people who would go home tired after 16 hours of working intensely all day, but they spun their wheels and nothing got done. They weren't working on the right priorities; they didn't have a clear-cut idea of where they had to go, what the vision was, and what they had to do to achieve it."

Esrey needed to get people focused, and he found information tools were able to help him achieve that goal. "You can drive a lot of effects with these systems," says Esrey. One step he took was to have the cash figures put on his system every day. It was an important signal, letting people know the importance of cash. "It's useful in terms of setting priorities."

Access to internal information continues to help Esrey focus people by prompting him to ask the right questions:

> For my next staff meeting at Sprint, I have a number of things I want to ask people about. I get the information off the system, make copies and notes, and use them to find out if people are still keeping their priorities straight. The system is a great thing. I can look and see how we're doing; and I can see that we're doing great on these 23 things and, on these 4, we're going the wrong direction. Then I can ask people about those [four specific issues] in the meeting.

Esrey's operating information is set up in a hierarchical way, so he is able to get varying levels of detail. The name, phone number, and electronic-mail address of the person who compiles the information is available on the system; if Esrey wants more detail or has a question, he can contact that person directly.

He is surprised at the impacts of calling those contact people. "I just recently started calling them. There have been some surprises. It starts to change the culture. It pushes things down in the organization to the people who really know, and lets them know that management is aware of what's going on and that we haven't lost touch."

Besides making people aware of areas of management's interest, there are other ways of focusing people on what's important. One way is rewarding them for work well done. "The system also helps you be more inspirational. It gives employees confidence when they know you care about what they're working on."

He provided an example of the motivational impacts:

> I saw a guy in the fitness center here the other day. He works at Sprint, and [on the computer] I just happened to have been looking at some of the things he's been doing. I said to him, "Hey, Tom, I see we're really making progress on your project." Well, you know, he starts thinking, "Hey, what I'm doing is important; somebody cares about it. Somebody's interested in it." You can relate a lot better to what people are doing.

Other tools serve Esrey in his efforts to continue to guide the maturing Sprint culture:

> We also use our DEC electronic-mail system a lot to comment on issues that we really want people to focus on. I can flip through information

and then fire off questions, responses, and comments through electronic mail, without the need for extensive meetings. In a couple of minutes' time, I can talk to 10 people on 5 different issues.

Electronic mail helps me to focus people on the issues that I consider important. They set their priorities by what I respond to. If I keep harping on the same issues, it sends a pretty clear message about what is important. If someone sends me an e-mail message on a bunch of issues and I consistently respond to a selected few, it doesn't take a rocket scientist to figure out that those selected issues are the ones which really have my attention.

Esrey believes that the way he uses electronic mail differs from the way he uses a paper memorandum:

In many cases, electronic mail is more of a dialogue. I think people do things in e-mail that they might not do in a memo. A memo is more like a formal report. E-mail can be both formal and informal. You get a lot of "Gee, I just picked this up," or "I just talked to so-and-so." You probably wouldn't get a memo or a report on those kinds of things. It facilitates the general flow of information.

There is a difference in the type of communication. I can tell that the people who send me electronic mail feel that they are dealing directly with me. They are sending it to my machine, and they know I am going to read it. They treat it differently from sending a letter that is going to be screened by a secretary.

Balancing Internal and External Attention

In a new corporate culture, people are often more concerned with internal, as opposed to external, activities. In the early stages of growth, people tend to fight internal fires and establish their territories—rather than think about what is going on in their marketplace or the outside world. In tandem with his efforts to focus people on the correct internal issues at Sprint, Esrey wanted to create a broader awareness of activities outside the company. He notes that companies cannot move into a top market slot without knowledge of what competitors are accomplishing. "I'd ask, 'Well, how are MCI and AT&T doing?' They'd say, 'I don't know.' And I'd ask, 'Well, how do you know we're going to be the best if we don't even know what our [industry's] standards are?'"

Esrey knows that as a corporate leader, he must practice what he preaches. Esrey uses on-line databases to stay abreast of external events. "The system goes in once an hour and checks companies in the industry that I want to follow: GTE, MCI, AT&T, and so forth. Now, if there's any news released over the news wire, it immediately shows up on my screen and I can push a few buttons and pick up the story. So anything that's happening in the industry that's significant, I know about it immediately."

Esrey had external information added to the internal financial data to reflect his managers' goals and competitive stance. This helped focus the attention of others on external events:

> You can't get anywhere without goals. So, on each one of those charts that I can pull up on the system, we added a place for an industry standard and our own goal . . . with a time frame on it. Now, when you talk to people, they say, "Well, here's the industry standard; here's our goal by December; and here are the programs that are going to allow us to get there." The system really helped with that process, combined with the discussions. The system reinforced our discussions.

This system worked so well in the early days at Sprint that Esrey is continuing and expanding his efforts in this area:

> The culture is starting to change, and people are paying more attention to external information. We're taking the next step to tie this to our quality efforts. We're starting to benchmark. Many people who are involved in the quality process are doing this. Benchmarking is a process of establishing a standard of what the best is. It may not even be in your industry. You find out who is the best in a particular area, such as customer service, and why. Benchmarking involves a detailed analysis of what you're doing, how you're doing, and what you could be doing.

Esrey relies on information systems for guidance in determining the appropriate benchmarks. "To set the benchmarks, I need to be fully aware of how the organization is functioning. Information systems help me to create a firm foundation for knowing why something needs to be done and how to improve results."

Paving the Way for More Change

Once a general game plan is established, Esrey must help people to focus their efforts on moving toward the goals. Instead of policing their actions, Esrey has adopted a coaching strategy that includes performance feedback loops. Esrey uses the computer to distribute performance information and let people know that he himself is focused on certain measures of performance.

The key word in this profile is "focus." Better information helps Esrey view his business more clearly, and it helps him guide people in the right direction. Esrey said, "Information systems help us track and explain the progress being made on the goals. Ultimately, this focuses people on what's important."

Esrey is able to guide people by communicating, via the information system, why and where change needs to occur. "Once you have [set benchmarks], you're in a position to implement major changes in your culture. You become convinced yourself about where change needs to occur, and the information systems assist you in getting buy-in by helping you share ideas with people. [The tools] help you describe more clearly the standards from other organizations and the measures of your progress in those areas."

EXECUTIVE SUMMARY

Esrey uses information systems to create feedback loops that report on targets and progress toward milestones. As a leadership strategy, he carefully creates information channels to reinforce the kind of managerial behavior he seeks from people in the company.

This approach is far more dynamic than the typical strategic plans, executive speeches, and performance-appraisal systems. The feedback he distributes through the computer continues to enhance Esrey's ability to provide detailed guidance to people at many levels on a daily basis. A high-resolution and dynamic management "control" system enables this corporate leader to rally creativity and energy in a fast-moving business.

By focusing people on what was important, both internally and externally, Esrey brought US Sprint a long way within a very short time. Now a respected competitor in the long-distance market, the company born just a handful of years ago is already moving toward maturity.

CHAPTER 13

Maintaining

Market Share

Richard Crandall

CEO and President, Comshare Inc.

When I selected interviewees for this book, I intentionally limited the number of executives from computer companies. I figured everyone would expect *such executives to use computers. But Richard Crandall, CEO and president of Comshare, reminded me that reality does not always reflect the expectation.*

He pointed to a small sign hanging over his computer workstation. It reads:

LE PATRON MANGE ICI.

The translation is "The owner eats here." Such signs are hung outside quality French restaurants to imply that, if the owner eats here, the food must be good. "That was a compliment given to us by an editor of a U.K. business magazine," explains Crandall. "It seems that rarely do you find a computer company that uses its own product."

By using computers, Crandall is doing more than signaling his faith in his own company's products. Crandall believes that computers play a significant role in helping him achieve one of his primary business goals: maintaining market share.

The Company

Comshare was founded in 1966 as a computer time-sharing business. As time-sharing was largely displaced by personal computers, Comshare had to change. It has evolved into providing executive information systems (EIS) software and services. "Our software provides executives with the ability to access, probe, and analyze information from a broad diversity of corporate and public data sources. The software integrates these tools with desktop functions such as electronic mail, reminders, and calendars," explains Crandall. Comshare also provides decision support software and services for human resources, and the retail and telecommunications industries.

This change in corporate focus paid off, and the company has been on a growth spurt. In fiscal year 1990, worldwide revenues increased 18 percent and earnings per share went up 39 percent. Offices are located throughout the United States, Canada, Europe, and Australia, with headquarters in Ann Arbor, Michigan.

Market Share

According to a leading industry watcher, Comshare holds a 53 percent share of the EIS market, and Crandall intends to maintain that market leadership. He considers this his prime executive challenge.

Crandall believes that Comshare must excel in eight critical areas in order to maintain and increase its market share:

- Block the competition
- Manage internal product development priorities
- Focus on customer satisfaction
- Focus on quality
- Create strategic partnerships in the sales process
- Retain top people
- Develop alliances with other vendors
- Create an environment for effective collaboration

Information tools help Crandall personally contribute to each of these critical success factors. His approach is to use the computers to create feedback loops that help management monitor key business indicators. By measuring performance in these key areas and providing that performance information to management, the attention of the entire company is channeled in the proper direction, which in turn produces the desired effects. In Crandall's own words:

When you measure something, it gets better. By tracking information on the EIS, we are communicating that certain things are important and that these issues are being watched. It's visible. It's not being buried in memos that most people are convinced executives don't read. The feeling is that the workstation is visible. . . . Therefore, if information about what they're doing is on it, people feel that it's probably being looked at. So they then believe they ought to look at it too, and use it as a management tool.

Critical Success Factor: Block the Competition

An essential component of maintaining market share involves knowing where you stand vis-à-vis the competition. As strange as it may sound, when it was a time-sharing company, Comshare was not so concerned about competition. "We never used to be very competitive. It wasn't necessary in the time-sharing arena. If you proved to the customer you could solve the problem, they didn't go out and find five other vendors to bid on the action. They said, 'Go ahead and do it.'"

Now that it has moved into the highly competitive software business, that picture has changed. "In the software world, competition is unbelievable; and now we've got to pay attention. Market share never used to be important to us when we sold exclusively to the end-user. But now, we have to appease the [customer's] data processing departments, who will buy more often from the market leader, because it's safer."

Comshare has to respond flexibly to strategic moves by its competitors. Since this is critical to success, Crandall built an information feedback loop—that is, a steady stream of information on competitors:

> I use external databases [to track the software market], and our treasurer also puts together a model of other software companies so I can track what's going on with them. We've got tons of information: P&L information, share-price movements, cash and balance sheets, debt to capital, and so on.
>
> Let's say I notice our receivables are stretching out. Well, is that happening to everybody else, or is something going on with us? I can ask the model. Or I may get a call from a financial analyst saying, "Why is your debt to capital where it is?" I check the model and say, "Well, here's where everyone else's is. What's the problem?"
>
> It gets me in touch with reality. You hear all this stuff about trends in the industry, and you get nervous about it. I can check the model and say, "Wait a second, I know what the industry is doing, and I can

see what is going on with us." You tend to start picking out bellwethers as well. I'll notice our performance is kind of tracking two or three other companies, and if we start diverging from them, I want to find out why.

In addition to tracking competitors' financial performance, Crandall keeps a close eye on the products that competitors are introducing:

Quite frequently, I'll access PR Newswire and Business Wire to take a look at press releases on our competitors. Then it's uncluttered by what newspapers do to it. You see product releases when they first happen instead of when they get picked up. In fact, an awful lot of software releases from vendors don't ever get picked up by magazines. If all you do is read magazines, you'll never see it. But if you're looking at the raw press releases, you get it all.

Compared to having information sorted for him, Crandall much prefers the "interactive navigation" of accessing such information himself. "Some [people use] clipping services, but I don't want to put someone between me and the information. I will read something in one article that will lead me to want to wander down that subject to another article."

Why are early warning signs on competitive actions so important?

One of the key things to maintaining market leadership is not letting a competitor of yours execute a successful flanking action by finding some niche to jump into that you haven't covered. If a competitor makes a new product announcement that moves them in a different direction and the press release doesn't get picked up, you may not find out about it until a month or two later. Or, you might not even find out about it until they get it into the marketplace.

The lead time is critical. In our industry, vendors regularly are advance releasing what they are doing by 3 to 12 months. You have to take advantage of that lead time if you want to maintain or grow market share. You need lead time to modify your own product plans in order to take a blocking action against your competitor. A blocking action might be a change in price or adding an additional feature to the product. You need time to make that happen. You also need lead time to change your sales pitch to accommodate the new differentiator that the competitor plans. Without the EIS, I quite frequently wouldn't have that lead time.

Critical Success Factor: Manage Internal Product Development

Managing internal product development priorities is Crandall's second critical success factor. It's fine to track the competition's products, but Crandall also needs to know what is going on in-house. He and his management must make shrewd decisions about which products to build. "Product development tends to be the core of what customers buy, so everybody likes to see what the critical success factors are for the development organization, and how they're doing against them."

Once again, Crandall built an information feedback loop in the form of a time line on product development. "This system tells me where we stand on all of the different versions of our software for each hardware platform. It tells me what's going on with each project. Then I can also get a description through the system. When is the commercial release scheduled? How many resources do we have working on it?"

Such information is critical to Crandall's ability to make planning decisions in the product development area. "We may decide that we've got to move around something. For example, DEC just announced it's doing something new with local-area network support, and we had that scheduled for two releases out. We had to move it up to one release out. But we're going to have to give up something else to do it." The time line allows him and people throughout the firm to look at inter-dependencies and see where adjustments should be made.

Critical Success Factor: Focus on Customer Satisfaction

Crandall says that his third critical success factor—customer satisfaction—is vital to his ability to maintain and increase market share. "The main differentiators in the '90s for software products will be quality and customer satisfaction," he said.

Crandall's definition of customer satisfaction includes the development of a working partnership with customers. These partnerships are strengthened in annual joint planning sessions:

> Approximately once a year, customers come and visit us in Ann Arbor to match notes on their future strategies. As they reformulate their plans for information technology, they like to make sure they've got our input and that they understand our directions. They want to keep their forward strategies and our forward product directions on track.

Since these are strategies (not just projects and tactics) they get decided at senior levels in the customer company. Since we're talking about futures, not the current offering, we don't use the sales force for that. That is an executive-level visit. I have to be directly involved in these discussions, along with my management team.

When customers come for these partnership planning sessions, they naturally have questions for Crandall. "They want to know if we're going to support this or that feature. Some of these things we've already decided to do, but I might not know what release it's in. Will it be out in a year, or will it be longer?" Crandall's information systems serve him well in this context. "I can dig through [the product time line system] and find out what's happening. It gives me an ability to respond quickly and accurately to customers in those planning sessions."

Accuracy and speed in answering these types of questions are important to the firm's credibility. Customers grow weary of empty promises about "vaporware" and never-to-be-seen product features. Crandall bolsters his credibility with customers by having incisive answers to their questions about upcoming products and enhancements.

Crandall also wants to make sure that others in the company are focused on customer satisfaction. Of course, he has built another feedback loop to do so. The system tracks customer complaints as a critical measure of how happy the end-user customers are:

I look at the number of problems that are settled in one day—that's the red bar on the graph. Then I want to know which ones are suspected bugs in the product—that's the white bar. The blue bar represents the movements out, meaning the problems that have been fixed. I use this to see how we are trending in terms of solving problems and to see what development group it's coming from if there is a problem.

Critical Success Factor: Focus on Quality

Quality is Crandall's fourth critical success factor. "Companies that have the resources and the commitment to go for quality will be differentiated from the thousands of 'garage-shop operations' and other companies who don't focus on quality, or who focus solely on price. We've already begun to see this in the automotive industry and consumer electronics."

Building an organization-wide commitment to quality is a monumental task, one faced by virtually every corporate leader today. Crandall elaborates: "Achieving high levels of quality is not easy. In order to get such a broad-scale involvement of people from many different areas throughout the company, you can't just write a memo and tell them to do it. They've got to buy in to the whole process. There's got to be very pervasive, constant communication on the subject."

To ensure that quality is a priority, Crandall and his executives track it on the computer:

> We have a whole set of metrics [tangible benchmarks] for quality, and we are distributing them broadly throughout the company, putting them in the hands of all the people that it takes to produce quality. We track quality all the way from development through release. We track such things as customer complaints, responses to those complaints, surveys of customer satisfaction, and so on. It is a very deep and broad database of information coming from all parts of the company.

Why use a computer to track data on quality? Crandall explains how the computer helps him build organization-wide commitment to quality:

> Everybody tends to think a little too positively about the results they're producing. If you don't look at the stark realities of performance in relation to goals, it's very easy to lose sight of where you actually stand. It's easy to have a difference of opinion between those who cause quality problems and those who have to experience them.
>
> Without the metrics, you get arguments. You get nonobjective opinions on how well or poorly we're doing. Sometimes people are just not connected with reality because they haven't been looking at specific information, or it hasn't been presented to them. The benefit of having metrics and reporting on them is that you get a common agreement on where you stand. By showing reality, you get a shared understanding.
>
> You could use paper to do such reporting, but it causes problems with delivery.

Why does the the on-line system motivate people more than paper? "With an EIS, you know where things are, and you know exactly how to get to them. The EIS also has graphical treatment that tends to accentuate the information. The convenience and availability of the information shouldn't be underestimated, because convenience and availability create visibility. People are more likely to see and respond to the measurement of [quality] goals when those goals are highly visible."

Critical Success Factor: Create Strategic Partnerships

To maintain market share, Comshare must obviously produce new sales, Crandall's fifth critical success factor. Crandall believes that the nature of a Comshare sale demands his occasional involvement. "We are selling to very large organizations, and the sell is an educational one, which involves strategic-level discussions—much like the annual planning meetings with existing customers. So, again, it is important to involve top executives in the process. We encourage the sales force to bring the prospective customer executives to Ann Arbor for head-quarters visits."

To participate, Crandall must keep up with a steady flow of new faces. "It's a continuous process; we have about five to seven head-quarters visits per week." These strategic sales visits are all tracked on Crandall's system. "It tells me who the company is, who the people are, what their positions are, and the date of arrival."

Not only does this tracking mechanism help Crandall prepare for visits with key prospects, but it also indicates business trends. "We've actually started using it as a leading indicator of business. If corporate visits started falling off, you think, 'What's going to happen to business four or five months out?'"

Crandall's tracking of headquarters visits has cultural impacts:

Getting the headquarters visits up on the workstations became a crucial mechanism for becoming more competitive. Everybody could see if we only had one visit this week, and it put pressure on people. I didn't want to know about all their prospects; I wanted to see those headquarters visits scheduled.

Once we got it on-line, we put a goal on it. You get x hundred bucks per headquarters visit for a nontechnical, high-level executive who's in attendance. We measured it right off the headquarters-visit chart. It got everyone's attention. Now it's part of the process. It's part of the culture for people to be focused on getting more such visits.

Critical Success Factor: Retain Top People

In this high-technology business, turnover of the high-potential people is a perennial problem, and Comshare is not immune. To retain top market share, you have to retain top people—hence, Crandall's sixth critical success factor:

> You can't succeed without excellent people. I teach some of the management training internally, and I put forth a question to people, "If you had to choose between starting a company with (a) the best product, (b) top market share, but not the best product, or (c) neither of those but the best team of people in the business by far, where would you start?"
>
> I tell them I'd start with the team of people. Without top people, you'll lose your position. If you've got the top group of people, it won't matter what you throw at them; they'll succeed. They'll overcome it. They'll give you the best product eventually, and they'll get you top market share.

Crandall and his senior executives attempt to minimize turnover by making sure that Comshare is rewarding and developing its key people. Here again they use their information system to measure key performance indicators. "We look at the turnover of people who were rated excellent in their job reviews in the last 12 months. It's the top-rated people who cost us the most when they leave." Crandall pulled up a screen on his computer to demonstrate. "I'll see things like this: In the U.S., we've got some 450 employees, of which 330 are top rated. Of the 22 that have turned over, July through November, five were top rated. So those are the ones I focus on. Where are they coming from? You notice here on the screen that they are all in sales and support, which is usual. Those people turn over more than those from other areas of the organization."

As with each feedback loop, Crandall looks at this information for two reasons: to keep himself informed, and to communicate to others that the performance indicator is important:

> I noticed that when we began to deliver this information to other executives, and when I began to talk about it in meetings, there was an increased focus on making sure that top-rated people got spoken to from a career-path standpoint. Sometimes executives didn't even know who these people were. There were records on it, but nobody was really looking at it.

We now have created goals which we track on the system. Executives are expected to interview a certain number of top-rated people each year with regard to where they stand in their current job, where they're heading, and whether we are doing the right management development things for them.

Critical Success Factor: Alliances

Given the complexities of providing the latest solutions to customers, Crandall believes that a key to retaining market share in the information systems industry is the development of alliances:

> An alliance is a relationship with a participant in the information industry. The alliance could be with a vendor of hardware, software, systems integration services, or public databases.
>
> The relationships are symbiotic. Alliances allow us to come to market with new, innovative product features that differentiate us from our competition. These are projects that we could not have done on our own. Therefore, the alliances contribute directly to maintaining market share.
>
> There are a lot of companies that are going to have to face this, whether they're in the computer business or not. It used to be that it was feasible to implement a full solution yourself. Today, with the complexity of what the customer is asking for, and all the technologies you've got to put together to deliver, it's almost impossible. We ought to be able to solve the customer's integration problems without acquisitions. [To do this] we need to have alliances with each other.
>
> With some allies, in addition to a manufacturing arrangement, there is also a marketing relationship where we are working together to produce sales. In that situation, we are able to take advantage of the reputations of both firms, which can shorten the sales cycle or give us a marketing advantage. This again, of course, affects market share.

Relationships with large allies are particularly important to Crandall, and he stays up-to-date on their progress. "We have a marketing arrangement with a large vendor, where they sell a version of our software. I'm interested in every prospect that they're working on. The people who manage that in Comshare have created reports for themselves, and I get those on my machine so I can see where we are. Normally, I don't track individual prospect status; but since this relationship is so important, I like watching the progress."

Crandall likes to keep up-to-date with product announcements made by allies:

I track what our large allies are announcing in terms of products. There are amazing things buried [in the news]. This week, one of our largest allies announced a layoff, and at the same time, they released a bunch of new product issues. The press covered the layoff and neglected the product issues. We have been waiting for one of the products they announced for years. None of the papers or magazines covered it. But it was available from a public data source that carries the press releases.

Crandall also likes to be proactive in his relationships with allies. He keeps up with the financial contribution Comshare is making to the alliance, and he lets the allies know about those contributions. "We are reselling a piece of an ally's software as part of the total relationship. I called the ally the other day after I had been browsing through the system. I said to him, 'Do you realize that, in the last six months, we've sent a quarter of a million bucks your way?' He said, 'You're kidding.' I said, 'Go check, and call me back.' He called me back a half a day later and said, 'That's astonishing.'" Calls like that build alliances that last.

In every aspect of his relationship with allies and potential allies, Crandall seems to have built an information channel that keeps him abreast. He tracks joint sales processes, ensures integrity in the handling of prospects, closely follows product announcements, and maintains a personal relationship with their executives.

Critical Success Factor: Create an Environment for Effective Collaboration

All these critical success factors are a responsibility of the entire Comshare team. Effective collaboration is essential to success in formulating and attaining objectives. Meetings are a means to achieving collaboration.

Meetings at Comshare are greatly enhanced by the information systems, according to Crandall. Many offices and rooms are equipped with large screens that display the information from the computer. "The EIS allows people to look at the same phenomena in a variety of different ways. That's what's different from paper. With paper, you can't work interactively. Because you can look *behind* the numbers [with the EIS], you get more shared understanding and buy-in."

The on-line system can keep up with the group's far-ranging creative process. If meeting participants go off into related areas, for example, the computer is flexible enough to move with them; paper is not. "On an ad hoc basis, you can jump into a subject and have instant access to the very latest information on that subject, with the ability to change and manipulate it. Often, in a group meeting, you'll start talking about one subject, and you'll drift into other, related areas. The EIS gives you the ability to jump-shift into a whole different subject that you didn't think was initially needed or related."

The system may even expand the creativity of the group, opening their minds to potential problems and alternatives. Crandall offers an example: "After grueling multiple passes at the budget, where we've finally got something on the screen we all agree with, I like having a management session. I say, 'OK, we've got the plan; we've got the budget write-ups; now let's do a potential problem analysis. What could go wrong with this thing?'"

Sometimes this kind of lateral thinking really pays off:

> We thought we'd just about exhausted everything after our last budget session. I was really just doodling with the system, and I popped into PR Newswire and it said, "Computer Associates makes an offer for MSA." Well, nobody had thought that one of our potential problems in the coming 12 months might be that Computer Associates would come after us. So that thrust us right back into the conversation, and we came up with some interesting strategies, which we executed.

New Feedback Loops

There are always new performance objectives for which Crandall has not yet set a goal. Because he wants participation from others in goal setting, the challenge is to use new information feedback loops in the process.

He describes his approach to this task. First Crandall has information on the topic dispersed to people via the system, and then ideas about the goal start to take shape:

> My observation is that, if you start looking at data, getting used to it, and asking questions about it, you start evolving a gut feel for where a goal ought to be. Once you get a goal in place, that communicates action to the organization. That changes culture. Then you start digging into how it would be reasonable to raise the sights of that goal. That's the beginning of understanding.

For example, we set goals for customer satisfaction in the area of our hot line. Customers who were not very satisfied received extra effort from us. A group of five senior executives, including myself, got together and evolved a measure for responsiveness to a call-in.

We started off by guessing [at performance goals]. Then we did a survey. We had our marketing department call out to a twelfth of our customer base every month and ask them what they thought of the hot line. We began tracking where they were satisfied, where they weren't, and how that correlated with the goals we set. Over a couple of years, we found we needed to stiffen up on some of those goals. We also found we couldn't meet them in some places, and we had to make changes.

Existing goals are constantly evolving:

Just recently, we became concerned that we were only tracking the people who used the hot line. We were missing people who weren't using the hot line at all, because they weren't showing up in the database. We recognized it because there was a discussion about one of our field office manager's perception of the hot line versus what our metrics were showing. There was a difference. There were customers in that office who weren't using the hot line at all because of some less-than-favorable experiences with it a year ago. So that motivated another metric, which is How many of our total customers have not used the hot line at all in the last three to six months?

This is an iterative process that goes on forever. You're always finding something new and modifying the measure. The important thing is that the measure gave us a basis for modification and improvement.

Information as a Usable Commodity

In Crandall's case "The owner eats here" because better access to information and people allows him to do a better job of running his company and holding on to a market leadership position in his competitive industry.

Crandall's own use of information systems keeps him informed and personally focused on key areas, and it helps him to guide others in focusing on strategic factors. Crandall builds feedback loops specifically to focus attention—his and others'—on key performance factors. By distributing performance information in a highly visible way, he lets people know what is important and where they stand on their accomplishments.

He believes that the computer is critical to this leadership strategy, because it makes access to information easier. "Because everything and everyone is so accessible, everything flows from that. You're more likely to look at information, and you're more likely to use it for communication. The system makes information a usable commodity."

Crandall believes that, by measuring performance, he can influence the organization's culture. He consciously designs the computer-based feedback loops at Comshare as a coaching technique, to motivate others to focus on quality and customer satisfaction. "I use [the computer] to come up with new measurements that I know people will pay attention to, which in turn influences corporate culture."

EXECUTIVE SUMMARY

Crandall's emphasis on making information a usable commodity, highlights the fact that information is valuable only when it is channeled, compiled, and distributed in such a way that people take action as a result. The more accessible and visible information is, the more likely people are to act upon what they see.

If this is true, then an executive must be careful to design information systems that encourage the right kinds of actions. By being conscious of the power of the computer to guide behavior, Crandall demonstrates a thoughtful, planned approach to the design of many feedback loops for each of the firm's key strategic objectives.

Thomas Stephens, chairman, CEO, and president, Manville Corporation, analyzes financial alternatives.

Bill Gantz, president, Baxter International, reflects on company performance and competitive information during travel.

Debbi Fields, CEO and president, Mrs. Fields Cookies Inc., uses performance information to focus and motivate employees.

Burnell Roberts, chairman and CEO, Mead Corporation, uses a group database to develop and maintain a network of international contacts.

CHAPTER 14

The Baking
Business: Bits,
Bytes, and Chips

Debbi Fields

CEO and President, Mrs. Fields Cookies Inc.

It was a clear, crisp November morning when I wheeled my rented Jeep into the mountain town of Park City, Utah. I passed the Utah Coal and Lumber Restaurant where two (live) horses were tied to a hitching post in the "parking" lot. Half a block away stands an unlikely neighbor. The building at 333 Main Street houses the heart of a bakery empire—the headquarters for Mrs. Fields Cookies Incorporated.

The company's executive offices are tucked beneath a shopping mall, where, of course, you can buy Mrs. Fields Cookies and La Petite Boulangerie bakery products (a bakery chain owned by the Fields organization). The headquarters location is a fitting symbol of the Debbi Fields management philosophy: Stay close to your employees and your customers. In fact, as part of their ongoing education, headquarters employees take turns working behind the counter of this particular cookie store.

Legions of Legends

The stories about Debbi Fields are as numerous as the chips in her cookies. The one that has truly reached legendary proportions is about

143

how her husband, Randy Fields, bet Debbi that she couldn't sell $50 worth of cookies in her first day of operations. Of course, she did, and the rest is a history easily gleaned from magazines like *Inc.* and *Esquire,* or from her book, *One Smart Cookie.*

Smart is certainly the right word to describe Fields. Her intelligence is of the practical variety. Debbi Fields knows how to make people happy. And that is her true "secret ingredient."

I'm a first-hand witness to this magic. The night before our interview, there was a knock on the door of my hotel room. I hadn't ordered room service, and I didn't know a soul in Park City. My opened door revealed a smiling deliveryperson holding a mammoth, beribboned basket filled with cookies and baked goods. The attached card read: "Welcome to Park City! Love, Debbi Fields."

That kind of attention to detail has made Debbi Fields famous. It has also contributed to her ability to manage approximately 600 stores in five countries as "one big family." Though some people persist in believing that Randy Fields alone runs the company, a meeting with Debbi convinced me otherwise. The Fields team produces the results.

Coaching as a Growth Strategy

Debbi Fields is fanatical about product quality and customer satisfaction. That fanaticism caused her to stop and take stock before expanding from her original one-store location in Palo Alto, California. How could she ensure that cookies baked by someone else would be up to her standards? How could she pass on the "magic" of her sales expertise? Maintenance of quality in the face of growth was the key to continued success.

It was also important, from Randy's perspective, that management controls be instituted. Reporting mechanisms were essential to tracking operations, and the ability to track operations governed the pace of expansion.

Fields knew she couldn't personally run every store, and the traditional approach of top-down corporate decision making and tight controls over people hardly seemed appropriate. Success meant being responsive to customers' needs and adapting to the local community. This led to a common management paradox: To build a customer-focused, responsive organization, she had to truly delegate authority. Yet Fields had to ensure that others would run her stores as well as she could. Her leadership strategy is conceptually simple but a logistical challenge: She wanted to be "present" in every store—if not physically on site, at least there in spirit.

Ultimately, one means to implementing the strategy proved to be the computer, which Fields uses to *coach,* not control, her store managers. All Mrs. Fields locations have personal computers, which are linked by phone lines to one centralized minicomputer in Park City. Software for the computers was developed primarily by Randy, with programming assistance from a small staff.

The computers help Fields spread her presence throughout the organization, sharing her knack for running a successful store. Her coaching via computer takes a number of forms:

- Advice on marketing and operating decisions
- Establishment and distribution of tangible, fair, and immediate performance goals
- Presence through communications
- Personalized recognition of both good and poor performance
- Tracking follow-through on commitments

Each form of coaching constitutes a business strategy.

Business Strategy: Advice

One of the most interesting computer applications is aimed at solving Debbi's problem of passing along her baking and sales expertise. Her years of experience and systematic approach to running a store are captured in an expert system that can be accessed through the store computers. The system factors in historical operating data to help employees make key decisions. With all it offers, the system is—in effect—Mrs. Fields-In-A-Box.

The expert system gives employees advice on issues such as how many cookies to bake, when to bake them, and when to do "sampling" (taking cookie samples out into malls or streets and offering them free to passers-by) or "bartering" (negotiating with customers at the end of the day to reduce the number of leftover cookies).

"The computer is like a box of consultants," explained Debbi. "I'm one of those consultants, Randy's one of those consultants, and the people who built this company are consultants. We tell employees: 'Based on history, based on what we know, based on standards, here are our recommendations.' The system helps with their decision making, and it helps to maintain the culture of the organization. I want people to have guidance and support as though we were there to help them."

Employees are by no means forced to use the system to make decisions. The computer simply makes suggestions. Debbi explains: "Our job is not to tell people how to run the business. It's their job to run the business. Computers don't run the store; people do. Someone who has been with the store for a long time will use their own judgment because they have a feel for the business. But if a new manager walks in, they can't just instantly 'feel' it. You've got to give them some history."

"The machines can only know the past," interjects Randy Fields. "They do not understand that a bus just pulled up to the door."

Debbi went on to explain how the system makes suggestions. "The suggestions it offers the person running the store are ranked from the highest potential opportunity to the least. It shows people the most highly leveraged actions they can take." For example, if sales are down, the computer will offer a range of suggestions for getting sales back up. Based on the situation, it might suggest sampling or some other method for bringing sales back up to speed. Each of these suggestions is placed in order of its potential impact, from highest to lowest.

Debbi summarizes: "The expert system doesn't tell you what to do: It gives you insights into the business." This expert system gives store managers the feeling that Debbi Fields is available and ready to support them if they need her.

Business Strategy: Tangible, Fair, and Immediate Goals

What motivates people to seek help from the expert system? To know when they need help, people have to be able to compare their performance to an ideal or standard. Thus, another key aspect to Debbi's coaching is providing tangible, fair, and immediate goals.

"When people talk to me about 15-year plans, I just roll my eyes," says Debbi. "That sounds wonderful, but is it really realistic? What can I do about it today? What I did at our very first store was set hourly goals . . . because if you focus on this hour, this increment, this moment, you'll get to where you want to go."

The computer gives employees hourly sales goals to help them gauge their performance. These sales goals are based on past history for that particular store. The expert system takes into account the fact that it may be a holiday, or a school day, or a sale day. Concrete, reachable goals are essential to Debbi's management philosophy.

When people are running behind their goals, they can ask the computer for advice—while there's still time to do something about the situation. "There's nothing worse than closing a store and saying, 'Wow, I'm down $200 for the day. How depressing.' [With hourly goals] you can say, long before the day is over, 'I'm down $12 on the day so far. I can do something about that.'"

Fields summarized this particular coaching strategy. "The key was to teach people, to empower them, to let them know that they *could* really do something about [problems]. We challenged them to go out and sample if that's what they needed to do. . . . Do whatever it takes to get back on track. Conversely, when they were on track, they felt great."

This coaching strategy will only work if the goals are set properly. Too low, and they become meaningless. Too high, and they become demotivational. To ensure fair goals, Fields does time-and-motion studies to check on what it really takes to accomplish all the tasks associated with running a store. Once standards are set, they are incorporated into the software.

> Every year, things change. You add something that makes the business more complicated, and you haven't given the manager credit for that. Or there might be opportunities for greater efficiencies. So I go to the stores and I challenge our systems. I open, close, and run the entire operation to find out if I can do what I expect others to do.
>
> I go out and do it myself because I'm not as skilled. When I place muffins into muffin pans, it's going to take longer than it would take a baker. But I want it to be that way, because if there's a new person coming in, you don't build your standards to the most efficient. You need to give them flexibility.

By going out and doing this work herself, Fields builds credibility with employees; and she has a benchmark for rating performance. "That way, I can always say, 'Hey, listen, I know you can do it.' Because people will sometimes say, 'I can't.' And I'll say, 'If you can't, then show me why you can't, because I can show you why we can.'"

Of course, while she is out in the field conducting these studies, she gets a tremendous amount of input from employees about the way the system should be designed. "The systems are always in a state of refinement. When I go to the stores, I ask them, 'What do you think?' And they tell me. Sometimes they say, 'Debbi, I hate this program. I think we could be more organized.' And while we're standing together in the freezer, we'll figure out a better arrangement."

Thus, the information system has become a two-way channel for communicating expectations and performance opportunities.

From Cookies to Croissants

In addition to helping employees, the expert system has also enhanced Debbi's mental framework for understanding how stores operate. "The baking standards don't change. But as we develop new products and as we have our store management place more emphasis on sales, we change certain rules in the system. The expert system teaches me, too. It teaches me new ways to think about problem solving and store management."

The expert system became one medium by which Debbi learned and launched an entirely new business. In 1987, the Fieldses purchased the La Petite Boulangerie bakery chain from Pepsico. The challenge of maintaining the Mrs. Fields quality standards across dispersed locations is the same. Debbi and Randy are taking the same systematic approach to setting up the stores, except that this time, the process is more complicated. Debbi explains one aspect of the challenge:

> I've been very involved in setting up the bakery software. It's a much more complicated system. So the key is to make it as simple as possible. We have 13 kinds of cookies at Mrs. Fields and we make 7 flavors each day. But with the bakeries, we're talking about 50 products.
>
> You've got to keep things coming out of the oven fresh, all day long. You're dealing with more products, more variety, more potential problems. You've got to understand baking time lines. What cooks first? How does it go in the oven? Where does it go in the oven? How do you transfer it out and keep it fresh? It's a very challenging business, but it can be computerized.

This exercise—learning the new business while developing the expert system—brought Debbi very close to an entirely new population of employees. The new expert system was another extension of her presence, and it helped her influence the standards for a new company as it came into the corporate family.

Business Strategy: Presence Through Communications

The expert system helped Debbi address her first two "presence" objectives—giving advice and setting immediate goals. But she uses different information tools to address the remaining three strategies.

Her third strategy—being present in the stores, and available to the people she leads—isn't easy to achieve in such a geographically dispersed organization. Even though she spends a great deal of time on the road visiting her stores, her face-to-face time with employees is limited by the size and dispersion of the company.

Fields finds a voice message system to be valuable in connecting her with her "family." She says: "Phone mail is wonderful because you hear emotion, and because you're in touch with people you don't know. If I didn't have phone mail, my secretary could take all my messages. But then I'd never know who these people are. I'd never know what they had to say to me. I think that's impersonal."

Even though Fields likes to hear people's voices, that fact doesn't preclude her use of electronic mail as well. "I constantly send [electronic-mail] messages to store managers, and everybody has access to sending a message to me. That's very important to me because sometimes there are people who have problems and concerns. They're frustrated, and that should be heard. And there are people who have great ideas, people who just want to say hello, or who just want to know I'm there."

Usually, Fields's secretary picks up her electronic-mail messages and prints them out for her, always sending a quick response to let the sender know the message has been received. "Every person who logs on gets an instant reply from me saying, 'Debbi's got it.' My secretary handles that. If I'm gone for five days, I don't want these people sitting there waiting for a response." But her secretary doesn't screen her messages. "I don't want my messages to be screened. Even if my secretary takes care of fixing a problem, I want to know about it. I'll even know when there's a problem such as, 'Debbi, I didn't receive my insurance form.' My secretary immediately handles it, and I have a copy of the message. Of course, sometimes I'm the only person who can handle a particular problem."

Through both types of communication tools, Fields makes people throughout her 600-store organization feel that she's close by.

Business Strategy: Recognition—Good and Bad

Her fourth "presence" strategy involves personally recognizing both good and bad performance. Again, she wanted to do so without any semblance of top-down control.

Because Debbi wants to manage employees without breathing down their necks, the recognition process involves the sharing of information. "If I have information about someone's performance— either good or bad—I want that person to either have it before me or have it at the same time I get it. That way, if it's good, I know they are beaming with joy, just waiting for me to acknowledge their terrific performance. If it's not so good, I know whether they have chosen to act upon it and correct it."

A tool that aids her in this ranking process is a spreadsheet:

> I use Lotus 1-2-3 to rank people and their performance. I look at people by all of the food-group categories. Who sells the most cookies? Which district manager sells the most muffins? I then rank those people from top to bottom. I post the results on the system so they get a perspective of, 'Hey, I feel great. I'm wonderful.' But the people on the bottom are important too. If everybody is positive in muffin sales, and there are just two district managers who aren't, then there's an anomaly. I use that information to help them improve their performance.

Fields summarizes her open approach to performance monitoring. "I'm not a numbers person, but what I believe in is good feedback and letting people know where they rank in relationship to everybody else." People throughout the organization know that Debbi knows them personally, and cares about their performance. Once again, she is using the information systems to make her presence felt.

Business Strategy: Follow-Through

Debbi points out that recognition is only the first step in a business improvement process. "You've got to recognize the great performers. Then you've got to identify all those individuals who've chosen not to follow through on the key components of the business and find out what they're doing about improving their performance. You need to know their plan of action and get agreement on a time frame for fixing the problem." In other words, the result of a coaching session is often a commitment to improve some aspect of business practice. Once Fields has worked with employees to identify areas for improvement, her fifth "presence" strategy is to ensure that people follow through on their commitments.

Fields uses a commitment-tracking system to keep her on top of what she is expecting of others. "I keep all my notes to myself in Lotus Agenda. It tracks all the things that I've asked people to do, and it serves as a reminder; it's a call to action." By tracking promises, Fields not only discovers whether or not commitments are being met, but she also becomes aware of the demands she is making. She finds that it is easy to expect too much of people when you're not keeping track of all the projects they're working on. "I sometimes ask myself, 'Oh my gosh, am I pushing them too hard?' Sometimes you overcommit people. Suddenly you realize that maybe the reason they're not successful is because you've given them too much work."

The system gives her a summary of all the deliverables that everyone owes her. "It shows me how much I've got on people's plates. This allows you to constantly see what you're asking of people, and it's in front of you each day. Boy, it's really insightful. Now, basically everyone who works with me is on it. We can Agendacize together! It's been a great tool."

Fields knows that good coaches must set an example for others by impeccable follow-through on their own commitments. Thus, she feels it is just as important to track her own commitments as it is to track the commitments of others. Fields also uses the commitment-tracking system for this purpose. "When people ask me to do things for them, I plug all that in. The key is to keep my little list small," says Fields, laughing.

Though she may joke about keeping her list small, she takes her commitments seriously. "I used to wake up in the middle of the night thinking I had forgotten things. I don't do that anymore since I have this tool. Everything I have to do, even my notes, I put on Agenda. So I don't worry. If I don't do it, it's because I choose not to. There's nothing worse than telling someone you're going to do something and then forgetting it."

With so many commitments and demands on her time, it is essential that Fields set priorities. The commitment-tracking system helps her do that as well:

> I was a "to-do" person. I absolutely used to be among the trophy winners of the to-do lists. Unfortunately, I learned the hard way that many of the things on the to-do list didn't really accomplish a result. They were really a waste of time.
>
> I try to teach people that it's a big mistake to put down what you want to *do*. What if you're crossing off a lot of things that are not important to your company or your boss? Instead, think about what you want to *accomplish*. Then be the driver of those accomplishments. It's a real change.
>
> Agenda has helped me do that because it pops up only what I consider to be the priorities. What I love about this system is that it sorts things for me. It balances my thinking style. I love detail, but I don't want to get bogged down in detail. The machine sorts through the detail for me, highlights the most important points, and helps keep me focused on the right things. Because it keeps me focused, it helps me keep the organization focused.

This fifth strategy brings Fields's presence to the project level. People knows she cares about their milestones and deliverables, and she brings her "family" together with a clear sense of corporate priorities.

The Attributes of a Good Cookie Coach

"I like to challenge people, and I like watching people take on more responsibility. I am constantly coaching. People don't always like what I say. It's always easy to tell somebody how wonderful they are, and that's very much a part of my personality. But it's also part of my job to specifically identify what they could be doing better."

Fields takes her coaching job seriously. She characterizes two aspects of effective coaching:

- First, coaches must have the right information in a timely fashion to be well-informed leaders.
- Second, coaches must be creative in helping people identify solutions.

Geographic dispersion makes these challenges more difficult for Fields. In each of these areas of personal effectiveness, Fields creatively tapped the power of the computer to improve her capabilities.

Knowledgeability

Employees know that they have access to Debbi if they need her. But simply being accessible to employees isn't sufficient for excellent coaching. Fields must be well-informed if she is to be trusted and respected by her employees and if her presence in the stores is to have a positive impact on results.

This first attribute of a good coach is a real understanding of business operations. For this, Debbi accesses internal databases. "I stay on top of the key pulse points of the business. I make sure it's heading in the right direction. I hate *reacting*. And it's something that happens in business. As much as possible, I want to be proactive."

Data is not enough. Fields must filter it and decide what problems she wants to tackle. "The problem is that there are so many things to work on. There are so many problems and so many opportunities. Which ones do you do first?" Together, the Fieldses found a clever aid. "Randy approached that challenge with volume weighting . . . [finding the] biggest bang for the buck."

A volume-weighting model assigns values to specific variables in an equation. Based on the mathematical equations, the model can sort through information and point out the primary areas of concern. "Now I can see that if I fix these three stores, it will solve 50 percent of my problem. For example, let's say I see that my cost of goods is too high. I can immediately pull up the cost of goods for all of my stores, and it shows me which ones I need to fix."

This type of information is logged in daily by employees at the stores and archived at the Park City location, giving Debbi the latest information available. "We just started using this tool; and frankly, it's the best thing that ever happened to me. You naturally feel more effective. You're focusing your attention and your people's attention on things that will get results."

Once she identifies the key issues and people that need her assistance, Fields reaches out to those people. In addition to her long-distance access to people via electronic mail and the voice message system, Fields believes in face-to-face contact. She logs hundreds of thousands of miles a year traveling to stores. "Ask my people. I drive them crazy. I spend a lot of time on the road. What the computer does is give me information so that I'm better equipped to know the manager of the store."

By dialing into the Park City computer while she is traveling, Debbi pick ups the precise information she needs before visiting a store. "I download [operational information] on my laptop when I'm traveling. It can give me a daily report on how every store in this company performed yesterday. Sales, customer counts, and so on. I look at keys that I think are vital to the business."

Such up-to-date information is important to the coaching process. By arriving well-informed, Fields can use precious time with employees to discuss solutions to problems rather than discussing what the problems are. "When I walk into a store, I already know how it's performing. It's absolutely clear that nobody can tell me something in operations that I do not know. That knowledge helps me gain credibility with employees. And I give managers straight feedback on where they stand. I want them to hear it directly from me, so that it doesn't come down through three levels that, 'This is what Debbi said.'"

Debbi also uses this operational information in the office. "It's so fast. I can punch up a store automatically. So when someone calls and says, 'Debbi, did you see what I did yesterday?' I can punch in their store number and say, 'Wow! Isn't that impressive?'"

Debbi could delegate the work she does on the computer to an assistant, but she feels it would make her less effective. "It's just so much easier for me to use it myself. I can query it and ask questions. It's very different from looking at a piece of paper. I can look at things the way I want to look at them. After asking questions, I can do my own evaluation."

In this application, the computer helps Fields make the most of her face-to-face presence when visiting the stores or in conversations with her people. By being well-informed, she focuses on areas that most need her help, makes better use of her time with people, and leaves them feeling that she is close to them and their business operations.

Creativity

Second, a good coach must come up with creative solutions to problems—or, more proactively, create ways to tap future opportunities.

In addition to looking at data about what happened yesterday, Fields uses computers to help her brainstorm about what might happen tomorrow. She uses a simple but valuable off-the-shelf expert system for thinking through issues and opportunities:

> I've got another program called The Idea Generator. It challenges you to think. You know how sometimes you're stuck on a problem? Well, it doesn't give you answers; it just asks you questions. Then it helps you come to better conclusions, because you have to think through the whole scenario . . . the good, the bad, the what if's, and the ideas you might be overlooking. It's given me a real good perspective when I'm stuck or if I'm basing a decision too much on my emotions.

Of course, when you feel as strongly as Debbi Fields feels about many things, the inevitable occurs. "There are times that I just feel strongly about an idea, but I haven't thought it through enough. Then I like to go and use my idea generator just to help me think of new ideas, new innovations, and get unstuck. Then there are times that I'll just make the emotional decision anyway because I *believe* in it!"

She may be strong-minded, but Fields certainly is not close-minded. She pushes herself and tests her assumptions, using the computer to bring objectivity to her thought process.

Interwoven Organization and Systems Design

From the outset, Randy Fields helped Debbi design an organization that could meet her objectives for quality through her "presence" in every store. The distance between Debbi Fields and her store managers may be wide in terms of geography, but it is short in terms of access, reporting levels, and management knowledge about operations.

Debbi wanted close contact with the people in her stores, which translates into fewer reporting levels. Far earlier than most executives, Randy Fields knew that computers could help shape flatter, more responsive organizations. By giving top management the controls it needs to ensure success and providing employees with the information they need to make decisions, computers provide a link between management and operations that precludes the need for multiple management levels.

"We have basically four reporting levels," Debbi explains. "The managers of the individual stores report to a district sales manager, who is responsible for about six stores. Those sales managers report to regional directors. Each regional director is responsible for anywhere from 30 to 60 sales managers. The regional directors report to the director of operations, who in turn reports directly to me."

With such a flat structure, some people might anticipate that management would become overburdened, but this is not a problem. In fact, because the computer provides information to all levels of the Fields organization, people are encouraged to make decisions and solve problems at much lower levels rather than having to get approvals or resolve issues through the chain of command.

Debbi and Randy's objective was to create an organization in which middle management spent much of its time focusing on people, rather than being bogged down in control issues. Randy helped her design systems that shifted middle management's attention away from administration and more toward the customer. "I frankly don't want to rely on middle management to inform everyone," says Debbi. "I think middle management is important, but I think they should be focused on developing people, maintaining our image, and bringing in new customers. I want to get them out of the mode of control."

Middle managers at Mrs. Fields Cookies need not be concerned that their positions will be replaced by computers. Instead, the computers at Mrs. Fields have been set up to support the functions of middle managers, freeing them to do the more interesting work that computers cannot do:

> We set up our information systems so that managers know that the company is working for them. They're working to improve the company, and, conversely, they need to know the company is working for them. I believe in generating systems that provide great feedback and simplification, so that we can focus on what we do best. We give managers systems to help with the kinds of things they don't want to bother with, such as inventory control and paperwork for new hires. They don't *want* to spend their time on control when they can be doing more important things.

Debbi Fields believes that, in the future, most organizations will be designed in a similar fashion to Mrs. Fields Cookies. "The future is to do more with less. You'll have much less bureaucracy and much more timely information, faster response rates, and higher customer expectations. The customer is going to expect more and more."

The New Style of Executive

Randy Fields believes that flatter, more responsive, less bureaucratic organizations will change the role of top management. "Right now, about 5 percent of what executives do is inspiration. Ninety-five percent of what they do is sell ideas down the system. The use of expert systems and artificial intelligence will obviate that."

Randy speculates that, in the future, "Huge ranks of middle managers who only process data from the left in box to the right out box will probably be virtually eliminated. People will handle exceptions and rule determination; they really won't handle process work. That whole service cadre will have fundamentally redefined jobs."

Randy believes that Debbi is a pioneer not only in her use of computers, but more broadly as a new style of leader. "Jobs for executives will be much more in the style of Debbi—motivational, inspirational, and conceptual," says Randy.

Given Randy's description of Debbi's role, I asked Debbi about her vision for the company. Her response perfectly illustrates Randy's point: "I don't have a vision. I have very clear views of what needs to be done for the consumer and for our people, and I haven't achieved them yet. People feel so compelled to say they have a 'vision.' The real question is, 'Do they have a *view*?' Are they willing to live or die for it, no matter what? I'm willing to do that."

Debbi Fields creatively uses computers to enhance her ability to "mentor"—to pass along her views in ways that motivate others. "The computer keeps score for me. It tells me who's winning today and who needs help. It's my recognition tool, and it's a tool to help with a pep talk. Without it, I don't know how I'd function. I can't call 600 stores a day. I'd lose control of the business. All of the stores are like my little family; and, without the computer, I'd feel totally disconnected."

EXECUTIVE SUMMARY

Fields emphasizes her coaching (not controlling) responsibilities as a leader and how she uses every available resource to be continuously "present" in every store—working alongside her people for their mutual success. There's no question that Debbi Fields would be a good coach with or without computers. But it is also true that computers significantly expand the depth, breadth, and reach of her natural coaching abilities.

The expert system is a medium for putting her knowledge at people's fingertips. And other information tools help Fields identify areas of importance to the company, focus on the people who need assistance, track the commitments they have made to improve performance, and then recognize their successes.

Fields has built systemic ways of motivating and rewarding the people in her organization. The success of her coaching is not dependent upon her physical presence. Rather, she has used the computer to put mechanisms in place that incorporate her approach but do not require her constant involvement. With this approach, she also avoids the need for vigilant middle management to oversee the actions of others. Through a broad array of information tools, Fields has improved her personal coaching capabilities and has maximized the impact of those skills across an entire organization.

PART SUMMARY

Throughout Part IV, we have discussed an emerging style of leadership. In organizations of the past, the motivation of others relied largely on charisma or punishment. Coaching is an approach that goes beyond reliance on charismatic or punitive leadership. Coaching encourages people to internalize approaches to problems and opportunities, thus making success less dependent on the leader's constant influence and presence. In other words, coaching builds and develops self-sufficient people.

In order to make these types of lasting changes, leaders must first gain the trust and respect of the people they are coaching by being well-informed. Then they must find ways of leveraging their coaching efforts—they cannot serve as effective coaches to large numbers of people on a daily basis through conventional face-to-face meetings alone.

These leaders use a variety of information tools to stay informed and gain the respect of the "teams" they coach. Internal and external databases, financial models, electronic mail, voice messaging, and spreadsheets all help these leaders to gain the kind of knowledge that allow them to ask the right questions.

These executives leverage their coaching efforts through information tools as well. By creating performance feedback loops in the form of expert systems and internal distribution of performance data, they are able to guide people in spite of spatial and temporal separation.

With the assistance of computers, these leaders influence and motivate people in positive, creative, and systemic ways.

V

THE
LEADER
AS
CHANGE
AGENT

Shifting Power
and Responsibility

Part V

When circumstances create crises or opportunities, an organization must often respond by making immediate and significant changes. This goes far beyond the concept of continuous improvement, that is, of doing a bit better what the organization did in the past. Rather, flexibly responding to changing external conditions often demands fundamental transformations in the way the organization works.

Executives serve as the architects of such change. In addition to *responding* to crises or opportunities, they must *anticipate* them. By anticipating change, leaders can mold and shape their organizations in ways that allow them to respond ever more quickly to the dictates of business, social, and political influences.

How do leaders create organizations that embrace change instead of shunning it? Shifting power and responsibility further down in an organization is one way that leaders make organizations more fluid, flexible, and open to change. By empowering people at lower levels, executives enable organizations to deal with more variety. Organizations can respond more fully because the people making decisions are closer to the problems and opportunities. In addition, the organization can respond more quickly because people making decisions are not constrained by a bureaucracy.

All the executives in Part V faced the need for major change within their organizations. Each responded by creating systems and procedures that put power into the hands of people who could best resolve issues and problems. Though he was not facing a crisis of major proportions, Ron Compton recognized the need to make Aetna more fluid, flexible, and responsive. Changes in the financial services industry underscored the need for the company to be "quick, flexible, and right." Compton employed an impressive array of information systems—at both the personal and the organizational level—to aid him in his role as an architect of change.

Competition from small regional competitors who were able to stay close to customers drove Frito-Lay's decision to decentralize decision making. Michael Jordan describes how information systems support and enhance his ability to shift responsibility to field operations and how this shift helps the organization respond to unique local markets.

162

The most dramatic need for change occurs during an emergency. Bob Wallace faced a crisis of staggering proportions after two takeover attempts at Phillips 66. The organization could not afford to wait for decisions to be approved through successive levels of a bureaucracy. He determined that the only way to weather the storm was to downsize the company and then put power in the hands of the line managers who made daily operating decisions.

Wallace faced the familiar conundrum of shifting power and responsibility downward, while maintaining management controls. Wallace describes how information systems enabled him to empower line operations while improving the executives' ability to manage and set strategy for the organization. The changes that Wallace made in the face of a crisis not only enabled the company to get back on its feet, but also prepared it to be a more highly adaptable organization in the future.

CHAPTER 15

Quick, Flexible, and Right

Ron Compton

President, Aetna Life & Casualty Co.

Ron Compton, president of Aetna Life & Casualty, is a charismatic person with substance—qualities that don't often come in the same package. When he talks about something, you believe it can indeed happen.

However, talk of making huge conglomerates "quick and flexible in responding to changing conditions" and "right in making key decisions" is a bit hard to believe—even when the message is coming from Ron Compton. Large corporations remind me of ocean liners. They have a purpose, but it's unlikely that they'll hold their own in a speedboat race.

But Ron Compton is refuting my ocean-liner analogy at Aetna. He has a plan for making the company "quick, flexible, and right."

Compton explains the importance of this mission:

When guiding a corporation, you have to recognize that the future is virtually unknowable. If you want a company that is going to deal successfully—not defensively, but opportunistically—with a fundamentally unknowable future, what would be the characteristics of that company?

First of all, you have to be quick, because lead times are down to nothing. You're also going to have to be flexible, because what works today won't work tomorrow. And you're going to have to be right; you can't afford to be wrong.

Disadvantages of Size in an Unstable Environment

When I interviewed him for my previous book, Compton was the president of American Reinsurance Company (American Re), a subsidiary of Aetna Life and Casualty. Since that meeting, he has ascended quickly through the executive ranks to his current position as president of the entire Aetna financial conglomerate, which has in excess of $81 billion in assets.

Compton took this new position during a period of considerable instability for the financial services industry. Insurance claims are increasing in number and size because of increased costs in a number of areas. Medical advances are expensive; automobiles are more complex and, hence, more costly to repair or replace. Assets are down because of a collapse in the real estate market, a weak stock market, and the demise of the junk-bond market. And insurance premiums are vulnerable because of increased competition from deregulated and diversified banking and brokerage firms, as well as political pressure to regulate the insurance industry.

To respond to these environmental challenges, Compton knew he would have to make the company responsive. But *quick* and *flexible* were not appropriate adjectives to describe Aetna at the time Compton took his position. The internal decision-making process was not up to speed to meet the increased demands of the external environment.

Furthermore, people within the company were not always working together for common goals. "You don't have the feeling of a single family [in such a large organization]. What you have are four or five families. And with four or five families, you get a couple of feuds. They're all well-meaning and they love each other . . . until the chips are down. Then, they love themselves a little more," Compton explains, laughing.

Divisions were separate from each other, operating autonomously and not taking advantage of synergies and each other's strengths. They looked after the needs of their division, but not necessarily for Aetna overall. Thus, some of the advantages of size were lost, while the disadvantages remained. The results were reflected in many areas, including productivity and customer service. Compton says, "When compared with the rest of the industry, our productivity and customer service were pretty good. But they were still not what Jim Lynn [Aetna's chairman] and I wanted them to be at all."

In other words, Compton faced a paradox: He wanted the company to work toward similar overall goals, to turn size into an advantage. But their businesses were quite distinct. Clearly, better alignment and streamlining were needed. But how do you get everyone headed in the same direction when people have differing lower-level objectives?

Compton notes that scale significantly exacerbated the problem:

> This is a *big* place. Aetna has 44,000 people. So the first thing you have to do is figure out how to deal with the sheer size of it. You can't directly reach 44,000 people. You try to influence key people, and you try to influence the policies and decision-making process in order to make them consistent with the overall goals of the organization.
>
> I think [the problem of scale is] also a function of the diversity. At American Re, there were really only two businesses, and those two even overlapped. Here, that's not true. The businesses are very distinct from one another, even in their distribution systems. So you have to figure out how to knit the company together in order to achieve the goal of quick, flexible, and right.

Somehow, Compton and Lynn had to get lower-level objectives aligned with the overall strategic direction of the company. They had to establish a unifying theme and teach people to accomplish their diverse, unique, individual objectives within that theme. "It's the same problem as in philosophy—my old field—where [it is said that] anything that is universal is meaningless. As executives, we have to make general statements in order for them to be applicable to everyone in the company. But the more general the statement, the less meaning it has for the individual. So how do you knit people together if the general statements have no meaning?"

To meet the challenges with which they were faced, Compton and Lynn first directed the focus of the company toward a unifying theme. "The first thing we did was to introduce the notion of quick, flexible, and right as sort of a 'corporate character' goal. We did that with speeches and my appearances at the Aetna Institute training programs. We pounded on the theme that this company was going to be quick, flexible, and right. We even put it in our annual report."

Once the theme was established in peoples' minds, tangible steps had to be taken to achieve that goal. Part of the action plan included building a corporate-wide focus on the few critical areas of the business that demanded attention. This focus was to be directed with a management approach developed by Compton: the Aetna Management Process (AMP).

"We're AMPing That One!"

The AMP process had a history dating back to Compton's tenure at American Reinsurance. At American Re, Compton was instrumental in designing his own executive information system (EIS). In doing so, he went through a process of identifying critical areas of the business and then worked directly with his information systems staff to ensure that they delivered a system that gave him direct feedback on his objectives.*

Compton describes the experience:

> When I sat down to design what I wanted from my [information] system at American Re, I did it by looking at the critical success factors of the business. Some people call them levers, and some people call them drivers. Out of that came the feeling that the company was not paying enough attention to these things, and I began to wonder why. It occurred to me that either people didn't understand what we were there to do or they hadn't really sat down and figured out what it takes to get it done.
>
> Half of our problem was that people thought we were there to sell reinsurance. We weren't there to sell reinsurance. We were there to make money. Of course we had a lot of other objectives; but if we didn't make money, we weren't going to be around to do all those other wonderful things.

At American Re, Compton designed a system based on critical success factors. This system helped him focus people on key areas of concern. The process of designing his *computer* system at American Re gave Compton the kernel of an idea for a *management* system for Aetna. He developed a simple, yet elegant, step-by-step approach to teaching people how to focus on critical areas of the business. That approach was the AMP, which is described in Figure 2. "We now

---

*For a more thorough account of Compton's success at American Re, see Dean Meyer and Mary Boone, *The Information Edge* (Homewood, IL: Dow-Jones Irwin, 1989), pp. 234–238.

FIGURE 2
THE AETNA MANAGEMENT PROCESS (AMP)

1. Identify your mission in highly specific terms.
2. Identify critical success factors associated with that particular mission. Again, specificity is of the utmost importance.
3. Scan and describe factors in both the internal and external environments that impinge upon those critical success factors.
4. Identify gaps between where you are and where you want to be.
5. Set measurable objectives for closing those gaps.
6. Set action steps and a time line for each objective.
7. Put a system in place to monitor performance. (This system may or may not be automated.)

---

have a new verb around here: 'to AMP,'" says Compton, smiling. "When I say to someone, 'Are you getting something figured out for *XYZ* problem?' they'll say, 'Don't worry, Ron, we're AMPing that right now.'"

By helping achieve alignment of objectives and purpose, the AMP approach is helping people at Aetna make "right" decisions. As people begin to work in the service of similar overall goals, the company is improving its ability to respond more quickly and with greater flexibility to changes in the external environment.

Communicating the AMP Message

For AMP to work, the process has to be communicated, and people at every level of the company must acquire new management skills. Coaching the entire corporation became a key leadership challenge for Compton.

Of course, Compton used conventional means of employee communications. He got out and made numerous face-to-face appearances to explain the AMP. In addition, he helped design a training program that teaches the AMP skills to key people in the organization. Compton appears in person for the classes for VPs. For levels below that, he appears in a videotape at the beginning of the course. But in such a large organization, there is a limit to the number of workshops that can be given. Compton needed a way to infuse the AMP discipline into a far broader cross-section of employees than conventional means of communication would allow.

In this context, Compton's creative thinking about information systems is paying off. In fact, Compton is quite adept at using technology in support of his objectives for the AMP, both at his level and at lower levels. He is relying on two types of information systems to disseminate the AMP message:

- A database that provides feedback on critical success factors
- An expert system that will guide people through the process

The AMP Information System

Compton remembered how his use of the information system at American Re helped to focus other people on his key goals. To repeat this success in such a large and diverse setting was much more complex. It was not a matter of tracking a few company objectives, but rather a complex hierarchy of interrelated critical success factors.

When he got to Aetna, Compton participated in the customization of an EIS. The system was specifically designed to track the critical success factors defined by the AMP process. The new system allows him to track the corporate-level critical success factors, across all Aetna's businesses. "The EIS consists of three things. The first is management numerical data, the second is interpretation of the data, and the third is a [progress] tracking system for the key issues the company is working on."

The information system contains a combination of tables, graphs, and text:

I learned something from my experience at American Re. I used to tell people that I wanted information in graphical form because it is a universal language. Everybody understands color and shape. But I forgot that if you don't put the [textual] interpretation with it, you can't sort out all of the different opinions of the people who put the information together.

> The interpretive material in [the information system] allows people who report to me to look at the reports about operations in their areas and tell me which interpretations they don't agree with and why. The people who report to them have participated in that interpretation.

Compton says the system gives him indicators of how people are performing on the corporation's critical success factors. He provided an example of the type of information the system delivers to him:

> One of the critical success factors in this business is price. Therefore, I need to know what rates we think we need, and what rates the regulatory authorities are going to let us have.
>
> Suppose we need to charge 6, and the regulatory agencies are only willing to let us charge 3. Then you have a gap. There are several potential gap closers. Either we are going to have to operate with less money, or we are going to have to get out of the business, or we are going to have to convince the regulatory authorities to let us charge more. The question is What are we doing to close the gap?
>
> The system highlights the gaps, tells me how we are doing, and it shows the potential gap closers.

The information system has been in place for less than a year, but Compton says the results are already apparent. "The main difference is that people are now able to answer more of the questions we ask. And they have questions of their own. Instead of simply giving me data, people are now giving me information on what the data mean. They figure it out, and then they tell me. Telling me is an afterthought. The real issue here is getting those managers to think about their businesses and explore what's going on."

Compton elaborates on what happens when he watches key indicators. "To me, the success of a system like this is characterized by the fact that people are more in command of their businesses. I don't want to have to ask the question What are you doing about this? That means people aren't doing their jobs. In an ideal world, executives wouldn't have to ask any questions."

Executives at Aetna know what Compton is watching. Therefore, they are beginning to respond in a proactive way. They make more decisions and adjustments ahead of time, instead of using excuses to respond to questions after the fact. Compton explains that he is trying to move the company toward perfecting this process. "In that ideal world, the information an executive would get would be so complete that the questions wouldn't *need* to be asked. The perfect situation is when a piece of data pops up, the division head looks at it and says, 'This is going to raise a question in somebody's mind. Therefore, it's raising a question in my mind.' So he answers the question. Then, when I get the data with the question and the answer, I know he's thought through it."

Training others to anticipate questions is an important goal for Compton. In a business of this size, one or two people cannot possibly keep tabs on everything. Delegation is an imperative. On the other hand, Compton and Lynn need to retain control of the overall business and assure the board that the proper actions are being taken. This creates a common executive paradox: Delegation is quickly undermined when the boss meddles in the details.

Compton provides an example of how the system provides information without undermining the managers:

> Let's say someone has a critical success factor to raise prices by 6 percent, and at the end of the year prices are only going up by 4 percent. When I hear it's only 4 percent, I simultaneously want to know that a total and complete analysis has been done of why that's the case and what corrective actions have been taken. So when I get that 4 percent piece of data [on the system], it contains a full explanation of why it has occurred and what they're doing about it.

Through his personal use of the computer, Compton sends signals to people about what concerns him. And by requiring their analysis of the data along with the facts, people develop the habit of thinking through business problems and solving them on their own. Compton believes that the AMP approach and the accompanying executive information system will help empower people to make better business decisions and align corporate and lower-level objectives, thus melding the company into a single unit and allowing it to respond flexibly and quickly.

President as Personal Tutor

Getting people focused on the right issues is only part of Compton's challenge. In addition, he wants everyone to acquire the AMP management skills. He wants people at all levels of the company to apply the seven-step AMP approach to their own personal objectives.

Aetna invests heavily in training. It developed a management competency training program associated with the AMP. Training, of course, is just a beginning. People must incorporate new skills into their daily management practice. This is when coaching becomes important. Obviously, Compton can not personally coach everyone in the day-to-day application of the AMP to their jobs; yet this, essentially, is what is needed.

Compton figured out a clever answer to this problem. "I am having a knowledge-based expert system built which will be used for many, many applications. The expert system will contain all of the knowledge that is imparted in the AMP workshops. The expert system is a training device that will teach the seven-step AMP checklist."

According to Compton, the AMP process—captured in the expert system—will help people take large, amorphous organizational goals and break them down into more tangible and meaningful objectives. "Let's say we establish a mission statement for the overall organization for a certain level of profitability. Now it's up to all of the different parts of the business to figure out what their piece of that mission is. Then, through the AMP, they determine what it's going to take to meet that goal."

Compton explains how the AMP will be incorporated into the expert system:

> You can take any subject, and the expert system will run you through the AMP and ask you all the appropriate questions. It will create a file that captures the information you put in as you are answering the questions. Then the expert system will compile the information. When you are finished, you will be able to print out the entire AMP analysis on your chosen subject.
>
> So, through the expert system, people will learn about the process; they will think through a problem; and then, at the end, they will have something that they can hand to someone else for discussion.

Once people go through the AMP, they have a clear and concise statement of their goals and objectives, and they have articulated the process by which they will attain those goals. Then Compton's executive information system provides him with a feedback loop that tells him how well people are performing on the goals they set for themselves.

Compton is personally involved in the design of the AMP expert system to pass along the tenets of his personal management philosophy to thousands of managers. By allowing him to reach out with his message to Aetna employees at all levels, Compton's expert system will help him communicate his overall vision in precise terms. At the same time, the AMP teaches people about establishing and measuring their own critical success factors.

Will it work? "Absolutely," says Compton. "This expert system is a real people developer. It will help people to have a concrete understanding of how their critical success factors relate to the company's overall goal of becoming quick, flexible, and right."

Compton's Critical Success Factors

So far, the product of Compton's leadership strategy is a company that is more focused on corporate goals and one that translates these goals into specific individual critical success factors.

While the organization continuously improves these skills, Compton continues to work on his own personal critical success factors. By applying AMP to his own job, Compton is able to describe in simple terms his own objectives. He feels he must:

- Do an excellent job of picking and developing people.
- Know with great precision what he wants from them.
- Communicate clearly what he wants to them.
- Be a superb listener and analyzer.

Critical Success Factor: Developing People

With regard to his first objective, we have already seen how Compton's information system and the AMP expert system are designed to help develop Aetna's management talent. The computer allows Compton to avoid extensive questioning of his people, because it provides the information that he would normally have to seek from them. "The executive support system provides feedback to the top executives who are running the business. It is a feedback mechanism to help accomplish one thing—to assure us that the managers of these businesses are managing the critical success factors of the business." He has also been applying his attention and information systems to the three other areas critical to success.

Critical Success Factor: Knowing What He Wants

Compton's second objective—knowing what he wants—requires reflection:

> There's some level at which you have to sit back and look at what your business is supposed to do. It's related to the AMP process. Jim [Aetna's chairman] and I know what we want this company to become. We know the level of profitability, we know that we want to be an international company, we know that we don't want to be in businesses that trap our capital. How do we know all those things? It's a complicated process, but it's a logical process.

How does he tackle these complex thinking tasks? "One of the ways that I think through what I want is by preparing option papers just for myself or to give to Jim. I think up all the possible options to an issue, list the pros and cons, and it helps me figure out a course of action." When putting together option papers (as well as speeches and presentations), Compton uses a word processor. "I take the laptop with me on the sailboat when I want to get something creative done. I use the word processor the way some people use a pencil. It's a creative tool. I'll use it to help support me while I think through a problem."

Compton doesn't want his administrative staff to run the word processor for him. "I have to prepare these papers myself for two reasons. First, the information is often confidential. Second, and more importantly, I use the tools as an aid to my thought process. A word processor allows me to think my way through things. I can look at something and change it, and then look at it again."

Can't you change things as easily on paper as on a computer? "I like it so much better than pencil and paper because, using paper, I'm striking things out, throwing things away, keeping doodles. This is neater, and allows me to think more clearly. Then I can come back, hand it to one of my associates to review, or have it printed out."

He also uses graphics packages and spreadsheets, depending upon the nature of the issue he is exploring. As an experienced user of these end-user computing tools, Compton has some interesting observations on the impacts of computers on thinking. "I'm just a regular guy. I struggle hard with putting stuff together. I don't sit around and think this stuff up in great flashes of brilliance. It doesn't just pop up like Mozart writing a symphony at recess in the fourth grade," says Compton, chuckling. He explains his use of the computer as a creative tool:

When I write option papers or other things on the sailboat, what I am doing is taking this great mass of right-brain, intuitive, creative stuff, and forcing it through a process that makes it come out more palatable and precise.

Tools such as spreadsheets, word processors, and even electronic mail match my cognitive style . . . my desire to blend the intuitive and the analytic. If you think of intuition as fundamentally a right-brain process, then what you're doing is forcing it through a filter to make it more logical.

I used to think managers who wrote their own stuff [on-line] were wasting their time. They're not. It actually takes less time than sitting there staring at your secretary or dictating to your machine. Very few people, and I am not one of them, can dictate on complicated issues with any precision. The stuff comes out like James Joyce.

He sums the advantages of the computer up concisely: "The computer is a creative tool to help me work through things, to help me shape them."

Critical Success Factor: Communicating Clearly

Compton's third objective is to communicate clearly what he wants, so that this huge, diverse organization develops shared goals. "I need an easy way of communicating with groups of people in order to knit the culture together. It's not enough to just reach a few people at a time. I have to leverage my communication efforts if I want to make such a huge organization operate as a single unit."

Compton emphasizes the importance of clarity in his communications. "People usually fail because they don't know what you want, not because of their lack of ability. People around here are terrific. If you can explain to them properly what you want them to do, 99 times out of 100 they're going to do it and do it in a quality way."

To be sure of clarity, Compton says, "I give almost all instructions in writing. Written instructions are just so much more precise than verbal instructions." However, formal memoranda are not the prevalent means of written communication for Compton. Many business issues are discussed informally, either over the telephone or in quick, informal messages. Compton prefers the latter and finds that electronic mail provides an easy, quick medium for informal messaging. "E-mail just beats the hell out of the typed, written, delivered, in-your-mail-folder thing. The flexibility and connectivity it provides are unsurpassed."

Compton elaborates on why electronic mail produces clearer communications:

> There's by far more precision in my communication on tasks, issues, and questions when I use e-mail. What really helps is that I can see, once I've typed a message, that I haven't said exactly what I wanted to say. In electronic mail, I have the option to edit it and change it around in order to be more precise. It also gives the person on the other end time to think about a response. Therefore, the response is also more precise and well-thought-out.
>
> I seek precision, but I also know that there has to be a great deal of flexibility in human relationships. But flexibility has a place. I think it's terrific to go out and build relationships with people face-to-face. But flexibility [in communications] is reserved for those personal relationships. Precision is what I want in communication about what's important to the business.

To knit together an organization, Compton needs to establish links with people at all levels of the company. Of course, this is difficult to accomplish in such a huge corporation. Electronic mail allows Compton's influence and connections with people to stretch far beyond the executive suite:

> Most of my electronic mail use is with my direct reports and other people I work closely with—accountants, lawyers, planners, and so on. But other people send me messages too. They know I'm on [the e-mail system]. I'll give a speech or a talk somewhere, and the next day I'll have three or four messages from people I've never heard of. I always answer them.
>
> Can you imagine somebody sitting down there who gets up the nerve to send a message to the president of this huge company, and then gets one back? I'll bet that every time somebody who doesn't know me gets a message back, a thank-you or something, I'll bet 300 other people will hear about that . . . talk about a machine for changing culture and for communicating! If that's what you want to do as a leader, electronic mail is a tremendous help.

Another tool Compton uses to reach groups of people is computer conferencing. "We've set up groups here on our computer conferencing system. It allows people to communicate with each other on specific issues. So, with a couple of keystrokes I can communicate with 14 preselected people who are interested in that topic."

As discussed, Compton uses option papers both to clarify his thinking and to communicate clearly with his chairman, James Lynn. "Jim responds well to work that is well-structured and well-thought-out. If you want to sell something to Jim, this is the way you do it. I'm working on an option paper now for a major organizational move, and it's important that it be done in writing so that Jim can look at the rationale. We need to understand each other very specifically."

In packaging his ideas to share with Lynn and others, Compton uses a word processing package and a graphics package that creates organization charts. "I'll give Jim an organization chart, an option paper, and the critical success factors. He likes to deal with things that way."

Communication tools allow Compton to reach many people in a large organization directly, instantaneously, and clearly. By creating such efficient and effective channels of communication, Compton is able to move closer to people and, as a result, closer to his goal of quick, flexible, and right.

Critical Success Factor: Listening and Analyzing

Compton's fourth personal objective is to do a good job of listening to people and helping them analyze the business. Compton feels that good listening encourages creativity. "In a meeting the other day, someone asked me, 'How do you make a company creative?' The answer just popped out of me: 'You don't. You just stop stamping it out. People already *are* creative.' If you're not a good listener, you're going to be stamping out some of that creativity."

One sure way to stamp out creativity is by cutting people off before you've heard them out. Compton feels e-mail helps him be a more patient listener. "Sometimes it's better for me to get feedback on e-mail. [When someone is] presenting me with an idea through e-mail I may be thinking, no, No, NO! But at least I'm not saying that to them. I'm not cutting them off prematurely. With the machine, I can formulate a more constructive reply, and ask more constructive questions."

When he *receives* messages in writing, Compton is better able to listen well, because the messages he receives are clearer. "You want to have people communicate with you in a thoughtful way? Get them to put the message in writing."

Time Management

Compton has ambitious personal objectives. Like all executives, he struggles with the problem of not having enough hours in the day. "Segmentation of time and focus are the answer to a job like this. You've got to segment your time; and while you're in a segment, you've got to focus on it."

Here, too, Compton has thought about how computers can help:

> A strong feature of e-mail is that you get to it when you want to get to it. It takes pressure off of me. It allows for a greater focus and greater concentration on the job. And for communicating, it's quicker and it's less disruptive. You do it wherever and whenever you want.
>
> If I want to ask somebody a question and it's Sunday, I can ask them the question on Sunday. . . . I kind of look at it as though that person is on the other end of the line all the time. Of course, they're not there every second, but they're much more available.

Compton is serious about making the best use of every minute. "I have a cellular modem on my sailboat now, so I have e-mail out at sea. I can take my laptop out on the boat and, without being plugged into shore at all—I mean really out in strange places like Great Salt Pond at Block Island or Newport Harbor—I can access the e-mail system and the calendaring."

Not only do the tools help Compton choose when and where he wants to work, they also allow him to get more than one thing accomplished at a time. While on the road, he is able to both meet with people and get work done that would normally be waiting for him back in the office. "If I'm away at a conference for three days, I'll get a lot of handshaking and backslapping done, but I've also got things to do back here, decisions to make. I can't afford to lose those three days. It's do it now, or do it later, but do it."

Corporate Guidance

Compton's leadership strategy can be described as having two components: a unifying theme of "quick, flexible, and right," as embodied in the AMP management discipline, and personal modeling of effective managerial behaviors.

To make "right" decisions, Compton must get people throughout a huge organization to align their personal objectives with organizational objectives. As they do so, a shared information system provides an overall sense of direction.

To make the company flexible, Compton must get people at all levels of the company to think critically and make well-considered decisions. Managers have the information they need to be analytical about their businesses, and they know what Compton is looking for.

And, to make the company quick, Compton disseminates information and tracks key areas of the business. This allows him to encourage people to be more proactive in their problem solving. Therefore, issues are being resolved earlier, making the company more responsive.

All these feedback loops reinforce a management thinking technique: AMP. In addition, the technique will be communicated via the expert system, which will help people focus on their most pressing priorities.

By aligning his organization, giving people the right information, tracking the issues that matter, and training people to be critical thinkers, Compton has begun to effect the kind of wide-sweeping change necessary for a large company that wants to compete in a fast-paced financial services industry.

In addition to using computer technology to help him spread the AMP message to others, Compton also uses technology in support of his personal objectives at the executive level. He uses a range of information tools to enhance his personal effectiveness. "[Quick, flexible, and right] applies to leaders as well. And technology is a major element of the development of these characteristics. There's no doubt about the fact that the tools I personally use help me develop those characteristics further—both for myself and for the corporation."

EXECUTIVE SUMMARY

With his scope in terms of both the range of tools and diversity of applications, Ron Compton is an unusually sophisticated user of executive information systems. His personal use of information systems helps him be more effective as an individual. Beyond that, he consciously designs information systems for others to use to maximize his influence on a large organization. Finally, his creative and forward-thinking use of computer systems helps him set an example for his entire organization in the development of innovative, strategic applications of information technology.

CHAPTER 16

Battle of the Bags

Michael Jordan

Chairman, Pepsico International Food & Beverages Division,
and Former Chairman, Frito-Lay

The adage "People are pretty much the same wherever you go" doesn't seem to apply to taste buds. Apparently, when you're talking about food, people are pretty much the same only if they live in the same geographic area. According to the people at Frito-Lay, Northeastern Yankees are crazy about Lays-brand Salt & Vinegar Flavored Potato Chips, but Southwesterners much prefer the barbequed variety.

The battle of the bags (of snack food, that is) has been heating up over the past decade. In the mid-1980s, local preferences for certain types of snacks became more apparent as new, specialized products appeared on the market. At that time, smaller, regional competitors with highly targeted products began chewing on Frito-Lay's heretofore barely challenged share of the snack-food market.

Frito-Lay's management recognized that, to maintain market leadership, the company would have to be more flexible in answering the competition and more responsive to the needs of market segments in its product offerings and sales and marketing efforts.

Responsiveness Through Decentralization

Flexibility and responsiveness are a tall order for a huge, centralized, functional organization. Frito-Lay is the largest manufacturer and distributor of snack foods in the world, with over $4.5 billion in retail sales in 1989. In a company of this size, information about local and regional preferences had to make a long, laborious journey from the supermarket to the executive suite. With a centralized culture, Frito-Lay found it increasingly difficult to keep up with the quixotic movements of its smaller, regional competitors, who were closer to their customers.

Michael Jordan, former chairman of Frito-Lay, explains the company's competitive challenge:

> We had to deal with much more specific areas. Instead of just understanding the Midwest, we needed to understand Kansas City. And within Kansas City, we had to understand performance in supermarket channels versus convenience-store channels, and so on. We had to be able to track the performance, and the responsiveness of volume to different kinds of programs, down to a very specific level to really understand the effectiveness and efficiency of the things we were doing in the marketplace. And we also needed to be able to track the information through the total cost system to ensure that incremental volume was producing incremental profit.

Jordan says that the need for flexibility and niche-oriented responsiveness made delegation an imperative. Decisions had to be made closer to the customer. "One of the things we've been trying to do is to get more people to make decisions lower in the organization so that we can respond to geographic variances. Delegation is not just something that's nice to do because you read a *Harvard Business Review* article this week. In my mind, it has become a business necessity."

In 1989, the decision was made to reorganize along regional lines and to delegate operational decision-making power and profit-and-loss responsibility further down into the organization. The company was divided into four regional businesses, whose vice presidents have profit-and-loss responsibility. "This is a real philosophical commitment to changing the organizational culture. We set up stronger regional management units, and we've identified people below the very top level who now have business and profit-and-loss accountability."

With this restructuring came a host of leadership challenges. The Frito-Lay management team had to convert a bureaucracy into an entrepreneurial culture, cultivating new attitudes, perspectives, and skills at every level of management. At the same time, it had to maintain alignment with the overall corporate strategy—without disempowering those decentralized entrepreneurs.

The Shift Toward a Culture of Entrepreneurship

Jordan notes that it is a big step from a top-down approach to an entrepreneurial way of doing business. "When you take the company apart and expect people to make well-informed, balanced decisions, that's quite a cultural change for a business where most decisions in the past were made by a handful of people at the top."

He explains the changes his operating managers had to go through. "In an organization like ours, people lived on functional goals. In a highly centralized, functional organization, you get very short-sighted and uneconomic points of view on a lot of projects. People don't really understand what drives profit in the business. Until recently, there was only one profit-and-loss statement for a $3-billion company, and it didn't really mean anything below my level."

The challenge facing the Frito-Lay executives was to take the people who knew their specific areas of the business and encourage them to look at things from a broader perspective:

> The whole point [of decentralization] was to make people accountable for the business. But we couldn't just hand them the keys to the car and say, "Go drive it." One person might know how to operate the brake, another might know how to operate the steering wheel, and a third might know how to operate the gear shift—but it isn't easy to have three people driving a car. . . . We wanted to make people more businesslike in their outlooks and more comfort: in dealing with profit-and-loss issues.
>
> That's more than simply learning how to read a profit-and-loss statement. It involves understanding the impacts of promotional programs on volume and spending and profit and making more accurate judgments by tracking impacts through a fact base. In the past, the organization did a very good job of managing budgets, but we dealt with business issues in very general terms.

In the past, people also tended to base their decisions and advocacy positions more on subjective judgments than on cold, hard facts. "We often found in this organization that, when you rely excessively on judgment as opposed to facts, you're never sure where you are. It's like driving from New York to California without a road map. You just take a series of random turns as you're trying to drive west. People had to have a road map for managing the business, and they had to have it in a fair degree of detail."

Coaching

Management can't mandate new skills and perspectives. A significant cornerstone to such a cultural change is coaching: The Frito-Lay management had to teach people to understand the business in finer levels of detail and encourage them to take on increasing levels of responsibility. To guide people who had just been empowered, management had to walk a fine line. "You have to provide the framework to exercise meaningful control without overcontrolling," explains Jordan.

Modeling Behavior

First, the management team had to model behavior by asking the right questions:

> [Coaching] starts out with a directional framework. We say, "These are the things that are important in terms of our hierarchy of objectives." Those goals get translated into plans and budgets that meet financial and marketplace objectives. As they go forward in implementing our strategies, we need to know how things are working in order to make the decision as to whether you stick with a strategy, or change it in mid-course.
>
> For example, let's say we decide to make a major push in the Southeast this year to get much more competitive on pricing and promotion. We think that's the right strategy when we set it, but we need some sort of test to see if it's working. What you try to do is ask the right questions to get people to look at the data the right way. After a period of time, they adopt that behavior and begin looking at the business and reporting it out in the way you need it.
>
> Then you step back and read the overall results as they analyze them. I view it as a modeling of behavior in specifics, and then a step back from that intense modeling behavior as it begins to take hold.

Informing the Newly Empowered

Jordan used Frito-Lay's operational databases to model the right behaviors in very specific terms and then equip people to make better entrepreneurial decisions. He considers the information system a key factor in helping people accept new responsibilities. "Flexible and dynamic internal databases give people the information they need to dissect results more thoroughly. They now see information broken down into finer and finer profit-and-loss structures. They had the numbers in the past, but nobody understood them."

These internal databases, for use by middle and upper management, helped foster an understanding of profitability and accountability. "I'm a great believer that a system doesn't produce thinking, but it stimulates and channels thinking. With the availability of data, we are able to force some more profit-and-loss accountability to lower levels in the organization. The [databases] give us the tools to decentralize, to force the decisions down, and to ask the right questions about profitability."

Is it working? Jordan provides an example of how the dissemination of this information is impacting the business:

> We are right in the midst of our preliminary plan reviews and targeting for next year. We had the headquarters marketing people present their ideas, which were not much different from past presentations. But then the field [sales] organizations, the decentralized profit-center people, came in and said, "No, we don't want to do it that way. We want more media on this product and less on that product, and here's why. We want some of the money taken out of consumer promotions and put into here, because that makes sense for our business. And we can show you why we think this, based on this year's activity."
>
> In the past, sales was only interested in sales volume. They wanted the sales target to be as low as possible so they could beat their plan and all their people could make bonuses. The marketing people, on the other hand, wanted a high-volume plan so they could justify a higher level of program spending. But no one in the old scenario was accountable for the final result or trading off these kinds of issues."
>
> What we found now is that there's a much more detailed grasp of how the business works than we've ever seen before. [The field salespeople] were better equipped to negotiate because they came from a fact base. They could specifically tell the marketing people why they thought an idea would or wouldn't work.
>
> By putting people in touch with the data, we empowered people. In the current situation, I spend less and less time going at the details and more and more time getting people to come back with a horizontal or diagonal slice through the data for strategic indicators. For example, I'll ask how we are doing in wholesale versus chains on an overall basis.

Informing the Coaches

Though the computer assists with coaching by putting the right information into the right hands, in a format that encourages clear thinking, Frito-Lay management must also personally guide and assist the people who have newly bestowed power and accountability. Thus, it is equally important for top management to access the information. They have to have the knowledge necessary to ask the right questions in a coaching session. "We have to show people the thought process by asking the right questions. We can't just ask them, 'Well, how did you do in Kansas City?' We have to be more specific and ask them such things as, 'Are the programs we have to differentiate supermarkets from wholesalers in Kansas City really paying off?' This forces them to go back and think about different ways of approaching the business."

Jordan uses his access to operational and competitive information as a means of staying informed for his coaching role. "If you've got a question about a fact, you can do a better job of coaching people on the decisions they make if you've got your hands on the data and can walk them through it yourself." He offers an example: "If I'm looking at a profit-and-loss statement for the western zone for Fritos Corn Chips and there is something amiss, I will get people to dig into things and explain why. And then over time, as they get more used to the numbers and what they mean, they start doing something about it [on their own, before I ask]."

Creating a Common Language

The system helps Jordan ask business questions in precise terms. The data is displayed on the system in a form that expresses his analytic approach:

> With standardized approaches or a common framework for understanding the business, you can encourage people to walk through a train of logic whenever they think through a problem. And they will learn over time how to manage profitability and how to balance cost, performance, and spending versus volume and profit tradeoffs.
>
> If we're looking at the performance of the business in very specific ways, we can develop a common language. We don't want everyone to develop their own analytical methodology, we want a common language for communication.

As a coach, Jordan encourages people to learn that language. "It's a managerial language that we're talking about—a way of communicating in specifics but with the right kind of intellectual and strategic framework."

Teaching a Proactive Approach

Jordan's coaching challenge wasn't limited to building the entrepreneurial perspective. Understanding and analysis of the business had to result in action. Successful entrepreneurs must act on their conclusions—and demonstrate their results to management.

In the functional, bureaucratic culture, people may have felt responsible for accomplishing tasks, but not necessarily for results:

> People used to say, "Don't ask me what I did this year; let me tell you what I'm going to do next year." There was a very low value given to following up and post auditing what had actually happened as a basis for planning new things. People just launched off on their new plans without post auditing the past.
>
> We also had a lot of churn in the organization—people changed jobs a lot. So the brand manager on Doritos brand Tortilla Chips doing the 1991 plan was likely to be different from the person who did the 1990 plan. He might say, "Don't bother me about that plan. That was wrong anyway."

Jordan felt that information systems could help him build a discipline of accountability for results. "When you're dealing in generalities, that type of attitude is hard to fight. But when you're dealing in specifics, you can get people to think in much more concrete terms and get them to analyze what went right or what went wrong as a basis for what we're going to do in the future."

Looking at operational data is not an isolated, monthly phenomenon at Frito-Lay. Jordan has played a key role in establishing widespread use of the information systems he helped to design. Looking at operational data is now a way of life. This ensures quick response to changing customer needs and clear accountability for results.

With accountability for results comes responsibility for problem resolution. Jordan wanted to coach people to follow through on fixing problems—before those problems reached the next level of management. He provides an amusing example of how information tools have helped him to encourage follow-through on projects.

In 1984, when he was president of Frito-Lay, if something stood out in a report he was reading, Jordan made a note. Later, he would slip into the marketing databases to see if people were following up on plans and commitments. "I didn't do any broad-scale investigative work. I'd just do stiletto-like follow-ups. I wasn't proficient enough in the system to use it for anything more than little spot checks. But it was effective," he says.

He tells a story of one such spot check of the head of sales and marketing: "He's a real character. He's a huge guy, and he carries his own personal swagger stick, which is a 36-ounce Louisville slugger bat." Jordan didn't let the bat stop him. "I asked him, 'How are we doing on that special pretzels promotion in Pittsburgh?' He said, 'What?' And I said, 'The marketing report said we were going to do this thing two months ago, and I looked it up [in the databases] and we weren't doing anything.' He went back to check on what I had asked. It was a way for me to get him to do more detailed follow-ups instead of generalized follow-ups on things. He also got on the database after that!" After that famous showdown, "Pretzels in Pittsburgh" became an organization legend. "It was a symbol of getting down to the nitty-gritty of what is going on."

Jordan believes that his personal access to the internal information system has helped him shift people's thinking from an observe-and-report-it mentality to a fix-it mentality. Because they know that he has a detailed view of operations, they now anticipate the types of questions he will ask. Now they are not only following through on commitments, but they are also taking on increasing amounts of responsibility for fixing problems. "Before, we were in the position where profitability was an observed phenomenon, as opposed to a managed phenomenon. People said, 'Well, we were behind plan last month because distribution and selling costs were too high.' And that's it! But now they are beginning to say, 'Here's why they were too high, and here's the factors that were one-time affairs, and here's the ones that were performance problems, and here's what we're going to do about it.'"

Synergies and Alignment

Though management sees the new, profit-center-structured organization as key to responding more quickly to the marketplace, it does not want decentralization to eclipse common, overall organizational goals.

There are clear economic advantages associated with scale and a functional organization structure. These were Frito-Lay's traditional strengths, and they didn't want to abandon them.

Thus, in parallel with his strategy of decentralization, Jordan wanted to set a clear, unifying strategic direction for the entire organization. To do so, he pursued two leadership strategies:

- Formulating strategy at the top
- Building teamwork from the bottom up

Formulating Strategy at the Top

"Strategy in our business is not so much going off on major, different initiatives that we've never done before—although we have some of that in a product area, especially when we're trying to penetrate new channels. Rather, strategy generally focuses on growing volume [in existing market niches]."

Jordan's competitive weapons to increase volume included new product introductions, advertising programs, and promotions. But each of these costs time and money. To decide how to spend the corporation's finite resources, Jordan had to ask questions such as What's regionally important? Which competitive activities should we respond to? Where should we put more media money?

He summarizes: "It's the balance in resource allocation that is one of the most important aspects of strategy."

Adjusting Filters. To make these multimillion-dollar decisions, Jordan and his management team have to maintain a detailed understanding of the operations of the company.

> To do proper resource allocation, you need to be in touch with both the marketplace numbers and the financial numbers. If you have a feel for what's happening in the business in specifics and what's happening to the profit-and-loss statement, you can make judgments about directional shifts or shifts in resource allocation.
>
> If I'm generating a hypothesis about the business, by going into the numbers [on the computer] I can see how we're doing and get a feel for whether I need to send someone out to chase an issue. If you're going to develop hypotheses about the business, you need to test them in facts.

With the up-to-date information he receives from his information systems, Jordan has much greater flexibility in decision making regarding resource allocation. "This year, in responding to some major competitive incursions, we [shifted our direction and] stepped up our competitive response funds. Unless you have a good feel for how the numbers behave, it's hard to make those kinds of judgments and directional shifts."

By "numbers," Jordan does not mean the high-level summary reports typically presented to executives. "When you've got 26,000 people, it means that the top 15 or 20 executives are very knowledgeable and very bright, but they are isolated from what's really happening in the business and they're certainly isolated from the numbers."

In the past, Jordan and his team were forced to rely strictly on summary reports:

> We used to have a lot of people in the staff organizations spending their time saying, "What happened?" They took data from all of the different sources and tried to position it for senior managers.
>
> But their vision was very incomplete, and they added their own interpretation. I wasn't sure I necessarily wanted that interpretation. Often you don't agree with the way someone else looks at things. When people are trying to sell you on a point, they will use only the data that they like. That's the traditional situation with any advocacy position in a corporation.

How does he now overcome these distortions? "I like to get in touch with the numbers. I prefer looking at raw information to continually accepting someone else's conclusions about what the data means. I wanted to get the staff people out of the role of aggregating and interpreting actual results."

Instant Actuals.   Another issue is response time:

> When I was trying to generate hypotheses before, I'd scribble a note asking the question and send it to the guy three levels down, who would then get two or three people to do an analysis. Then it would be checked by his boss, and then his boss, and so on. And then about a month and a half or two months later, I'd get this report back: "In Response To Your Question." By that time I might have forgotten what I had asked, or I might not have phrased the question right in the first place. I'd get what I asked for, but not what I wanted. It was very awkward to try to penetrate strategic issues.
>
> I needed what we call the instant actuals. If you're generating hypotheses from actual results, then you can send people to work on major

issues. So you have a value-added staff position instead of just a journalistic or reportorial role.

Therefore, Jordan and his top management team wanted to personally get into the details—in specific areas of interest and in a timely fashion. And they wanted to get this information without disempowering their newly empowered managers by looking over their shoulders.

Internal databases provided Jordan with those "instant actuals." He calls the database system his insight tool. He is able, using the system, to get a view of information that is unfiltered by the bias of others and one that allows him to get a quick feel for the numbers. "With [access to internal data], I can browse through the raw data and develop hypotheses and draw conclusions."

But pulling together the massive amounts of information needed for these instant actuals presented a real challenge. The 10,000-person Frito-Lay sales force calls on 400,000 stores a week. In the past, with that degree of complexity, it was impossible for top management to track closely what was happening at the regional and product levels. Hard details of manufacturing were known, but other aspects were "visceral and interpretive," according to Jordan.

> Sales volume was a black box. If you put money for advertising and trade promotion in on one end, volume came out the other, with no exact idea as to what happened. We had some ideas, but we couldn't really pin it down.
>
> We didn't know whether a price-off promotion on Ruffles brand Potato Chips in Dallas was cost-effective and where it was cost-effective. It might work at Kroger, but not in a local market chain. We didn't know any of these things. We just didn't have the analytical capability to master it.

To capture the masses of data at the retail level, top management gave hand-held computers to the entire 10,000-person sales force. Each day, the sales force sends data about the performance of the various trade brands (via phone lines) to mainframes in Dallas. The information is then sorted and redistributed to various areas in the organization, including top management.

Jordan is able to access the sales information directly. His system combines internal sales data with external competitive information on market share and pricing. The system then condenses the data to provide highly specific information to top management. "With the hand-held computers and our ability to look at that data through the system, we finally have been able to evolve the tools to really penetrate into marketplace performance and understand it in very fine detail."

The systems allowed him to kill two birds with one stone. First, he was able to do a better job of developing the hypotheses, because the information on the system was dynamic and instantly available. Second, after he developed the hypotheses, he was able to make "value-added" use of his staff's time in working through major issues and initiatives.

Ultimately, such increased knowledge leads to better strategy formulation at the top of the organization. And, by accessing internal sales information himself, Jordan is able to get the type of detailed information he needs—without micro-managing people who are down the line.

Strategic Hypotheses.   As he shifts more toward strategic issues, the ratio of Jordan's attention to external information will change:

> As time goes on, I will access the system less regularly for that detailed [internal] information. I won't have as strong a need to pull apart performance to see if people have met their commitments, because we hope to institutionalize that process. But I will always use the system to formulate strategic hypotheses. I'll always need to ask questions such as I wonder what's happening here? or Are we really making progress here? or Which are the key markets, and what are competitors doing?
>
> What I'm already beginning to do is to move away from driving specific performance and management behavior, and more into strategic issues. Soon, I'll no longer have to be the role model on how to take the business apart; I'll be spending an increasing amount of my time testing [strategic] hypotheses.
>
> The information I now access in order to drive performance is on a huge database that integrates all of the internal financial information and external marketplace data. Right now, at least 40 percent of what we do involves looking at the *external* information. But [as I focus more on strategic issues], that percentage [of external information] will increase.
>
> I believe the computer will, for me, become more of a personal thinking tool as opposed to an operational control tool. As that occurs, the external information will become more and more important.

Building Teamwork from the Bottom Up

Although competitiveness required local flexibility and responsiveness, some business decisions had to be made with consideration of the total corporate perspective. Teamwork across geographic boundaries was required to achieve Jordan's strategic goals.

Part of the answer to retaining a spirit of teamwork in spite of decentralization was the organization's structure. The company is now structured so that functional managers have both regional and national authority and accountability. Therefore, according to Jordan, people take into consideration both the impacts on the region and the impacts on the company as a whole. "For example, the manufacturing organization is a national organization, but it has a vice president who is responsible for the manufacturing plants in a specific region. He reports to the regional general manager in a dotted line. But he's really part of that regional management team, and at least 50 percent of his performance is measured in terms of the total regional results, not just manufacturing results."

But structure alone wasn't enough. Jordan used information to reinforce the corporate view and help people throughout the organization function as a team. For example, marketing information is shared across the regional profit centers. So, if a promotional idea or campaign works well in one region, another region can borrow that idea. "They're all tied together, and they have a shared language for understanding each other."

The sharing of information has also unified headquarters groups. "We have a large group of people in headquarters—1,500 people, 1,800 if you include Research and Development. They are very strongly functionally oriented, with some pretty significant cultural walls between each of the functions. They're large, and somewhat baronial."

Jordan wanted to ensure a horizontal flow of information. "Information is power in a complex, fractionalized environment. So instead of having each of these somewhat isolated functions doling out information from one function to another, our information system is making it available to all of them simultaneously. In my mind, that can go a long way towards breaking down the negotiative nature of tasks and problem solving in this organization . . . you know, the classic 'I'll show you mine if you show me yours.'"

By using a common information system, a common language develops across functional and geographic walls. "You start speaking from a common script. I can be talking to someone in San Francisco, and that person can pull up on his screen exactly the same profit-and-loss statement or volume chart that I've got."

The Results

With the proper organization structure in place, supported and enabled by a networked information system, Frito-Lay is beginning to see results:

> Several years ago, Frito-Lay decided to do more to maintain its leadership position and high profit level in the snack-food market. We knew that we would have to grow the category with a lot more initiatives in the marketplace. We measure our initiatives by the number of business propositions that flow through the system—such as new flavors and new products.
>
> We had a major thrust to try and do a similar thing before [we had information systems to support us], and the business got out of control. We tried to introduce 85 new line items in 1986, and the business was chaos. We introduced many more than that in 1989, after we had the systems, and we were very successful.

Jordan is sanguine about the contribution of the system to building this successful culture of innovation and entrepreneurship:

> These systems were absolutely necessary to support a major strategic change in the business. . . . We have gone from having 120 marketplace initiatives a year to 350 to 400 a year, and that number is rising. In fact, we've almost doubled our real growth rate over the last three years. We couldn't have done that without being able to manage the business in detail.
>
> To make all of that happen, you had to empower people to make decisions and take accountability for results. Unless we had the systems, the whole place would have cratered trying to do all those things. [With the decentralization enabled by information systems,] we were able to manage an increasing level of activity and decide which [initiatives] were working and which ones weren't, and very quickly alter our strategy and do mid-course corrections. We were able to manage three or four times the amount of activity in the marketplace.

Jordan knew he had to be personally involved in the design of the information systems used by himself and others. "I feel that if I personally hadn't led the process at the detailed level, that we wouldn't be this far. I can see that, as we go forward in changing the organization and the culture, we could not have done it without putting people in touch with the data and putting those of us at the top of the organization in touch with what subordinate layers are doing, without trying to overcontrol them—without having to flow every decision up to us."

Jordan is optimistic about the continuing role of information systems in strengthening Frito-Lay's position in the snack-food market. "I think we have a great opportunity here to make significant impacts through both my personal use and the organization's use of information systems."

EXECUTIVE SUMMARY

Michael Jordan gives us an understanding of how information systems can help management decentralize an organization and shift it toward a culture of entrepreneurship. The Frito-Lay management team made a decision to change the organization structure, and then supported that decision by dispersing the necessary information to line, staff, and upper management. As a result, Frito-Lay has evolved into a less bureaucratic, more flexible, and more responsive organization.

CHAPTER 17

Overtaking

Takeover Attempts

Robert Wallace

Former President, Phillips 66

The year was 1984. T. Boone Pickens moved stealthily and mercilessly. Phillips Petroleum Company was his target. A second attack came only three months later, when Carl Icahn made a hostile tender offer for the company. The battles were long, leaving a weary and weak survivor. Throughout the struggles, Robert Wallace had been heading up the Petroleum Products and Chemicals Group at Phillips.

The company emerged in shaky condition. "Phillips was in a very perilous state," says Wallace. "We had tremendous debt. It jumped from $3 billion to $9 billion—$9 billion! Our interest payments were $900 million a year. That's over $2.5 million of before-tax income every day."

Wallace describes the devastating effect this debt load had on the company. "At that point in time, the company was literally one step from Chapter 11. We knew it. All of the market had written us off, our stock had plummeted, and all of the analysts were predicting either collapse or ultimate takeover."

As if the takeover attempts were not enough, market circumstances conspired against Phillips as well. Just as the company emerged from the corporate raiders' grasp, bleeding debt, crude-oil prices fell, and the market became even more volatile. At this point, management had every reason to feel desperate. "There was a strong sentiment in the company at the management level to get rid of everything downstream," remembers Wallace. "There were great

196

arguments. Some people were saying, 'Let's liquidate, get the cash, pay off the debt, and at least we'll survive.'"

Wallace surveyed the littered battlefield. "I stood there looking at all that, and I knew what I had to do. I was fighting for the survival of the whole thing. And so I had to fight for change . . . change in how we thought about the business and how we managed the business. I had to make it more effective, to get rid of the bureaucracy. I didn't know if I had the wherewithal or the knowledge, but I did have 35 years of experience."

Wallace developed his vision around a primary goal: streamlining operations and leveraging staff groups. As the first step in streamlining, in 1985 he made the decision to combine the Petroleum Products and Chemicals Groups into a single entity: a corporation called Phillips 66. Wallace became president and retired the two group executives. "I needed to immediately downsize the organization in order to make it more efficient. By getting rid of the group concept, we could significantly downsize staff support through consolidation," explains Wallace.

The Functions of Staff: Decision Support, Control, and Innovation

Wallace knew that simply cutting staff costs was not enough. What about the work all these staff people were doing? Wallace understood that staff people were making contributions in at least three general areas:

- Decision support
- Control
- Innovation

Wallace knew that if he reduced staff, under a typical scenario, he would also be reducing the decision support to the line organization. "In times past, the whole decision-support mechanism was staff controlled—pricing groups, planning groups, strategic groups," he recalls. "All of those staff groups were built around supporting the decision-making process—ensuring that the guy on the line out there making the final decision had the necessary information."

Staff is also in a position to see across line organization boundaries. They could trace the implications of a decision "upstream" and "downstream" and see corporate synergies. Wallace did not want to lose this integrative function in the downsizing.

Wallace notes that the second reason for staff groups is management control. This function, he says, accounts for much of the growth in the size of staff (versus line) groups. "Most corporations' idea of decentralization in the mid-'70s was to transfer down as much information as possible so you could make decisions closer to the front line," says Wallace. "But executives were worried about control mechanisms."

He uses the example of accounting to illustrate his point. "As corporations shifted accounting out, decentralized it, there was a concern about adequate controls. So the first thing companies did was to put a controller at the end of the stream—he's the furthest guy out. Then the division levels wanted a duplicate controller to interface with the field controller. The same thing then happened at the group and corporate levels."

Companies ended up with what Wallace calls a tiering effect. "Companies had anywhere from four to seven tiers. As that occurred, costs went up, not down," he says. "The only way you could justify decentralization was a hypothetical concept that we're going to get a better decision-making process by pushing information out to the line and letting the people make the business decisions. We rationalized the fact that we were carrying excess overheads because of the tiers we put in to protect ourselves. We said it would still work out. But that didn't happen."

By the early 1980s, staff-to-line ratios had increased dramatically, notes Wallace. "Sometimes these percentage changes were phenomenal. The worst part was that you were adding high-priced people."

Up until the 1980s, Wallace says management was very protective of these control mechanisms. "As you start eliminating staff, your controls sag. And certainly if you're in a perilous period of time, you're cautious about that. Management will typically concentrate on trying to get rid of the guy that's making the widgets and not tinker with their control mechanisms very much." However, in 1984, tiers of staff were a luxury Phillips could no longer afford. Wallace wanted to retain controls while he cut staff, but he wanted to avoid past mistakes.

He also worried about innovation, the third function of staff. "I don't want to minimize this. Staff people provide about 90 percent of the innovation in any organization. But the more you have them involved in decision support and in the control-mechanism functions, the less you have them available for doing the innovative things."

A Vision for Reconstruction

Wallace recognized that he had to take a whole new approach: to regroup, reorganize, and reshape. "I looked at this not from the standpoint of just how to get rid of staff people, but how to eliminate redundancies, unnecessary jobs, and the strictly support positions. At the same time, I needed to transfer more authority down to the operating levels so that the company would not only be more efficient, but also more effective."

The key word here is *leverage*. Wallace wanted to get maximum benefit from the staff functions Phillips could afford to keep, while moving support and control functions from staff to line. In parallel, he wanted to get the most from senior management by flattening the staff structure and empowering operating managers to run their pieces of the business.

In summary, his leadership strategy embodied six points:

- Cut staff significantly.
- Focus remaining staff on innovation.
- Flatten the staff management structure.
- Provide decision support directly to line.
- Move management controls from staff to line.
- Build a culture of synergistic teamwork.

In 1982, he had read an article about Ben Heineman's use of information systems at Northwest Industries; in 1985, he remembered that article. As he surveyed what the raiders had wrought, Wallace recognized that information systems might be the tools he was looking for to pull the company back together. He envisioned a system that would provide real-time information to people at all levels of the corporation, including executives. "Heineman had developed a system that allowed for delivery of database information to top management. That's as far as Northwest Industries had taken the concept. I felt, right from the beginning, that if you could deliver the information to top management, then you could take the same information and deliver it anywhere throughout the organization."

By delivering information to the entire organization, Wallace expected three results:

- The elimination of redundancies in staff support groups. Staff people would no longer be required to deliver information to front-line decision makers or filter it up to top management. Thus, staff people could focus more on innovation.
- The lessening of senior management's fears about losing control mechanisms. Senior managers would be able to get the information they needed without extra tiers of management or staff.
- The delivery of the right information to the right people. "When staff groups are making the decisions, it's impossible to maximize the value of information," explains Wallace. "Staff people are not in a position to understand the ramifications of a business decision as well as operating people. The operating person is running the business on a day-to-day basis and can interpret the dynamics of the marketplace much better."

If the system worked, Wallace expected that the ultimate result would be a tremendous cultural shift toward empowerment of front-line management. "The true power of this concept was that it provided an immediate feedback mechanism to the operating person making the decision. Essentially, he could begin monitoring himself. And that's the best way to make decisions—through self-monitoring." With empowerment comes accountability. Senior management still had a role in ensuring the performance of operating management and in solving some of the tough problems.

Wallace explains how the information system would help top management in this new, decentralized culture:

> At the same time, we could let senior management at various levels, including the very top of the organization, have a view of how judgments were being exercised. That way, if big mistakes in judgment were being made at the operating level, senior management wouldn't have to wait until the end of the month to get the financial statements before they spotted the problem. They would be able to look into the system and see the problems much earlier. That would relieve their concern about controls, and we could get around the problem of the tiering effect.

As the new culture encouraged line managers to improve their entrepreneurial judgment, top management could shift its attention from controlling and coaching to corporate strategy. Here, too, the information system would play a role.

In summary, Wallace had a vision of how to save the company: Cut staff, empower line, give top management direct feedback on line's performance, and then shift top management's attention to corporate strategy. The cornerstone to his entire leadership strategy was an information system that gave all levels of management access to the right data.

A Visit to the Board

With his concept in mind, Wallace set to work. First, he needed to rally his board to support his vision. "You've got to realize, here's this company—$9 billion in debt, $900 million a year in interest payments, crude-oil prices collapsing, the market volatility mushrooming overnight—and I go to the board and tell them that I'm going to develop a new concept of using information to more effectively manage the business!"

But the board was more curious about the concept than he had anticipated. Wallace explained to the board that he wanted to take operating data, format it into usable information, and deliver it—starting with himself and then working down through the organization—to where it was needed so decisions could be made closer to the front line.

Given the company's debt, the board was naturally concerned about costs. "At the time, most data processing projects had problems. And in our company, I will tell you, we've had a lot of problems. I'm talking about data processing projects that maybe had two- or three-year completion schedules, and we'd find out four or five years later that we had to abort them. When I started talking about information systems, frankly, there was an apprehension." Wallace promised the board that he would personally see to it that costs were controlled.

Wallace was a trusted friend of the chairman. Even so, the chairman had concerns. He was worried that the employees would become apprehensive, even paranoid, about the concept of management looking over their shoulders, waiting to drop the hatchet at the first sign of a mistake.

Wallace responded to the chairman's concern: "Well, if we try to use this system as just another approach to corporate control, you're exactly right. We could create a true disaster. But that is not our intention. Our intention is to use it as a management tool to delegate authority."

The board immediately gave him the go-ahead.

Next Stop: The Management Team

Wallace felt fortunate in that he was starting with a fresh management team—a new group of nine vice presidents. He described his vision to them, drawing them in and making them part of it. He emphasized the magnitude and the importance of the potential impacts. "I said to them, 'You realize we're talking about a change in how we do business, a change in how we think about the timeliness of information. To start out, we have to have certain generally agreed upon cultural understandings, because we're going to change the culture of our company.'"

The first point Wallace made had to do with the sharing of information. "I'm telling you guys right here today that everything I put on my machine, you can have on yours. With me, there are no secrets. Whatever is on my system, you are going to know." There were smiles all around the table.

He then proceeded to tell them that they were the masters of their own machines—the sole determiners of what information they needed to manage their own part of the business. This included what they needed to understand of other parts of the business. "All data in this company is a resource of the corporation," Wallace told them. "It is not privileged to any group, staff, or individual. So you're free to go pick it wherever you need it." More smiles.

He pointed out to them that they would have to use good judgment about not drowning people with data, and he emphasized the importance of letting the user decide what he or she needed.

Everyone left the meeting happy. What a terrific and brave new world they would build, where information could be shared and the boss held no secrets! But a few days later, something interesting happened. One of Wallace's senior officers asked to meet with him. The following scenario unfolded:

Senior officer: Could we amplify a little bit more on this sharing concept?

Wallace: Sure.

Senior officer: I think this is a wonderful opportunity for me to truly get the total look at the company, but I have a couple of concerns.

Wallace: What are they?

Senior officer: Does this mean that the marketing part of the business knows everything I know about my business?

Wallace: Exactly. If it's in the system, they will. I assume you're going to have information beyond what they're going to have. But fundamentally, looking at the total view of your operation, yeah, they're going to know.

Senior officer: I have a concern then. They may try to influence some of my actions as it might relate to them.

Wallace: Well, I hope they do! That's part of the game.

Senior officer: It seems to me that we ought to have a time difference. Maybe we ought to have a day's lead time.

Wallace: Wait a minute! We're talking about a whole new concept of management in which we're all one team, we're all sharing the information on a common basis. There will be no differentials in time. When you make a business decision, I don't want you to make that decision without full understanding of all of the implications on every side of you. Whether you're looking downstream or upstream of your activity, whatever you do, I want you to know what's going to happen from both sides . . . what the implications are. I hope the result will be that you will start really pulling harder together as a team, and we'll really start optimizing this total activity for the bottom line of Phillips.

To drive a cultural change, Wallace continually reinforced the free sharing of information.

Onward into the Organization

Remaining true to his "user-driven" vision, Wallace formulated a team to go out and talk to people to find out what kind of information they needed to do their jobs. "We asked them, 'What would be of value to you if we could give you anything you want? How can we enhance your running of the business? You tell us.' Many times, they weren't quite sure."

Despite the difficulties of getting people to articulate their needs, the team persevered—starting with the executives themselves. Once they were able to get people to identify their information needs, the team put together a tailored module of the information system. As the system continued to grow, it became obvious that line people, as well as staff people, needed more than just internal information. "No businessman can make a business decision without knowing both the internal and the external factors that affect it," says Wallace. "Some people may simplistically view external information as the pump price down the street at the Exxon station versus the Phillips station. That's important; we have that. But it's much, much broader."

Ultimately, the system evolved into a full tool kit with access to internal data, access to external data, electronic mail, spreadsheets, and word processing. As it evolved, the system cascaded down through the organization. As people began using it, results began to take shape. The benefits accrued in what might be roughly characterized as four phases:

1. Immediate improvements in top management's understanding of the business.
2. An increased focus on the bottom line at all levels.
3. A culture of teamwork.
4. Support for the evolving role of top management.

Improvements in Top Management's Understanding

The implementation of the information system began with the top executives. Thus, the first results were felt at the top. The initial goal of the system was to give top management all the control that they needed in spite of greatly reduced staff.

Wallace found that the information on computer not only substituted for staff information reporting, but it actually did a better job. It put the executives in much closer touch with the business. The payoff was immediate. "We were able to spot things we never would've known about. We'd see these things and we'd say, 'What is going on here? We've never seen that before!'"

Wallace notes that there were many examples of such "discoveries," but he settles on describing one about pricing. In one segment of the market, Phillips has 1,800 customers buying out of 240 different terminals. Before they had the executive information system, Phillips set what it perceived to be a competitive price structure. Pricing was decided by a centralized staff group at headquarters in Bartlesville, Oklahoma. Unbeknownst to the pricing group (and the executives), the customers were taking advantage of a lag in price changes on the part of Phillips. The customers saw that other prices were going up in their segments, but that the Phillips price remained the same. Obviously, they began buying as much as possible before the inevitable price change set in. "Let's say, conservatively, that you make within a period of a year 30 price changes. These guys in all of these 240 segments were smarter than we were. They were only looking at their little sphere; they didn't give a damn about the other 239."

Not only were customers smart about buying a lot on the way up, they also knew how to handle dropping prices. "They'd see the market tipping, and we were still lagging; and when we were slowly coming off, they would just shut off all purchases. For example, they really killed us on holiday weekends. They sucked their tanks down to very low levels, leaving us with high-priced inventory in our tanks. They then waited until we made the change to the lower price before they restocked."

The Phillips executive team was completely unaware of this practice until they personally started using their information systems. "We began to see these enormous spikes and shifts in sales. And it wasn't just in one segment. I'd be looking at one area and then I'd pick it up again in another. Then you started putting the pieces of the puzzle together."

Having this information produced immediate and forceful effects on the morale of the team:

> This, of course, created a euphoric feeling throughout the management team. All of a sudden everybody became caught up in this: "My God! I had no idea!" So now we were able to get more sophisticated in dealing with our customers. What we found on the system [about these pricing practices] actually prompted us to go out and talk with the customers in small groups. We went out to talk to them about how we had priced in the past, and how we would price in the future.
>
> Because the system showed us things we had never seen before, we were much better informed. This allowed us to communicate with our customers better. We didn't just go out and thank them for their business.

The system opened up an opportunity for senior management to do more than that. We were able to show them that we understood some of their concerns and problems. This, in turn, resulted in a whole new philosophy about customer relationships. It shifted us from being a little bit dogmatic in some of our approaches, to being much more sensitive to their needs and a much more valuable supplier to them.

This experience reminded the executive team of the importance of their personal contacts with customers. "Product quality alone may not be enough. You have to create a relationship with customers through effective communication and an understanding of their concerns, constraints, and opportunities."

The executives then began to explore other ways of using the computer to stay close to their customers. "We went so far as to interlock our system with our customers. We can deliver electronically to them some of the information we have in-house. Obviously, we aren't giving them confidential information, but we share with them general business intelligence that is valuable to them in managing their own operations."

In addition to sharing formal information, Phillips set up another informal link to customers. "We also connected customers to our electronic-mail system. That way, if I picked up on a useful piece of information, I could just send it to them informally through electronic mail. Because it was so easy, I communicated with them more often. I could send a dozen electronic messages a heck of a lot faster than I could call all those people on the phone."

As a direct result of the use of information systems, the executive team was in closer touch with business operations and with customers. The results were quite tangible. "As we got our systems up and operating, the performance of our company just ramped up like this," explained Wallace, as he inclined his arm in an upright position. "You just can't believe it. It became an overnight success story. Unbelievable. It was beyond even my wildest expectations. I have seen our system increase the profitability of Phillips Petroleum Company by $25 to $40 million a year in a matter of weeks!"

Focus Others on the Bottom Line

The next step was to share the improved bottom-line perspective with line managers throughout the firm. The challenge was to get all these managers focused on the key profitability opportunities.

This was a two-step process: First, the executives began to improve communication of their interests and concerns to the rest of the organization. Second, line managers were given the data they needed to run their piece of the business as the information system was rolled out through the company.

Communicating a Bottom-Line Focus. Even before others were given access to the information system, Wallace felt he could better focus people on the bottom line by communicating his interests and concerns. Wallace wanted to communicate his understanding of vital issues to employees and also let them know that he was more than just a bystander in the corporate race for success.

There are at least two ways in which leaders communicate their interests to an organization. First, by the way they spend their time and, second, through their direct communications with employees. "A high percentage of CEOs, not all of them, are spending more of their time away from the company," explains Wallace. "Trade associations take up 20 to 30 percent of their time, politics take up maybe 20 to 30 percent of their time, and maybe the shareholder constituency takes up 10 or 15 percent. That's pretty typical today in corporate America of how executives think about senior management roles."

This doesn't leave very much time for staying in touch with operations. "They think they only need to look at the statistics instead of watching the race. Therefore, they get their internal information from the financial statement." Wallace says that the fallout from this is that CEOs build up committees to handle the internal activities of the firm:

> I can take you to CEO offices all over the United States and show you what they're doing. It's tragic. Look at any major corporation today and how many committees it's got in charge of the business.
>
> Management committees are usually a bunch of guys sitting in a committee room. They're not running anything. Those same guys 100 years ago would have been running companies. But as the systems got bigger and bigger, they started passing off operating responsibility without doing all the things needed to make it work.

It is this committee mentality that separates CEOs from their corporations, Wallace believes. When committees become isolated, they focus on financials instead of people. They lose touch with employees.

Wallace referred back to the race metaphor: "I think this sends a wrong signal. . . . Employees say, 'Management is uninvolved, management is uninterested, and management shows no leadership regarding what I'm doing in this company. He only wants to know if I ran [the race]. Sure he'd like to know that I ran the mile in 9 seconds, but fundamentally he's not out there cheering me on. He only wants to know statistically what happened."

Information systems provided Wallace with a tool to combat the "report card" mentality. Through Wallace's direct use of the system, employees knew that he cared about what happened because he looked at results every day. "It's enough that you see things, that you notice . . . you care. And maybe that's part of the whole thing: the caring. We try to make a corporation out to be something that's without soul and purpose . . . without heart. I don't believe that."

As others were put on-line, Wallace was able to use his information system as a tool for communicating that sense of caring. "I can see what a guy's doing down there at the bottom of the organization [by looking at the reporting systems] . . . and [I can] send an electronic message to him saying something like, 'I just happened to observe the good job, and I want you to know that.'"

Are such actions culture changers? "You bet they are," he responds. "I tell people, 'I don't know how it is in other places, but I can tell you in Phillips in Oklahoma, the motivation from a raise lasts at best a month. But commendation and praise last an awfully long time."

The Roll-Down.   The elimination of many staff functions forced line managers to be far more independent. Empowering decentralized line managers to independently run their piece of the business was at the heart of Wallace's transformation strategy. Those close to operations better understand what needs to be done. They are closer to the customers and can react more quickly and flexibly to customers' needs.

What was Wallace looking for from empowerment? "How to get more value out of that front-end decision-making process. That meant a faster response time and better information when a person made a judgment," he explains.

To empower people, you must first inform them. Wallace believes that information has the power to maintain the "soul" of an organization—to connect executives to their organizations and empower the people who work there. He passes that philosophy onto his management team:

> Let me ask you something, gentlemen. When you go home at night and your kid comes in and asks, "Daddy, what did you do today?" I know you take a great sense of pride in telling them all of the great things you did, and all the great decisions you made, and the great impacts you had on the oil business, on society, and on America.
>
> But I want you to think about the guy that's working at our plant down in Sweeney, Texas, or some other town. He's an operator, or he's a maintenance man. And his kid asks him, "Daddy, what did you do today?" I want you to think about his answer. Did we give him anything to tell the kid? Does he really know what he did? Did we really share with him the kind of information he needs to say, "I'll tell you what we did today. . . ."

By allowing for the sharing of information and by keeping people in touch with the workings of the business and each other, Wallace believes information systems truly have the power to transform organizations.

As the system was made available to successive levels of management, the benefits multiplied. People understood their respective pieces of the business better, and decision making throughout the firm improved.

A Culture of Teamwork

For at least two reasons, a sense of teamwork was critical to recovery. First, morale had to be restored in order to effect the type of change that would turn the company around. Second, people had to work together to pull Phillips through the crisis.

"We all accept that as a word: team. It's a good buzzword. But that by itself does not make it happen. We've seen too damn many motivational speakers and quality people. Some of them do a great job, but a lot of them tell you all these great things and then you wonder, 'How am I going to implement that?'"

The sharing of information unified the company in a way that no motivational speeches or tactics could. Everyone became aware of operations upstream and downstream of their own. "People all over the company started looking at the whole row differently. There was a total change in how they thought—first of themselves, but more importantly of their role with respect to the others."

As a result, of their own accord, people began operating as a unit. "People throughout the organization started to work now more as a team," says Wallace. "We didn't say, 'Go out there and run pricing as a team.' It just happened. We just gave them the information to know whether they were killing the guy next door or vice versa."

The cultural change blossomed. Wallace reinforced it with other information tools. He wanted to open new avenues of communication with people at all levels and all locations of the organization. "Electronic mail is informal communication. It opened up a new communication link for us clear down through the organization. It gave us a new link to people. In 1985, we had about 450 users on the electronic-mail system. Of that 450, about 250 were in R&D and 200 of them were in information systems. Today, we have over 8,000 people worldwide on the system, and there are fewer than 10,000 exempt employees in our company."

The Evolving Role of Top Management

With the basic operations of the company back under control, Wallace and his executive team could turn their attention to other areas. Two issues seemed to require Wallace's personal attention:

- Getting the right people in the right jobs
- Formulating strategy

In each of these areas, Wallace again turned to the computer for assistance.

Getting the Right People in the Right Jobs.   In a streamlined organization, every person and every position counts. Wallace considered it his duty to be involved with placement decisions—both to get the right people on the job and to rebuild the company's morale through a fair appraisal system that rewarded results.

For this, he needed to be personally well-informed regarding personnel data:

> I wanted to be sure that people throughout the organization werc bcing fairly evaluated and being given the appropriate opportunities, such as development programs, for job advancement. In the information system, I could scan the entire exempt organization of Phillips Petroleum Company and look at people's profiles, their work history, and how they had been evaluated. I could pull that information up in seconds.

I could also see—for any group, section, division, or the company overall—how people were evaluated on a year-to-year basis, or on a five-year basis. It showed me who was the top-evaluated employee, who was the bottom, and all of the in-betweens.

Why wasn't his Human Resources staff doing all this analysis for him?

By looking at that information myself, it encouraged management people to be more sensitive about how they were treating people. When a new job opportunity came up, I wasn't limited to what some person brought me. They might have looked at two or three candidates and recommended one. I could scan through the system, look at more alternatives, and see if it was a good pick. I might think of some other segment of the business that we ought to cross-reference.

Was Wallace short-circuiting normal Human Resource processes? He describes it more as a matter of sending the right signals. "I rarely countermanded them. That wasn't the point. The point was to let them know I was involved in the process. That is the role of a leader."

Formulating Strategy. As the company started to solidify and return to profitability, Wallace could shift his attention from building an effective organization to strategy. To set the strategic direction for the new Phillips 66, Wallace felt it was important to be constantly well-informed about both internal and external events. "I think a business-man should know the environment every day before he starts to think. Most businessmen try to get it out of the *Wall Street Journal*. Let me tell you my philosophy on that. I'm by no means against Dow Jones, but that's last night's news at best. And I think the dynamics of the economic and political world are such today that you have to know what's going on. You've got to know it so you can help your troops know it."

The first thing Wallace did every day was to take a broad look at the environment by checking out the external databases on his system. "Is there anything out there I need to be aware of, anything that might impact this corporation today? What do I need to know right now?" As he spoke to me, he loudly snapped his fingers. Included in the external information that Wallace scanned was information on trade associations and congressional activities. "What are some of the key issues before the [American Petroleum Institute] today? I could pop in and actually see . . . what were some of the House bills that were up on the floor today."

Wallace believes that the value of external information will continue to increase for CEOs. "It will provide the sense of guidance and focus . . . strategic judgment of the longer range. And it will help in shaping philosophy . . . driving the business forward."

After assessing the external environment for the day, Wallace directed his gaze inward:

> I'd pop into the business reporting systems—not archived data, but the actual transactions of the business. I'd quickly scan such things as marketing volumes. If I saw something screwy, I'd pop into individual sections, but [if] generally everything checked out . . . I'd move on.
>
> I could spin through all of our global operations in a matter of minutes. I could actually see what was going on in all the operations—all the refineries, all the chemical operations. If there was something off, the people out there would explain it to me. They updated it every morning for me, and they added dialogue if necessary.

Wallace provides an example:

> Let's say that I looked at something and saw that the rate was off 35 percent. Well, even though I'm at the president's level, I'm not dumb. A 35 percent production rate is a hell of a lot of dollars. What I would find attached to those figures in the information system would be verbiage from the plant telling me why it's off, what actions were being taken to get it back on, and when I could expect it to be back up to rate.
>
> Before we had the dynamic information system, events like this were never picked up. Our previous information system was static, it gave you what *had* happened all the time. It couldn't tell you what *is* happening. We had reams of hard copy, but it didn't allow us to focus in quickly on what needed to be done. You simply can't get the information you need from historical operating reports. It doesn't allow you the speed and flexibility of a dynamic system.

By having such information on a constant basis, Wallace was better prepared to develop strategy and lead the people who worked for him.

Back from the Battlefield

As Wallace spoke, I glanced around his office. It occurred to me that the sculpture of the cowboy on the coffee table and the Japanese sculpture on his credenza were symbolic of his blending of styles. Having spent eight years working in Japan, Wallace had obviously been affected by Japanese management philosophies:

> I'm really committed to the concept that success is a thing that feeds up. This is the fundamental philosophy of the Japanese. In a Japanese organization, everything flows from the bottom up, not from the top down. Because ideas flow up from the bottom of Japanese organizations, people have a strong understanding and commitment to projects and their overall value to the whole operation.
>
> In America, we've operated on the authoritarian model for years. The senior management committee or the board makes the final decision: "Let's do it this way." Projects start from the top, and often the bottom of the organization is not involved until the program has already been approved and implementation is under way. So lower-level input to the project is limited.
>
> We're not going to change in America, and I don't think we should. I think we should take the best of both cultures. Information systems can help us transcend the authoritarian model. People who are well-informed are more involved and in a better position to give their input. What information systems allow us to do is disperse power to other levels of the corporation, without totally abandoning our management style.
>
> When you distribute information freely throughout your organization, you totally change your power base. In a way, you dilute it. You spread power much more evenly throughout your business. That is true participatory management."

It was this philosophy of leadership that convinced Wallace that he had to have personal involvement in the design and use of the information systems in his corporation. The system provided people at all levels with not only information about the company, but also external information about the world. Through it, Wallace broadened his own vision, the vision of his executives, and the vision of people throughout Phillips 66. By implementing the system, throughout the company, with an underlying philosophy of empowerment, Phillips experienced fantastic results.

Wallace's own words summarize the importance of information systems to leadership: "If the drive of the '90s is survival and the fundamental drive for executives is optimizing the effectiveness of the organization—I don't care whether you're using Peter Drucker's theories or [William] Ouchi's—if you don't have a good information system, you haven't got a chance of altering the effectiveness of the organization. Not a chance."

EXECUTIVE SUMMARY

This profile illustrates how profound and dramatic change in an organization can be facilitated through the design and use of information systems. Wallace knew that his direct involvement was necessary to make such a leadership strategy work. Through the marriage of his operational expertise and his personal understanding of the capabilities of information systems, Wallace was able to effect an impressive turnaround at Phillips 66.

PART SUMMARY

All of the cases in Part V illustrate how information systems can help executives orchestrate change in their organizations.

The need for change was driven by opportunity or crisis. The way these leaders chose to respond was through empowerment of their people in one form or another. Empowerment came by sharing information and coaching people to take on more responsibility, and by reinforcing decentralization efforts with access to information.

This part shows how computers can be used as levers of cultural change. A common tool chosen by all of these leaders was interactive access to flexible and dynamic internal databases by people at a variety of levels in the organization. Other tools included external databases, expert systems and electronic mail.

By making their organizations more flexible and responsive, these leaders helped their companies respond to immediate opportunities and crises. But, more importantly, the systems they put in place have changed the very fabric of their organizations. Because they opted for systemic change rather than "quick fixes," these leaders have created lasting effects that will serve their firms well in meeting the future demands of a constantly changing external environment.

VI

UNDERSTANDING

AND

ACHIEVING

THE BENEFITS

OF

EXECUTIVE

COMPUTING

Part VI

At this point, you may be wondering how all this information might pertain to you. Your business problems, challenges, and opportunities are unique. You cannot directly transplant the applications described in the profiles to your situation and expect the same results.

The profiles showed that, when applied properly, information tools can serve as valuable, effective leadership tools. The key phrase is "when applied properly." Uses of computers are highly individual. The value you receive from a computer is directly related to the importance of what you use it for.

To gain the benefits of a computer requires a bit of time and thought. You need to think through your particular business objectives, and carefully select the appropriate tools. Your participation is essential to making the tools part of a new way of doing business for you and those with whom you work. Part VI will assist you in this thought process. It provides you with two ways of thinking about your own potential applications.

First, we must clear the way for a fresh look at executive information systems. Chapter 18 examines some of the common myths surrounding EIS, and shows how the profiles in this book refute them.

Chapter 19 outlines a framework for understanding the benefits of executive computing, and it presents examples from the profiles. I have said that the main hurdle to computer use by executives is the fact that executives don't know what computers can do for them. Chapter 19 gives a full description of those benefits and describes in detail how computers relate to executive work. It is intended to trigger your imagination, as you think about your own business needs.

Chapter 20 describes a method for analyzing your individual business priorities and for selecting the appropriate tool for your current leadership challenge. It is a semi-structured approach that will help lead you to tools that match your business objectives.

CHAPTER 18

The Barriers Holding Executives Back

Myths and Realities

Early one morning in Albuquerque, New Mexico, I awaited my introduction as the keynote speaker for an executive breakfast meeting. As the clatter of knives and plates died down, the person introducing me said, "Ms. Boone will talk to us today about executive computing, *a term many of us have long considered to be an oxymoron—sort of like* airline cuisine.*"*

My host's comment encapsulates the widely held belief that executives won't, shouldn't, or can't use computers. The executives profiled in this book disprove this notion. Nonetheless, a spate of myths have developed regarding executives' willingness, and even ability, to use computers. Some myths have arisen out of ignorance; others have grown out of genuine concerns on the part of executives and their information systems support staff.

When I ask executives who do not use computers what is holding them back, here's what they say:

- Someone else can do all this for me.
- I don't want to give up my secretary.
- I can't type.
- I might make mistakes.
- I'm too old to learn.
- I'll just work all the time if I have a computer nearby.

Information systems professionals and other observers add three more obstacles to the list:

- It's too hard to learn.
- Executives are afraid of looking foolish.
- We haven't found the "perfect" executive system yet.

I call these obstacles myths because they mask a deeper truth. When carefully interviewed, executives eventually see that the real reason they're not using the computer is because they don't believe it will help them. They do not see a connection between what computers do and what they do as executives.

However, neither executives nor their information systems staffs generally appreciate this simple truth. Both groups have seen executive reticence or, perhaps, executive information systems that have gone unused. They really believe their chosen myth explains the problem.

This chapter probes beneath the surface of each of these myths, to clear the way for an objective look at what information tools can do for executives.

Someone Else Can Do All This for Me

Many people (including executives) believe that assistants should perform any work that an executive might do on a computer. This attitude arises from the belief that computers are administrative tools.

Executives who do use computers are not short on support staff. They simply do not want someone else to operate the computer for them. There are two basic reasons why. First, they say that many of the benefits they experience could not be realized without hands-on use of computers. Second, they strongly believe in setting an example for others. By using the computer themselves, they have learned its benefits, and they want these benefits to spread quickly throughout their companies.

Here's what computer-literate executives say about turning over operation of the computer to someone else:

My dependence on others would increase.

Sometimes the information I'm working with is confidential.

It would take longer to get things done.

I couldn't get as much done.

I can't transplant the filters in my head.

Others can't do my creative thinking for me.

I would lose practical knowledge about how computers can help.

It would diminish my ability to set an example for others.

My Dependence on Others Would Increase

The ability to work when and where they want to is by far the most prevalent reason that executives prefer to work hands-on. Richard Pogue—managing partner of Jones Day Reavis & Pogue, one of the world's largest law firms—gives a representative perspective on reducing dependence on others:

> If I have to communicate by using my secretary, well, she's wonderful, but she's got other things to do. If she's off someplace, I can't do it when I want to. [Using the computer yourself] gives you a much greater feeling of control over your own ability to function effectively, quickly, and efficiently. You're not reliant on other people. You can communicate directly when you want, and to whom you want. You feel more in control of your own destiny.

Use of computers frees executives to accomplish meaningful work at odd hours and in a variety of locations, allowing them more discretion over when and how their work gets done.

Sometimes the Information I'm Working with Is Confidential

Though executives are usually interested in sharing information and keeping people informed, there are occasions when executives have to work with confidential information. Common examples involve personnel issues—in particular, compensation. In cases of confidentiality, executives have two choices: They must either do the work by hand or learn how to operate the computer themselves. If the confidential work is complex, computers can add a great deal of value by extending the executive's ability to reason.

It Would Take Longer to Get Things Done

Executives find the immediate availability of information to be tremendously advantageous when they are thinking about an issue. When they want to act, they don't want a bureaucracy to slow them down. Computers allow them to get things done in a more timely manner. Also, executives say that they might look at information less often if it were less convenient to get.

Even if people are available to help every minute of the day, it is often less efficient to have them do a job when executives can do it quicker and better themselves by using a computer. Executives are often slowed down by having to ask others to operate the machine for them or produce reports.

I Couldn't Get as Much Done

The previous section referred to an executive's ability to address tasks more efficiently when they use a computer. Executives also discuss the importance of time in a different sense: productivity.

Without their personal use of computers, executives feel that they would get less work done each day. In *The Information Edge,* Ron Compton (then president of American Reinsurance, now president of Aetna) said he would retire if they took away his computer.[1] I told him that now, retirement was not an option. He laughed and gave me a serious reply: "I don't think that anybody could work much harder than I work. I get home at least three nights a week at 10:30 or later. So, [without the computer] I would wind up doing less. I would do what I do more slowly, and with lesser quality."

Computers increase an executive's ability to think and create—that is, to do *their* work, not their staff's work. By using computers, executives are able to accomplish more.

I Can't Transplant the Filters in My Head

Successful executives have built-in "radar," or an intuition, for important or pertinent information. It takes years of experience and accumulation of knowledge to know what bits and pieces of information are relevant to a particular problem. This radar helps the executive navigate creatively through large amounts of information. It is true that an executive can partially impart radar to others, but it is impossible to ever fully transplant those years of experience and knowledge.

Some executives like to put their radar to work by browsing through external databases. These databases contain information on thousands of topics drawn from a plethora of publications. This voluminous amount of information can be accessed in highly specific ways. When executives look for information on a specific topic in such a database "search," they are using their own experience and knowledge to filter through that information. By accessing information directly, executives are able to make full use of the value of their mental filters, and discover things they otherwise might never see.

Also, as executives look through information, one idea leads to another. Therefore, they cannot always anticipate what direction a search will take. By accessing the computer themselves, they are better able to explore related areas.

Once they have used the computer themselves, executives feel more connected to what is going on both inside and outside their organizations. They don't want to lose that direct feel for what is happening.

Others Can't Do My Creative Thinking for Me

Assistants can help us with various aspects of the work we do, but it is difficult or impossible to ask them to think for us.

For executives who use the computer as a creative tool, turning over the keyboard to someone else would be the equivalent of an artist handing the brush to another person. Ken McCready (TransAlta Utilities) sums up the situation: "I don't delegate my own creative, innovative problem solving." Executives like McCready choose information tools to address problems that require their direct attention and action—not to support those tasks that they should delegate to others.

I'd Lose Practical Knowledge About How Computers Can Help

Rarely do you find an executive who doesn't want to understand computers. But for years, a computer was just a black box as far as most executives were concerned. They said information systems people didn't translate technical concepts well enough to give a feel for what computers can actually do. Randy Fields (Mrs. Fields Cookies) provides a powerful description of the result of this failure to communicate:

> [When] executives are not computer literate, they make some terrible assumptions about what computers are. The typical individual who runs a company doesn't use computers, does not understand them, and is intimidated by them. As a result, [that executive] basically abrogates an important part of the strategic direction of the business. . . . If he doesn't understand the technology that shapes his business—past, present, and future—how can he possibly be in control of his strategic direction?

Ellen Gordon (Tootsie Roll Industries) recalls how she felt before she learned to use a computer herself:

> As executives, we have to get with it or we're really going to be left out. It's even evident in the way contemporary language is changing in literature, the media, and newspapers. For example, in the '60s, I didn't know what software was. Somebody said they wanted to make an investment in computers. I asked what exactly they were investing in, and they said hardware and software. I asked them the difference, and I didn't hear the answer. It took me some years to figure out the difference.

Executives say they must use the computer themselves because they believe that their own use of the technology helps keep them abreast of the ways in which technology can be used to benefit the entire corporation. Without their hands-on experience, executives believe their ability to lead their organizations in exploring strategic uses of information systems would be diminished. Their experience allows them to assist others in understanding how computers can help. Consider the comments of Melvin Gordon (Tootsie Roll Industries): "Many times [I] say to somebody, 'Hey, that computer program you want for inventory control is going to take a year. Why don't you try Lotus 1-2-3 on this phase, then you can do the rest later.' And they say, 'Oh yea, gee, we hadn't thought of that.' Nobody can say [to me], 'Well, I can't do this because it's too detailed.' I say, 'Come on.'" Ellen Gordon echoes the importance of personal experience: "We'll have discussions in my office among my executives. Those that use computers are savvy and understand the conversation; the others don't. They sometimes can't even follow our conversation. And I think that chasm is going to get wider and wider."

There is no substitute for direct experience. By personally discovering the connection between computers and human minds, executives are far better equipped to make intelligent decisions about the direction of computing at their organizations.

It Would Diminish My Ability to Set an Example for Others

Not only does personal experience give executives a better understanding of what computers can do, but it also helps them avoid hypocrisy. Many executives expect others in their companies to use computers; some are determined to set an example for the rest of the organization by using computers themselves.

> I bought into the philosophy that technology could put us a step ahead of the competition. So I decided that if I'm going to preach that gospel, I ought to practice it as well. So I said, "Give me a PC."
> —RICHARD POGUE (Jones Day Reavis & Pogue)

> Look at the downside. If you don't use a computer, you're almost telling people who you're expecting to use a computer that, somehow or other, there's something wrong with it. . . . That's exactly opposite of the impression you want to give them.
> MARK EDMISTON (*The Cable Guide*)

> I think my own personal use [of a computer] has helped others in the company adopt it. They say, "Well, if Ken has the time to use it and can learn, maybe I should too."
> —KEN McCREADY (TransAlta Utilities)

Executives are the ultimate opinion leaders. Every one of the executives that I interviewed said that their own use of a computer influences use by others.

All of the reasons outlined in this section explain why executives want to use computers themselves, hands-on. However, there are situations in which executives may choose *not* to operate the computer. Executives sometimes have others operate a computer for them, particularly in a meeting environment. I don't want to discourage the use of a "chauffeur" when that is appropriate. But be careful. Until you have used a computer yourself, it's hard to know whether or not someone else can do it all for you. I liken the situation to the use of a telephone. It may or may not (depending on your style) be appropriate to have a secretary get another person on the telephone for you. But are you going to stand there and talk *through* the secretary? No. You're going to take the receiver and speak directly to the person on the line. For executives, the same is true of the computer.

I Don't Want to Give Up My Secretary

Another common myth is that the computer will replace the secretary. If this were to happen, the executive would lose the benefit of a number of paraprofessional services that computers cannot perform.

In fact, computers do not replace secretaries. Note that if executives are performing strategic applications on the computer, then they are not doing their secretary's administrative work. Even when executives use word processors or electronic calendars, their secretaries handle the administrative aspects of the work.

Nonetheless, the role of the executive secretary deserves a closer look because it is an important one, and it does change somewhat when an executive begins to use a computer. The executives I spoke with who use word processors, for example, use them strictly for "thinking" work. Once they have gotten their thoughts together, they then pass their work to a secretary for formatting and cleaning up. Deanna Marecz, secretary to Richard Pogue (Jones Day Reavis & Pogue), explains, "On Monday mornings I often find a floppy disk on my desk with all of the work he's done over the weekend. I go through the diskette, edit what he's typed, and print it out for him."

Barbara Schlaht, secretary to Thomas Stephens (Manville Corporation), explains how not doing drafts has changed her function: "He works on the plane, and he works at home. He'll bring his disk in and say, 'Clean this up for me.' [Not having to type drafts or take shorthand] frees me up to do my job. Now I can help with really big projects. . . ."

When executives are on-line, their secretaries are almost always on-line.* When secretaries are proficient computer users, many of them add the role of troubleshooting to their normal responsibilities.

---

*Of the sixteen executive computer users I interviewed, only one secretary does not use a computer. In my six years of dealing with executive users, she is the first executive secretary I have encountered who does not use a computer.

If the executive has a problem with the computer, the secretary is often the first line of defense for helping to solve the problem. One of the most active troubleshooters I met was Cindy Joyce, secretary to Ron Compton (Aetna). Joyce describes her role: "There are times I will help him troubleshoot things on the system. . . . When he gets stuck in the middle of something, he'll say, 'Cindy, I can't get this thing to work,' and I'll show him a way out." Joyce believes that computers have broadened her role. "I don't feel as though it takes away anything from me at all. If anything, it creates more interesting work for you, and it broadens your job."

Rachel Gardner, secretary to Richard Crandall (Comshare), points out that the troubleshooting role is challenging and enjoyable. "Technical knowledge . . . is a change in the secretarial role. You end up learning how the system works, and it's fun. You're not just a person who sits there and types. At one point, I was working on three word processing systems because I was doing some work for another executive. It's interesting to see how the different systems work."

At Mrs. Fields Cookies, the secretarial role has changed significantly throughout the company. Debbi Fields describes how her secretary, E. G. Perry, is much more involved in significant work: "E. G. is a good example. She does much more significant work because we both use a computer. She understands Debbi Fields; she understands the company. She has a big view of where the company is going."

Jackie McQueary, secretary to Bill Esrey (United Telecom and US Sprint), uses her computer to help her boss with follow-up. "If Mr. Esrey sends something to someone with a question on it, I take [an electronic] copy for follow-up. If I don't see the response within what he considers to be a reasonable period of time, I can send them [an electronic message] and ask when we can expect a response."

Like the secretaries who do *not* use computers, most secretaries who do say that they spend a majority of their time on scheduling and making travel arrangements. As Jeanne Winkler, secretary to Michael Jordan, (Frito-Lay) quips: "I spend most of my time scheduling. Actually, *rescheduling* is probably more accurate."

Some executives use electronic calendars. Secretaries have, in most cases, strict control over those calendars. I frequently heard secretaries say that, due to problems with doublebooking, they were the only ones who were allowed to change the electronic calendar. They added that electronic calendars containing all the executives' schedules made it much easier to schedule meetings.

It is amusing to note that computers have empowered executives as well as secretaries. As Cindy Joyce (Aetna) jokingly points out, "When your boss uses a computer, you quickly find out that you can't say 'It's the computer's fault' anymore!"

Computer use by secretaries and bosses seems to have significant benefits for both parties. They can stay in better touch with each other, and together design solutions to the problems of running an executive office. It's always been true that secretaries are an integral part of an executive's effectiveness, and computers haven't changed that.

I Can't Type

The myth about typing is perhaps the oldest and most popular of the myths about executive computing. This myth often hides other fears, concerns, and misconceptions about the value of computers. Here's what computer-literate executives have to say in response to "I can't type":

> You may not need to.
> I type with two fingers.
> Learn!

Only a few of the computer-literate executives I spoke with are really proficient typists; most "hunt and peck":

> I do a fast hunt and peck. You don't have to type. You learn roughly where the keys are. With the mouse and the [function] keys, you can do an awful lot.
> —BILL ESREY (United Telecom and US Sprint)

> I'm an awkward typist at best. I learned in grade 10, and I just barely passed the course. I was a good student except for typing and physical education. I'm not well-coordinated!
> —KEN McCREADY (TransAlta Utilities)

> I'd like to be a better typist. It doesn't bother me, though, or keep me from using [the computer]. I'm not a good typist. . . . So what?
> —SANDY SIGOLOFF (Wickes Companies)

> I don't type all that well. But I type as fast as I need to.
> —RON COMPTON (Aetna)

These executives are clearly saying that typing proficiency is not a prerequisite to using a computer.

On the other hand, a bit of typing skill is likely to speed things up. The fact of the matter is that typing is not all that hard to learn. The quotations that follow illustrate two simple ways of learning:

> I've only met one guy who couldn't type . . . a real senior guy. So I bought him a $49 typing tutorial [that runs on the computer]. I taught my kids to type that way.
>
> —RON COMPTON (Aetna)

> I bought a book called *How to Type in 24 Hours.* It took me six hours. I'm not the greatest typist, but I'll type an electronic message out to somebody.
>
> —ELLEN GORDON (Tootsie Roll Industries)

Typing does not have to be perfect. There is an unwritten code among executives about grammar, spelling, and punctuation in informal electronic messages. The following quotations illustrate this "computing code of conduct":

> You don't have to be the greatest typist in the world. You don't need to be spelling and paragraphing properly [for electronic mail]. It doesn't matter.
>
> —ELLEN GORDON (Tootsie Roll Industries)

> There's a rule around here. Nobody pays attention to spelling [in electronic mail]. You know, even if you see something, you don't go back and correct it. The idea is that you communicate. You don't worry about how it looks.
>
> —BILL ESREY (United Telecom and US Sprint)

For more formal documents, we've already seen that executives often have their secretaries clean up their rough drafts:

> I do the rough draft, and I don't even worry about the spelling. I put it in the out box and [the assistant] can fix it when she's ready.
>
> —MARK EDMISTON (*The Cable Guide*)

> I'm always behind on correspondence. So I'll take a batch of letters home, type out the responses on a disk, and bring the disk in. I don't format [the letters]. I give [the disk] to my secretary, and she looks up the address and adds 'Dear Roger' or whatever.
>
> —RICHARD POGUE (Jones Day Reavis & Pogue)

The simple fact of the matter is this: If an executive needs or wants to use an application badly enough, he or she will find a way. Robert Wallace, former president of Phillips 66, illustrates this point:

> We started out on electronic mail, and I didn't want it because I didn't type. I consented to it because it had some other benefits, like scheduling. But then I started finding mail messages on my machine . . . you know, the little sign, "Mail waiting." And so I'd pop into it. . . . In the beginning, believe it or not, I'd dictate a response through my secretary. But after a while, I'd just punch out a little cryptic note and push it through there and sometimes get an answer back in *minutes* . . . maybe from our guy in London. . . . So the value of mail really grew on me.

In the final analysis, poor typing is not a showstopper, it's merely an excuse for not using a computer. If executives say they are not using a computer because they don't know how to type, there are almost always other, more significant, reasons behind that excuse. Usually, the excuse masks an executive who doesn't see how the benefits of the computer outweigh the minor nuisance of typing.

I Might Make Mistakes

In the training stage or in the very early stages of use, executives may sometimes be concerned about losing work or destroying the work of others. But, in fact, it's not so easy to destroy the machine or the work. And it's also true that everybody makes mistakes—they're nothing to be ashamed of. Mistakes indicate that you're learning.

Thomas Plaskett (Pan Am) provides one example of a mistake:

> My son [used my home computer to] run one of those bulletin board services. [I use the computer too, for work, and] I let him have a chunk of the hard disk [for his bulletin board]. When I came home from a very long trip to Japan during the Northwest negotiation, I walked in the house and his face was white. Apparently there are good guys and bad guys who run bulletin boards. My son had installed a new board, and a Darth Vader type found a back door into the computer and scrambled my hard disk . . . three years of financial information. Luckily I had most of it backed up. So I gave [my son] that computer and I bought a new one.

One executive learning experience ended up on the pages of *The Wall Street Journal*. Richard Pogue (Jones Day Reavis & Pogue) came into the office one Labor Day weekend after he had first learned to use the computer. He spent three hours typing a speech on the word processor and then pushed a button and was unable to retrieve it. Fortunately, the next morning, his secretary pushed another button and found it immediately.

All the "mistake" stories executives told me had happy endings. Data was retrieved; no machines disintegrated. As Debbi Fields (Mrs. Fields Cookies) puts it, "Don't be afraid of blowing it up. I did, and I'm here to tell about it." Though fear may play a role in executive hesitancy, interest in utility and benefits should far outweigh the fear.

I'm Too Old to Learn

Some executives talk about how the next generation of managers and executives will be the ones to make use of computers. They believe that they are too old and set in their ways to learn new methods of doing business. But, if we wait for the next generation, organizations will lose much of the value that computers can offer today. And, in fact, much of the groundwork for the next generation must be laid today. Executives need to understand and use computers to be competitive, both now and in the future.

Only 4 of the 16 executives I interviewed are under 50 years of age. (See Figure 3.) It is meaningless to try to extrapolate statistics from such a small sample, but the point is that age has less to do with use of a computer than inclination.

Ellen Gordon discussed her experience at Tootsie Roll: "Some of our executives are very fast, and others are struggling. Originally, I

FIGURE 3
AGE OF EXECUTIVE INTERVIEWEES

Age	Number of interviewees
30–39	1
40–49	4
50–59	6
60 and up	5

thought [computer use] was going to be a function of age. It's *not* a function of age. We have people who are over 65 who are whizzes . . . and others who just can't get it. . . . We have one marketing person over 65, and he now teaches others how to use the computer." Tootsie Roll is not the only company in which an older executive has set the example for a younger one. One chairman said: "My president is a young man, 38 years old. He kept watching me use a computer, and the next thing I know, he has a computer on his desk."

Certainly, younger people have had more exposure to computers. But the young have no franchise on curiosity, creativity, and intellectual ability. All the executives I interviewed agree with me: CEOs will overcome age barriers if they see a compelling reason to learn how to use a computer. In fact, use of a computer can have side benefits for the elder executives in particular. One executive related this delightful anecdote: "When someone works on a speech for me, I have them put it in my word processor. Then I can arrange it and change it, and put it out at the last minute at home—*in whatever font I can read without my reading glasses!*"

I'll Just Work All the Time If I Have a Computer Nearby

Most executives already work too much, so it's easy to see why they might be concerned that a nearby computer will tempt them to work even more. Most hands-on executives are keenly aware of the problems a home computer can cause. For example, one said: "I'm sure my wife sometimes finds the computer at home to be a pain in the neck. Most of the time, I try to pick a time [to use it] when she's doing something else."

The computer may not be the culprit. In fact, without a home computer, some executives would find themselves spending more time away from home. One executive admitted, "I've had some complaints about working on the computer too much at home from time to time. But, on the balance, it hasn't really been intrusive. I think it's true that having a computer keeps me from having to come back to the office."

I was interested in how executives manage to balance their home lives with their home computers. Many of them take pains to keep from overdoing home computer use, as evidenced by the following comment: "Do I drag myself up and go compulsively to the machine at night? No. If I don't want to go to the machine, I don't go to the machine. If I don't want to go to work, I don't go to work."

Some are careful in their choice of on-line time:

"When I'm with my family, I have to really be with my family. I love to be with my kids. But I take full advantage of when they are sick and tired of playing with me [laughter], and I take advantage of nap times. Being with me all day is quite boring [laughter]. I use the computer [at home] early in the morning or when I can't sleep."

"When the kids were at home, I'd always bring the portable home and put it on the dining-room table while everybody was watching TV. My wife and I have been married 36 years. We went to nursery school together. We have an understanding. She knows there are times when I really need to do it. I don't abuse it."

A lot of executives have gotten around complaints at home by getting their spouses and families interested in using computers as well:

"My wife didn't make use of it for a long, long time. But recently she's been using it more and more. She uses it for some writing and some genealogy. She volunteers for a number of organizations, and one of them has some material she's been transcribing for them."

"My wife is using it to plan our daughter's wedding in November. She's keeping lists on it."

"Usually when I get home, my wife and my six-year-old daughter have already had dinner. I ask about school, and then she and her mom will head for the tub, and that's my signal that I can go work. I'll go down to the basement and start getting set up. My daughter comes down from the tub wrapped in a towel, and it's computer-game time. She pulls her chair up to mine, and we've got a whole series of games to play. So it's a business tool, but it's also something she and I share. We love to go to the computer store together to buy new software."

On the other hand, some family members remain unenthusiastic about the prospect of using the intruder:

"I tried getting my wife to put her bills on there. Didn't work. Then I said, 'How about putting it up for your Month-At-a-Glance?' She said, 'I use my Filofax.' Then I said, 'Well, what about using it to type letters?' She said, 'I like to write personal letters.' "

"I've asked my wife to send me electronic mail messages from home so we won't be playing telephone tag, but she won't. The kids will, though."

Ron Compton (Aetna) points out that there isn't always a choice in the matter of working outside the office. When I asked him about the fact that he takes a laptop with him on board his sailboat, he responded: "I don't *want* to work on the sailboat. Who wants to work on a Saturday? But they didn't ask me that when they gave me this job."

Overall, the problem of long executive work days is unquestionably linked much more closely to personality and business environment than technology. It is not clear that executives work longer hours because they have computers; however, the computer does present a powerfully attractive means of getting those few extra hours of work done.

Some executives seem to be able to incorporate their computers into their family lives better than others. It is important to keep in mind that the computer *can* be an intrusion, but, by the same token, it doesn't *have* to be an intrusion. Having a computer in the home calls for the same consideration required in having a television or a telephone.

It's Too Hard to Learn

This is the first of three myths that are primarily held by people who aren't executives, especially those in the information systems profession. Ease-of-use has been a controversial issue in the area of executive systems. Many say that executives will not use computers unless they have very simple interfaces. For example, a tag line for an article in a popular business magazine read: "Now, specially designed systems are so simple that even CEOs can use them."[2]

Though such attitudes are often expressed tongue in cheek, when it comes to computers, many people are almost insulting in their assessments of executives' learning abilities. I'm always astonished that people underrate executives' ability to learn. Robert Wallace (Phillips 66) shares my sentiments:

Ease-of-use is not an issue. The executive user, even though he is uninitiated to a computer, is not unintelligent. He's hyperintelligent. Our thought processes are fast. What got us to the top of our organizations is our ability to take information from many different sources, assimilate it, and focus on a conclusion. So it just takes a matter of hours before we can learn to do things. Why is it any different on a computer?

[Computer] systems are very simple. They're not like going and doing computer programming or something. . . . A lot of [information systems] people that I've run into underrate or underestimate the user's capability, and they build too many bells and whistles into the system. They build systems that are intellectually below the user's ability. And that's a big mistake.

Some things on the system are just trite. The executive doesn't like it. I spoke with an executive at one of the largest insurance companies, and he said, "Great system. But it's got too much trash on it. Amber flags coming up, and junk like that. I don't need that stuff." It gets in the way.

Ron Compton (Aetna) also mentions how simplistic user interfaces can get in the way once an executive crests the learning curve: "The first thing I do in [my word processor] is get rid of that help screen at the top. It takes up too much room on the screen."

It is even possible that simplistic interfaces have been responsible for slowing the evolution of executive computing in two ways:

- First, for fear of scaring the executive, information systems people may demonstrate only simplistic information retrieval capabilities. This encourages executives to continue to view computers as a convenience—as merely a means of getting information faster and more conveniently packaged. By demonstrating only the simple, systems people reinforce the myth of computers as administrative tools and discourage executives from learning more about computers.

- Second, the emphasis on simplicity has caused much of the research in executive computer systems to be channeled into making computers easy rather than focused on applications that augment the executive mind.

Of course the second implication is more serious than the first. Ease of use is not the primary factor in the executive's adoption process—it's easy to blow up balloons, but executives don't sit around in offices doing that. Executives don't do things because they are easy; they do things because they produce results. Consider the example of a formula 1 race car. No one ever told a performance driver that it would be easy to operate a formula 1 car. Can you imagine suggesting that he or she take a Chevrolet Caprice out in the next race because it would be easier to drive?

We make an investment in learning to operate a machine or a tool based on what it will return to us in performance. Executives who say they want easy systems may do so because they don't understand the power or capacity of the computer to perform. If they view the computer as a convenience, they perceive the payoff as relatively low. Consequently, they expect it to be easy to learn. But if they are convinced that the computer can extend their capacity to think and reason, then they are much more likely to stretch themselves to learn it, use it, and benefit from it.

Because they understand the powerful benefits of extending their ability to think and handle complexity, executives who already use computers say they are willing to invest in a learning curve. But that investment must pay off. Software for executives should accelerate the thinking process.

Ultimately, as executives become more savvy about computers and their capabilities, I believe they will demand more functionality, and they will be extraordinarily creative in designing their own applications. Executives will recognize that computers can assist them in ways that technologists may not anticipate. As this occurs, I believe executives will get more and more impatient with "friendly" interfaces, unless these interfaces are also fast, intuitive, and powerful.

An interesting observation on ease of use surfaced in the course of the interviews. Many executives are already recognizing that it is more important that software be easy to *remember* than easy to *learn*.

> If you don't do things on a repetitive enough basis, you forget and you feel sort of dumb. But we all do that. You forget . . . if you haven't used it for three weeks. It's amazing.
> —BILL ESREY (United Telecom and US Sprint)

> I'm gone 50 percent of the time. [In the time away, you] can forget a lot of the nuances of [the computer]. The longer you use it, [the more] it's just automatic and you find a greater degree of comfort with it. I can get locked out of it, but I can get back in now without kicking it!
> —BURNELL ROBERTS (Mead Corporation)

> When you really get the use out of [a computer] is when you have a need to be proficient. If you put the thing down for a week, you have to plan that you're going to be frustrated about 25 percent of the time.
> —SANDY SIGOLOFF (Wickes Companies)

To date, most software has been designed to be easy to learn as opposed to easy to remember. It is a subtle but important distinction. Software should have an intuitive component so that executives can use it after periods of absence.

In designing software at Mrs. Fields Cookies, Randy Fields (chairman) has an interesting philosophy regarding the user-interface issue:

> Our definition of software is that it has to be user-easy, not user-friendly. By that, we mean that it should represent an analogous system to something that someone already knows. The easiest way to teach someone is by analogy, not by teaching them a new thing. Because people are innately intimidated by machines, it's best if the machine works as they do, not vice versa. So we prefer no graphic interface, no icons, no mice, no things that people don't use. We prefer form-based systems.

Dr. Douglas C. Engelbart pioneered the use of information tools as thinking tools. The software and hardware that Engelbart invented is not necessarily easy to learn, but it is extremely easy to remember and extraordinarily fast and flexible. Engelbart designs formula 1 race cars for the mind. Unfortunately, many of his original design ideas were watered down by ease-of-use enthusiasts.

Engelbart stresses consistency as a means of helping the user remember commands. Ideally, commands mean the same thing across different tools. The way the user puts information into the computer is consistent. And commands are structured with verb-noun grammar to match the English imperative form (for example, *delete word* instead of *word delete*).

The idea of consistency may not seem revolutionary, but I am repeatedly surprised as to how inconsistent software can be. Many types of software use inconsistent vocabulary—even within the same piece of software. My electronic calendar is an example of bad design. If I want to print a single day from my calendar, the command is *list*. But if I want to print the entire month, the command is *print*.

Syntax is also a frequent design problem. Users are often asked to use menus, function keys, or different keyboard combinations to give commands in different places within the same piece of software.

By focusing on consistency and the way the mind works rather than worrying about ease-of-learning, Engelbart created tools that move at the speed of thought.

Whenever possible, impediments to learning should be removed, but not at the expense of diminished functionality or logic. In the early stages of executive computing, I expect ease of learning to remain a controversial issue. However, people who are designing software for the executive would do well to follow Engelbart's example by remembering the high intellectual horsepower of the target audience.

There is an ever-present tension between friendliness and functionality. Computers should be designed to be as easy to use as possible *for the level of performance expected.*

Executives Are Afraid of Looking Foolish

Many people are absolutely convinced that executives don't use computers for one reason: fear of looking foolish. Though there may be a certain amount of apprehension associated with learning something new, I don't believe that fear of trying something new is a serious impediment to the acceptance of computers by executives.

Executives face much more significant threats than a computer— meeting payroll, labor disputes, bankruptcy, international terrorism, and environmental catastrophes, to name just a few. Sandy Sigoloff's experience could hardly be added to this list: "I bought this laptop to travel with, and I found it very frustrating when I couldn't remember all of the commands. So you bang it, you hit it, you push every damn combination [laughter], and the guy next to you on the airplane is looking at you saying, 'Right, right' [laughter]."

Though this example trivializes the "fear" myth, the fact remains that there are a couple of grains of truth to examine. Several of the executives mentioned to me that they believed their peers were concerned about appearing 'secretarial.' This results from executive perceptions of computers as administrative tools. There is no question that new concepts and ways of working produce a certain level of discomfort. But the level of this discomfort has been greatly exaggerated in the case of executives and computers. Such minor apprehensions fade quickly once executives are familiar with the significant ways in which computers can help them.

We Haven't Found the "Perfect" Executive System Yet

This myth is particularly popular among information systems professionals. They tell me that before they will be ready to start executive computing, they need to clean up the corporate data or that they haven't approached their executives yet because they are searching for the perfect executive system.

However, the corporate data will never be perfectly clean. In addition, an executive may not need perfection to accomplish his or her goals.

Also, there is no such thing as a perfect executive system. In fact, an executive may not even need access to organizational databases. I have a friend, Tom Lodahl, who likes to say, "Personal computers are personal!" And it's true: What one executive loves, another wouldn't think of using. Witness some of the contradictory comments I received:

- If I could only have one tool on the computer, it would be a spreadsheet.
  - I don't get into spreadsheets, but lots of other people do.

- We don't use voice mail here. We use electronic mail.
  - Instead of using electronic mail, I use voice mail.

- With the model, we can do what-if's in our meetings.
  - I don't do modeling. Our system is not for what-if. Our system is for what-is.

- The word processing function is very, very useful.
  - I don't use the word processor.

Executives, as a group, use an incredibly broad variety of tools. Most of them, as individuals, use at least two different tools, and sometimes as many as five or six. The executives that I interviewed for this book use the diversity of information tools listed in Figure 4. They probably use even a few more that I didn't hear about.

The diversity of the tools executives use confirms the need for a broad definition of *executive information systems*. In other words, there is no perfect system for executives. Each individual selects tools according to his or her specific business needs.

FIGURE 4
TOOLS USED BY EXECUTIVE INTERVIEWEES

Electronic mail	Commitment tracking systems
Voice message systems	Expert systems
Outline editors	Internal databases
Word processing	External databases
Graphics packages	Personal databases
Spreadsheets	Group databases
Audioconferencing	Models
Videoconferencing	Project management systems
Computer conferencing	Reminder systems
Videotape	Spell checkers
Cellular phones	Facsimile
Calendars	

It is interesting to note that, in the past five years, an evolution in executives' use of information tools has taken place. When I interviewed executives for *The Information Edge,* most executives picked one tool and, for the most part, stuck with it—even when another tool might have been more appropriate. Now executive computer users are learning additional tools and applying them more selectively and judiciously.

This evolution is important because it indicates that executives who use computers are becoming more sophisticated in their knowledge of computers. Clearly, the benefits they have experienced from their early use of single tools are sufficient to warrant investing time in learning new concepts and new types of software. If the past few years are any indication, we can expect executives to continue to expand the number of highly specialized types of software in their repertoire.

Individuals must match their own objectives with an appropriate set of tools. Executives should start out by identifying their business objectives, picking their top priority, and selecting a tool that helps with that priority. It's best to start small and evolve. Employing a business-driven approach (explained in more detail in Chapter 20) increases the odds that an executive system will be of strategic value.

Chapter Summary

This chapter has examined many of the popular myths about why executives don't use computers. The executives quoted in this chapter provide rebuttals to those excuses, and they refute common misconceptions about executive computing. It is important to dispel these myths, because they have been largely responsible for the slow growth of executive computing.

But a simple fact remains: Few executives use computers in meaningful ways. The real cause, I believe, is a perceived lack of linkage between the tools and executives' jobs.

There is no intrinsic value to simply using a machine. If executives see no relevant benefits to computer use, then they are completely justified in not using a computer. To be used, computers must contribute in significant ways to top-priority business objectives that executives personally care about. It is not surprising that more executives have not adopted computers when most know so little about the benefits of computing. Only when they see the connection between their jobs and computing should they make the investment of time and effort required to learn to use a computer.

What, then, are the benefits that justify the learning curve? Parts II–V provided compelling examples of how computers can meet specific executive objectives. The profiles illuminated why these leading executives use computers hands-on. The benefits they are receiving are summarized in the next chapter.

NOTES

1. Dean Meyer and Mary Boone, *The Information Edge* (Homewood, IL: Dow-Jones Irwin, 1989), p. 238.
2. *Business Week,* June 27, 1988, p. 84.

CHAPTER 19

A Summary
of the Benefits

The profiles describe, in a business context, the ways in which leading executives benefit from the use of information tools. This chapter gathers together the various threads from these diverse profiles.

Chapter 18 argues that the primary reason why so many executives do not use computers is a lack of understanding of the connection between information tools and their personal challenges as leaders. This chapter directly addresses that objection by answering the question What can computers do for me?

This chapter is important as a precursor to selection of your own system. First, it will help broaden your view of what is possible. A narrow view may predispose you to accept others' descriptions of what computers can do for executives—particularly those applications that have been widely advertised in the trade press, such as on-line access to operational reports. Understanding the diversity of potential results will encourage you to ask not only What can I do with a computer? but also What do I need as a leader? It establishes a broad scope of discussion for the needs assessment process. Second, you can use the list of benefits presented in this chapter to target areas of your own interest. Third, by looking at benefits before you look at the information tools that generated them, you will develop a feel for the process of translating business needs into information solutions. (The process for analyzing your needs and determining relevant solutions is described in Chapter 20.)

Executive computing allows leaders to:

- Leverage time
- Be well-informed
- Communicate

- Coach
- Shape culture
- Enhance personal thinking

The leadership benefits were gained with a variety of information tools, each tailored to the setting in which they were applied. Each benefit is equally valuable, although some will be more relevant than others in the context of a specific business situation. In essence, the framework of benefits presented in this chapter provides a stepping-stone between business requirements and information tools. You may not identify precisely with a particular executive's business situation and personal leadership strategy. Nonetheless, you may be seeking a similar kind of gain in leadership effectiveness. This taxonomy of benefits may help you clearly state what it is that you want from a computer. This chapter is arranged in the same order as Figure 5, and it includes descriptions of each of the benefits and examples.

Leverage Time

I've never met an executive who believes that there are enough hours in the day. Gargantuan demands are made upon executives' time. David Diamond, author of *The Wall Street Journal Book of Chief Executive Style,* put it nicely when he said: "If there's one trait that binds CEOs, it's an innate ability to use their time with precision to accomplish several tasks in the time it takes the rest of us to accomplish one."[1] Necessity is the mother of invention.

Although time is the scarcest executive resource, I was concerned about including the theme of effective time use because I was afraid it would be misinterpreted. So often I hear executives say, "I don't have time to save time!" Already, too many people view computers as a mere timesaving device. I didn't want to reinforce the administrative, or "efficiency," view of information tools.

There's no question that executives can save time by using computers. Almost all the interviewed executives mentioned that the computer adds minutes or even hours to their productive time each day. But there's more to managing time than simple efficiency. As management guru Peter Drucker writes: "Effective executives know where their time goes. They work systematically at managing the little of their time that can be brought under their control."[2]

FIGURE 5
HOW COMPUTERS HELP EXECUTIVES

Leverage Time
Improve responsiveness
Work independently of time and location (perform
asynchronous work)

Be Well-Informed
Stay up-to-date
Increase depth of knowledge
Adjust filters on information
Absorb information quickly

Communicate
Be accessible
Improve the clarity and consistency of messages
Personalize communication with others
Improve listening abilities
Be more persuasive

Coach
Build credibility as a leader
Track commitments
Balance the need to know with the need to delegate
Broaden peoples' perspectives
Teach critical-thinking abilities

Shape Culture
Focus people on what's important
Measure performance on selected goals and objectives
Pick, promote, and reward the right people
Flatten hierarchies and empower people

Enhance Personal Thinking
Manage complexity
Think creatively
Balance logic and intuition
Improve clarity of thinking
Improve group thinking processes

Executives need to be able to work when and where *they* want to. To best leverage their time, executives need to reduce their dependence on other people's schedules. Here, computers can help. Computers give access to the tools and information executives need whether it is a Saturday afternoon or a Monday morning or whether they are in their offices or flying on a corporate jet.

In fact, the need to leverage time proved to be one of the most common reasons executives felt they needed to use the tools hands-on. In this regard they frequently mentioned the need to work *asynchronously*—that is, to collaborate with others without being in the same place at the same time.

Robert Wallace (Phillips 66) noted that *managing* time is more important to executives than *saving* time. "The computer saves each of our executives 30 minutes to an hour and a half a day, because information is so readily retrievable. We don't call up a secretary, we don't go rummaging through files. We can pop up information instantaneously. It saves us a lot of time, but that's not the true value. The value comes from being more effective."

The profiles contained many examples of how executives have used computers to help free them to some degree from the tyranny of time. Their use of computers and communication tools enables them to be more responsive and to perform work when and under what circumstances they wish.

Improve Responsiveness

Because direction often emanates from the executive suite, it's easy for executives to become an organization's bottleneck. Ron Compton (Aetna), illustrates the bottleneck phenomenon:

> Let's say I have something really short I want to get to someone in writing. I could dictate it. Then two hours later, Cindy comes into the office, picks it up, types it, and inserts it into the green folder she places on my desk twice a day for signatures. (And I've tried not signing things; people resent it.) Now I have to sign it, then she has to send it out. It is now six hours later.
>
> She's not the problem; I am. In fact, many times I'm only in this office for an hour a day. With electronic mail, I can turn around to the machine and go *bang*, and it takes me maybe three minutes to ask [or respond to] a question. And all the person on the other end has to do is to type two keystrokes to respond to me.

Dictation and other activities associated with formal correspondence simply take too long. Executives find that information systems allow them to respond more quickly to the demands made on them. By using computers, executives have found that they can avoid situations where decisions are delayed because of a need for their input.

Work Independently of Time and Location (Asynchronous Work)

As Drucker points out, *control* over one's time is critical.[3] Control is most difficult to achieve when your tasks are dependent upon others' schedules. The important contribution of the computer to leveraging time is the way in which it supports asynchronous work.

To review, the definition of asynchronous is not coinciding in time.[4] Quite often, executives find that the free time they do have occurs in off hours—early mornings, late evenings, weekends, while traveling, or on holidays. By having access to people and information around the clock, executives can make much better use of the time available.

There are two types of asynchronous work: thinking and communicating. When an individual or group of executives is thinking through a problem or opportunity, breaks in that thinking process can be quite disruptive. In fact, quite often executives schedule their thinking work outside the distractions of the normal business setting. The asynchronous access to information that computers allow enables executives to avoid interruptions and to work without regard to the availability of others.

The second type of asynchronous work is communication, and it constitutes a large part of an executive's job. By making people accessible at all hours in all parts of the world, information tools allow executives to accomplish work in a very flexible time frame. Later in this chapter, under the heading of "communicate," you will see examples of asynchronous communication work. For now, this section will explore the use of computers for asynchronous "thinking" work.

"A lot of the value [of computers] is their ability to let us work on our own time," explains Burnell Roberts (Mead). "I can work in an independent time frame. I come in on Saturdays and may need some information then. If there are certain key data that are pertinent to the work I'm doing that day, I can just pull up the information on the computer and use it. I don't have to wait until Monday morning. You know, most of the [weekdays are] *so* busy. Much of what I do is after five in the evening. The computer gives me greater freedom of work time."

These off hours may be critical to success. For lack of uninterrupted time to accomplish projects, opportunities may be delayed, canceled, or never initiated.

Travel time is often used by executives for thinking work. Wilbur Gantz (Baxter) gives an example of leveraging the travel time of an entire group:

> The last trip to Europe, we flew over on the company plane. There were four of us on the plane, and we had a computer with us; we spent time going through some of the numbers. People are less impatient in this kind of setting, and of course, there are fewer interruptions. We could have taken paper printouts, but we literally would have had to have taken five mammoth books of reports. But that inconvenience is less important than the fact that we could never have gone through all of the information as effectively using paper. We were asking lots of questions, interacting with the model. We couldn't have considered as many alternatives, and it wouldn't have produced the same result.

Gantz and the others were able to work with the information they needed, despite the fact that they were thousands of miles away from assistants and stacks of paper reports.

Asynchronous work is not simply a matter of better utilization of off hours. Thinking work requires immediacy. When you have a question or idea, having to wait for a piece of information can interrupt the thought process. Immediacy is also important to group work. When a group of executives is working together, they quite often need access to specific information. In the past, they might call on assistants to pull together the facts relevant to their discussions. Now, with convenient access to virtually unlimited amounts of information, individuals and groups can work independently of their assistants or make use of their assistants in more productive, value-added ways.

Leveraging executive time can add minutes or hours to an executive's day, speed and improve decision making, increase the amount of work an executive is able to accomplish, and allow executives better control of their time. Given most executive lifestyles, the time flexibility provided by computers can be tremendously valuable.

Be Well-Informed

To be respected and effective, leaders must be well-informed, in great detail, and with split-second timeliness, about a wide range of topics. Executives need to stay current on both internal and external information, increase their depth of knowledge on a variety of topics, adjust filters on information they receive, and absorb all this information quickly. As the pace of change within organizations and throughout the external environment increases, this challenge only gets tougher.

In spite of the mass of information pouring onto executives' desks, executives may not have the ability to keep up. In large organizations they often become isolated. Even in small organizations, executives can't stay on top of every detail; they must rely on others to filter and channel information for them. As Tom Peters says in *Thriving on Chaos*, "In the office, whether you are chief of a big organization or a small one, you are shielded from the truth by a bewildering array of devices, prudent or malicious, all designed to 'save' you from trivia and complexity so that your mind can be clear as you confront the 'big picture' decisions. Instead, your mind is likely to be empty of all but pre-packaged data, leading you to make uninformed decisions."[5]

No matter how trustworthy and honest people try to be, whenever they "package" information, they do so within the limits of their own perceptions. It's impossible for human beings to be totally objective. Therefore, executives tell me they need to find ways of doing "reality checks" on the information they receive. Some executives believe they should steer clear of numbers and details, but most would like to "get their hands dirty" more often if they could afford the time or knew where to get the information.

As Tom Peters rightly points out in *A Passion for Excellence*, one important way of staying in touch with reality is to simply get out of your chair, walk around, and talk with people.[6] But it's impossible to talk with everyone in large organizations. Therefore, executives need to *augment* their face-to-face contact with employees. I emphasize the word *augment* for an important reason. Many people fear that computers will gradually become so full of information and so easily accessible that executives will not get out of their offices and visit people face-to-face. That has not been the case with the executives I know. They highly value face-to-face encounters, and a number of them spend a great deal of time out of the office with their people.

Though executives want to know as much as possible about what is truly going on in their companies, they must have some filters on information. They can't possibly absorb all the details of a company. But they need the flexibility to periodically remove filters (to look at raw information), and they need to periodically create their own views of information (to construct their own selection filters). Being able to adjust filters on information is one of the primary components of being well-informed. Once filters are adjusted, executives can use the new information to work cooperatively in coming to a shared understanding of reality and what needs to be done.

Information systems help executives retrieve information in ways tailored to the question at hand—not just in standard reports, but in up-to-the-minute and detailed views of specific aspects of an organization's operations. Information tools allow executives to gain a greater depth and breadth of knowledge about what's going on in and around the firm—the competitive, regulatory, and economic environment—without getting buried in detail.

Stay Up-to-date

The shaping of perceptions and decisions must be based on the latest information. New events can alter situations dramatically in short periods of time. Executives must stay up-to-date on a variety of business, political, and social issues.

Many of the interviewees use external databases for the purpose of staying up-to-date. There are literally thousands of database services available on just about every imaginable topic across every type of industry, worldwide.

Executives also like to stay up-to-date with internal information. They frequently mention electronic mail and access to internal databases as means of tracking internal events. By staying in touch with people and keeping up-to-date with internal and external information, executives are able to enhance their effectiveness greatly.

Increase Depth of Knowledge

Even as the range of internal and external topics upon which they must be versed gets broader, executives must concurrently find ways of increasing their depth of knowledge. Many do not want to lose touch with details.

All executives receive summary reports. But summaries do not enable the executive to take a look at a "deep slice" of the organization. Summaries provide a little information on a broad range of topics, but they lack depth of knowledge in particular areas.

Ron Compton (Aetna) once had a mentor who told him: "Every now and then, take apart the numbers for yourself." Compton heeded that advice while at American Reinsurance, but he has had less time to do this since he has been at Aetna. "I can still take apart the numbers in this company to a certain extent, but it's more difficult. That's one of the reasons why I wanted this electronic system. [With it I can rebuild] the corporate model so that I can start accessing at least part of it and asking some what if's."

Adjust Filters on Information

Executives need to avoid isolation from the real world, both inside and outside the organization. Of course, there are multiple realities in organizations. I hasten to make this point because I don't in any way want to give the impression that computers contain "the answer" to anything. But they can help executives form different perspectives about the world around them.

Consider the basic problem: There is far more information available to the executive than he or she can possibly manage. As a result, filters are established to help executives get only the information they need. Filters generally take the form of people who select, analyze, and format information for consumption by executives. The permeability of these filters is an important variable. It is all too tempting to allow people to filter out too much information when there is so much to be dealt with. It is also easy to fall into the trap of trying to manage all the information by not letting others filter enough.

Perhaps more important, executives must recognize the simple fact that filters exist. Everyone has a unique way of perceiving the world, and these differences add a great deal of creativity to corporate thinking.

Though a diversity of perspectives is valuable, it has its dangers. People filter information on its way through the organization and put their own slant on its interpretation. As they do so, they both add value and distort the executive's view of reality. There is no question that executives need the interpretations and insights of others to help them construct their view of reality. But they must simultaneously, as much as possible, try to recognize the wisdom and limitations of both their own and others' perceptions.

Executives need ways of fine-tuning perceptions. It is precisely for this reason that their ability to adjust information filters is important. To examine questions raised by summary reports, they need to make their own determinations and judgments based on unfiltered information—information that has not been diluted, summarized, or interpreted by others. Thomas Plaskett (Pan Am) explains: "When somebody else does the financial analysis, they don't always see it the same way that you do. An executive gets a piece of paper from an analyst, and what he or she is really looking at is what that analyst sees in the numbers. I find that, occasionally, I want to look at some of the numbers myself [in a spreadsheet], and put my own twist on the analysis."

Information tools can give executives direct control over removing or constructing filters on the information they receive. Bill Esrey (United Telecom and US Sprint), is among those who directly access computerized databases to reconstruct filters on internal operating information:

> This is how you really get a feel for what's going on, rather than simply looking at numbers or statistics. It gives you the pulse of the organization. You suddenly have flows of information that are coming directly from the responsible individuals. The information has not been sterilized by a flow up from the organizational depths. Information that is received in other ways is often subjected to overzealous editing, or it becomes politicized. [Computers] give you an ability to overcome some of the isolation that you feel or that others might want to subject you to.

Esrey uses a variety of tools to overcome isolation, including access to internal and external data and electronic mail.

The need for unvarnished views also extends to the external world. Sandy Sigoloff (Wickes) describes his desire to look at things from his own perspective. Once Wickes was back on its feet, Sigoloff was particularly interested in reviewing external information on acquisition possibilities. He wanted to know about the management of the target company, its investment strategies, its past performance, and the possibilities of a product fit. Using the modem attached to his computer, he personally dialed into external databases. "I tend to ask lots of questions, and I tend to want to know a lot of things that may or may not come in a format [that I'd receive from others]," explains Sigoloff.

"It may be only what you might call nickel-knowledge [little bits of information]. But I'm a nickel-knowledge person. I like to know a lot about little things, because they make an interesting web at times. I find that very useful."

Absorb Information Quickly

Having discussed the need for information—internal and external, summarized and in raw detail—another problem becomes apparent: the executive's finite ability to absorb information. Computers can augment this limited human capability.

For example, Michael Jordan (Frito-Lay) says:

[Because of the computer] I'm able to go through a lot of stuff in a very short period of time. It's more than simply being able to find things quickly. For example, I've been out of the office for about three weeks straight, with only one day in the office. Tomorrow morning, I can review the last four-week period very quickly on the computer. The computer helps me get back up to speed. In the past, I would have had to ask for this and that, and, in fact, a lot of the stuff that's on the system is not available in standard written reports.

Other executives point out the advantages tools such as outline editors and commitment-tracking systems offer when one needs a quick perspective on volumes of information.

In summary, many executives use computers to stay well-informed. Their computers help them stay up-to-date, increase their depth of knowledge, adjust filters on information, and absorb quantities of information. Executives use information tools to develop independent perspectives about what is going on both inside and outside the organization.

Communicate

Central to the job of management is the ability to communicate. The need to stay in touch is particularly pressing for the people who lead organizations. By improving their communication, executives can affect almost every aspect of the work they perform.

Executives must be able to communicate freely with others at various levels and locations in the organization, and the messages they construct need to be clear, consistent, and convincing. For these reasons, many executives want to be directly involved in constructing the messages they send. In communicating with people inside and outside their organizations, executives must also listen well.

Executives are using computers to link themselves with their organizations, thus building a new level of connectivity.

Be Accessible

You can't communicate with people if you can't reach them, or if they can't reach you. Accessibility is a fundamental component of an executive's ability to communicate effectively. Accessibility can be limited by geographic and temporal separation, especially in large organizations. How does an executive communicate with thousands of people, perhaps spread among different time zones? Information tools allow executives to work closely with a global network of colleagues in spite of their hectic schedules and geographic separation.

Accessibility is particularly important in an organization that spans many time zones. Executives frequently mention the difficulties of managing global operations. Robert Wallace explains how he overcame the time-zone problem when he was at Phillips 66· "My initial response to electronic mail was, 'I don't need it. I've got a good telephone system and an excellent secretary.' I was really a doubting Thomas, but here's what I found. The ability to have quick, concise communications with people in your company through electronic mail is incredible. You can talk to London, Tokyo, or the office down the hall with the same ease. And you don't have to labor over the formalities of a letter or a memo."

In addition to providing a message system, the computer can be a way of extending the executive's availability by serving as a proxy. For example, Ron Compton's (Aetna) expert system will enable him to reach people directly throughout a very large, dispersed organization.

As companies grow larger in both numbers and geographical scope, executives will find themselves stretching more and more to stay in touch. Information tools can help them stay connected to their organizations and to significant people outside organizations.

Improve the Clarity and Consistency of Messages

To be effective, the executive must frequently communicate with many audiences, in writing or orally. Any discrepancies between messages lessens the executive's credibility throughout the firm. And, even if discrepancies are not directly noticed and criticized, the conflicting signals will lead to uncoordinated actions and less effective implementation of the executive's strategy. To counter such risks, executives must be certain that the messages they send are clear and consistent.

Information tools allow executives to tailor their communications so that they say just what they mean. For example, Thomas Plaskett (Pan Am) says that by allowing him to manipulate his text, the word processor helps him to formulate and structure his thoughts. Consistency is easily attained because of the way in which word processing information is stored on his computer disk. He can easily find and use material he has created earlier and include it in new messages he constructs. Because he doesn't have to completely rewrite messages each time, they are more consistent.

The written word allows for more clarity than the spoken word, and the ease with which written messages can be sent improves dramatically with electronic mail. All the executives who use electronic mail or word processing to improve clarity said that the ease with which they can change information encourages them to edit their communications precisely.

Personalize Communication with Others

Some executives are content to have others design communications for them. Others want greater control over the way their messages are designed, and they interject themselves into the communication process. Unless they are personally involved in the design and delivery of the messages that they send to their organizations, these executives believe that they run the risk of appearing less genuine or of losing control over the content of the messages.

Having less control over the design of messages reminds me of the uncomfortable situation of the White King in Lewis Carroll's *Through the Looking Glass,* when Alice takes over his writing:

> Alice [who was invisible to the King and Queen] looked on with great interest as the King took an enormous memorandum-book out of his pocket, and began writing. A sudden thought struck her, and she took

hold of the end of the pencil, which came some way over his shoulder, and began writing for him.

The poor King looked puzzled and unhappy, and struggled with the pencil for some time without saying anything; but Alice was too strong for him, and at last he panted out [to the Queen], "My dear! I really *must* get a thinner pencil. I can't manage this one a bit; it writes all manner of things that I don't intend."[7]

Communicating personally with thousands of people is critical to Thomas Plaskett's ability to regain employee trust at Pan Am. Plaskett feels his use of the word processor in constructing speeches, letters, and other messages to employees makes him better able to be personally involved in the communication process.

Senator Gordon Humphrey also believes in the value of personally constructing his own written and oral communication. He likes to express himself in both an accurate and personal way.

Some executives prefer electronic mail to memoranda, because they feel the electronic medium is more personal. Burnell Roberts (Mead) explains: "I like to access my own [electronic] mail because, for me, it has the immediacy of a phone call or a personal conversation. . . . By accessing mail myself, it eliminates layers, and I get all the information straight on. And people address it that way; they feel more directly connected to me."

To those who ask if computers make communication less personal, Compton (Aetna) responds: "People say to me [he mimics a deep, serious voice], 'Well, you know, Ron, the problem with electronic mail is that it does away with the personal involvement.' But it doesn't! Of course, not all of my communication with people is done this way. You have to build trust and a personal relationship face-to-face, but there's no reason in the world that you have to maintain it by calling the same guy eight times a day."

Improve Listening Abilities

Though clarity, consistency, and personalization are important aspects of *sending* messages, executives are also concerned with their ability to *receive* messages. The ability to receive and incorporate feedback from employees completes the communication cycle. To perform this leadership function effectively requires good listening skills.

Leaders must be willing to listen to bad news as well as good news. In fact, according to Warren Bennis, author of *On Becoming a*

Leader, leaders should actively encourage reflective "backtalk" and dissent: "Leaders need people around them who have contrary views, who are devil's advocates, 'variance sensors' who can tell them the difference between what is expected and what is really going on."[8]

Leaders can encourage dissent by keeping others well-informed. Sharing information with people encourages their development as independent thinkers and gives people a fact base from which they can argue intelligently. Sandy Sigoloff (Wickes) explains: "[The computer] gives the person you interact with the knowledge base to disagree with you, and the more disagreement you can have to evaluate a problem, the more likely you are to get a successful answer."

Be More Persuasive

Many people visualize executives as commanders or directors. But it is also true that executives often play the role of persuaders. Executives must be effective in presenting to and convincing others, both inside and outside the corporation.

By better equipping executives with the ability to think through issues before presenting them to others and by giving them the ability to represent information in a variety of ways, computers help executives be more persuasive.

Organizational Communications

The need for improved communications was a common theme among the interviewees. They realized that it is the executive's responsibility to design and implement the communication pathways, or "nervous system" of an organization.

Richard Pogue talks of the importance of connecting newly acquired offices to "the system." In particular, electronic mail serves as a vital link between people at all levels of Jones Day Reavis & Pogue. Likewise, at Aetna, electronic mail serves as a linking mechanism among nodes of the organization.

At Phillips 66 and Frito-Lay, information systems simultaneously provide vital feedback to both corporate managers and those in the field—that is, to both the "brain" and to other parts of the organization. This type of feedback enables these organizations to operate in completely different (in their cases, decentralized) ways.

Instantaneous feedback can have tremendous impacts in the area of quality. As Robert Wallace (Phillips 66) puts it: "Quality is not just a buzzword. It's a fact of life. It's a part of the nervous system. Do you feel a tingle? And if you feel it, you've got a problem."

Likewise, at Aetna, Mrs. Fields Cookies, and Frito-Lay, the computer draws the organization together as one entity and improves the feedback mechanisms at many levels of the company. By consciously designing the nervous systems of their organizations, executives in the future will be able to "feel the tingle" earlier and earlier, allowing them to respond to problems and opportunities faster.

Although the goal of improving their ability to communicate was common, each of these executives used, within his or her own context, a unique subset of the information tool kit, to stay in touch with internal and external communities.

Coach

Executives cannot run organizations alone. They must delegate to multiply their effectiveness and to allow the work to be done by those closest to the action. Delegation also cultivates executives' lines of succession.

Delegation means much more than a simple passing of the baton. People must develop professionally to be ready to take on more responsibility. But executives can't command people to develop themselves. Rather, the relationship between an executive and employees involves a subtle and delicate form of education. Good delegators teach people the relevant skills and help them to accept more responsibility. In other words, good delegators must be good coaches.

Good coaches are well respected and well-informed, and they proactively expand the perspectives of others. The leaders in this book use computers to enhance coaching skills by building credibility with the people they lead; tracking the commitments those people make; tracking performance discretely, without disempowering; enhancing people's perspectives; and teaching critical thinking skills.

Build Credibility as a Leader

A prerequisite to effective coaching is respect for the leader. People simply will not follow or learn from someone who lacks credibility.

Being well-informed is a cornerstone of credibility. People are more likely to respect leaders who are out in front of the group they are leading in terms of strategic direction and knowledge of facts.

The credibility issue is heightened in the case of a merger. People who are new to an organization are often skeptical about a new leader's ability to manage. The executive has to very quickly gain employees' respect through a demonstration of knowledge and competence.

Bill Gantz (Baxter) faced such a challenge after the merger of Baxter and AHSC. He built credibility with the people who didn't know him by being well-informed and prepared for meetings. Before meetings, he accessed both internal and external databases. This helped him to ask more intelligent questions of the people he was coaching.

Mark Edmiston (*The Cable Guide*) and Debbi Fields (Mrs. Fields Cookies) also mention the importance of preparing questions in advance of the coaching process. Edmiston explains that his preparation prior to meetings enables him to move right to the core of a matter, avoiding time wasted asking the person to explain what happened. Because he already knows what happened, meetings are more focused on solutions rather than problem statements. Fields describes a similar process when she talks about the preparation she does prior to face-to-face store visits.

Asking people pertinent and well-designed questions is an effective way of helping them learn. By staying on top of the internal and external environments, executives can do a better job of coaching.

Track Commitments

To be effective, coaches must also find out whether or not people are delivering on the commitments they make during the coaching process. If an executive sees that a person is not meeting commitments, that is a likely signal that the person needs more help. Sometimes, in such situations, the executive will see that people have been asked to do too much. Debbi Fields (Mrs. Fields Cookies) explains that by using a hypertext system to keep up with the commitments of others, she is able to see how much she is asking of others. If people are overloaded, she takes action to correct the situation.

Richard Crandall (Comshare), Michael Jordan (Frito-Lay), and several other executives mention the value of tracking commitments. If commitments aren't tracked on a consistent basis, people wonder how important it is to get commitments accomplished. By helping executives to know what they're asking of others and by paying attention to the fulfillment of commitments, information tools can help executives guide their people.

Balance the Need to Know and the Need to Delegate

Executives realize that they must track performance and stay informed to lead. Executives need to know the details of what is going on—if they don't, they lose the respect of their employees and it is more difficult to guide them. But if executives are too intrusive, people will not feel empowered and take on responsibility. To be a good coach requires an open, honest relationship. This is unlikely if the boss is seen as intruding.

The need to know and the need to delegate are paradoxical. Executives must simultaneously balance their tracking and controlling activities with delegation and empowerment. Rosabeth Moss Kanter encapsulates this balancing act in one of the leadership challenges she sets forth in her book, *When Giants Learn to Dance:* "Know every detail of your business—but delegate more responsibility to others."[9]

To maintain the delicate balance between delegation and control, executives use computers to gain access to the information they need about performance. In this way they can track work, without stifling the efforts of their people to gain autonomy. For example, Mark Edmiston (*The Cable Guide*) tracks key indicators of performance on-line; this leaves him comfortable with his circulation manager's work, without examining details such as expense accounts.

Debbi Fields (Mrs. Fields Cookies) explains that sharing information with people helps her balance her need to acquire information while empowering others. Because they receive performance information prior to her meetings with them, they have time to prepare. In similar fashion, Robert Wallace (Phillips 66) believes that the sharing of information makes people feel less intruded upon.

When both executives and employees have access to performance information, each group feels better informed. As a result, executives don't have to constantly ask for detailed progress reports. And employees don't feel as though they're being watched by executives— they know that they have the same information the executive has.

Broaden People's Perspectives

Part of the coaching role involves broadening peoples' perspectives to help them see a larger business horizon. In *The Information Edge,* Lee Paschall, former CEO and chairman of American Satellite, describes this challenge. He was managing a young company that needed to shift its thinking from internal issues to the competitive market.

> After I started sending out information from the [external] database [in messages to other people], I began to notice a greater awareness of the outside world. Up until that time, the company had an inward focus. They were struggling to make the company profitable and to make it grow. I tried to encourage them to be less myopic in their vision. An executive helps bring the company to maturity by forcing its employees to think about something other than tomorrow's work day.[10]

External databases are not the only tool for enlarging perspective. Ken McCready (TransAlta) says an outline editor helps him show people where their contributions fit into a "hierarchy of ideas" at TransAlta.

Ron Compton's use of internal databases to track Aetna's critical success factors also conveys to people a larger context for their efforts. Through this system, they can see how their individual and collective efforts fit the organization's objectives.

Quite often, organizations get caught up in "fire fighting." By thoughtfully following a broad variety of external and internal events, top executives can help make people in their organizations more aware and give them a context for the work they perform.

Teach Critical-Thinking Abilities

Coaches often want to teach people to think through problems and apply critical-thinking skills. In essence, the ultimate goal of coaching is to work yourself out of a job. If you are a good coach, people progressively become more self-managing. The clearer the thinking skills of subordinates, the lighter the coach's work load.

Ron Compton (Aetna) will teach people an approach to priority setting and problem solving through the AMP expert system. Through the use of that system, people will learn to anticipate the kinds of questions Compton might ask about a situation.

Michael Jordan (Frito-Lay) provides another example of teaching critical thinking abilities. Jordan uses the computer as a modeling tool to help him teach others how to take apart the financials of the business. He sees internal databases as a means of "stimulating and channeling thinking."

By sharing external and operating information with employees and reviewing the same information themselves, Compton (Aetna), Bob Wallace (Phillips 66), and Bill Esrey (United Telecom and US Sprint) are able to teach people to think through problems more fully and ask themselves questions before information is passed to a higher level in the organization. All three use internal and external databases to teach people how to take apart problems. As a result, in addition to raising problems, people are also beginning to give fuller explanations of why the problem occurred, what measures have been taken to correct it, and how the problem will be avoided in the future.

Shape Culture

Edgar Schein, author of *Organizational Culture and Leadership* defines culture as "a pattern of basic assumptions—invented, discovered, or developed by a given group as it learns to cope with its problems of external adaptation and internal integration."[11] Organizations adopt patterns of behavior and beliefs that allow them to adapt to events that happen both inside and outside their boundaries.

There is some controversy about whether executives shape corporate cultures or whether corporate cultures shape executives. Joseph Campbell, the well-known author of numerous books on myth and culture, believed that culture emanates from leaders. "There's an old romantic idea in German, *das Volk dichet,* which says that the ideas and poetry of the traditional cultures come out of the folk. They do not. They come out of an elite experience, the experience of people particularly gifted. . . . These people speak to the folk, and there is an answer from the folk, which is then received as an interaction. But the first impulse in the shaping of a folk tradition comes from above, not from below."[12]

I believe that the same phenomenon is true in organizations. Leaders—through the many decisions they make about organizational structure, language, values, methods, and systems—have tremendous power to shape and meld organizations. Attempts been made to more explicitly delineate those actions that can and do change corporate culture.

Edgar Schein describes the essence of leadership as the "manipulation of culture." Executives are often hard-pressed to determine the ways in which they can actually go about deliberately changing an organization's culture, and Schein is tremendously useful in that regard. He suggests that the following executive actions play a primary role in shaping organizational culture:

1. What leaders pay attention to, measure, and control
2. Leader reactions to critical incidents and organizational crises
3. Deliberate role modeling, teaching and coaching by leaders
4. Criteria for allocation of rewards and status
5. Criteria for recruitment, selection, promotion, retirement and excommunication.[13]

Coaching appears as Schein's third leadership action. The theme of shaping culture is closely related to the theme of coaching (which the preceding section discussed); in fact, coaching influences corporate culture.

Computers can contribute to other leadership actions in Schein's framework as well. Information tools have helped a handful of executives focus attention on what's important; measure performance on selected goals and objectives; and pick, promote, and reward the right people. In addition to employing the actions on Schein's list, executives have pursued cultural change through structural change: They flattened hierarchies and empowered people.[14]

Focus People on What's Important

People want to do a good job and be productive. But, even in small organizations, they can be working frenetically and still not be accomplishing what top management wants. To work well together, people have to share a common language and a common understanding of an organization's direction. Focus and alignment are the keys to directing the efforts of an organization.

Schein's first point that what leaders pay attention to shapes culture is relevant to unifying employee focus. Leaders communicate what is important in a variety of ways. Ron Compton, when president of American Reinsurance, mentioned that even the simple act of looking at information had impacts on focus. "When I'm looking at the cash figures then *everyone* is looking at the cash figures, and the numbers start to rise because we all focus on it. It's a tool in establishing culture."[15]

Other profiled executives described scenarios in which information systems helped them to promote shared understanding, and focus people on what is important.

Meetings are an important vehicle for the coordination and development of strategic initiatives. As such, they represent leveraged opportunities for getting groups of people to focus on issues of importance. Bill Gantz (Baxter) took full advantage of meeting environments to focus people on shared direction. He discovered that the use of what-if models in meetings encourages the development of a common perspective on problems and solutions.

It's not just a matter of letting people know what you want them to look at; the coach may also help people see *how* to look at things. By created standardized approaches to viewing information, Michael Jordan (Frito-Lay) believes people have started to view the business in similar ways.

This focusing effect is not limited to operating statistics. Debbi Fields (Mrs. Fields Cookies) wants to focus people on accomplishments rather than "to-do" items. She uses a hypertext tool as a means of encouraging people to work on top-priority outcomes instead of a list of tasks.

Information tools help executives establish shared language, common perspectives, and consistent facts as a basis for discussing and agreeing on plans.

Measure Performance on Selected Goals and Objectives

Schein also points out that what leaders measure can influence an organization's culture. Performance measures show people what matters and thus help executives shape culture. By creating feedback loops in their organizations, executives let people know what is being measured, why it is being measured, and how those people are performing in relation to those measures.

Richard Crandall (Comshare), explains that if he wants something to improve at Comshare, he measures it. Comshare executives track metrics of quality on dynamic internal databases. These management feedback loops encourage people to improve their quality efforts.

By measuring and posting performance results, which she tracks on a spreadsheet, Debbi Fields (Mrs. Fields Cookies) accomplishes two management objectives. First, she teaches people to be proactive, because once they see their performance rank dropping, they want to take action before they hear from her. Second, she identifies people who may need more coaching.

Robert Wallace (Phillips 66), says that better tracking of information encourages better accountability. Like Fields, Wallace saw proactive attitudes result from his measurement of performance. People not only explained what went wrong, but they also compiled information on correcting problems and preventing problems from recurring.

In fact, the use of information systems can be quite synergistic with TQM (Total Quality Management) programs. TQM stresses the importance of 100 percent, first-time quality. To achieve this, it is important to communicate those high standards in a tangible way to people throughout the organization. Bill Esrey (United Telecom and US Sprint) says he is using information systems to advertise benchmarks for performance.

Pick, Promote, and Reward the Right People

Picking, promoting, and rewarding people relate to point 4 (allocation of rewards) and point 5 (criteria for selection and promotion) on Schein's list. Like Schein, Tom Peters stresses the importance of executive involvement in personnel issues. "I strongly urge that any boss get personally involved in every promotion in his organization, even those three or four layers down."[16]

Information systems can help involve executives more fully in the process of picking, promoting, and rewarding people.

Ken McCready (TransAlta) has a spreadsheet containing information about all the managers at TransAlta. The spreadsheet tracks their department, their rank, and their promotability. He says the spreadsheet helps him "compare and contrast" individual performance.

Executives also use information tools to ensure that they are rewarding people in fair and equitable ways. McCready uses his spreadsheet to track compensation. "Before I present something to the compensation committee of the Board of Directors, the vice president of Human Resources and I get together and look at a spreadsheet I've prepared. The spreadsheet tracks previous increases, where individuals are in the ranges, and how the ranges stack up. I use it to think through individual compensation and bonuses."

Robert Wallace (Phillips 66) explains that his direct access to personnel information influenced the Phillips culture by making his managers more sensitive to the whole selection process.

Richard Crandall describes a similar effect at Comshare. He added turnover information about top performers to the information received by his executives. By highlighting turnover measures, Crandall refocused the attention of his top management team on retaining key performers throughout the company.

Ron Compton (Aetna) finds videotape to be an aid to his ability to participate in the personnel selection process:

> I just hired a new top executive. I was videotaped talking about the job. That was played to all the potential candidates for this job by a head-hunter. Then he taped interviews with the potential candidates before we ever met the people. The committee here reviewed these tapes.
>
> When we met them [face-to-face], we were way ahead of the game. We knew the fundamentals—you know, how many kids do you have, where are you from, and so on. We got down to the substantive stuff immediately.

By staying abreast of compensation and other personnel information and through the use of communication tools, executives are able to contribute more to the selection, development, retention, and promotion of people within their organizations.

Flatten Hierarchies and Empower People

If there were a wall spray-painted with 1980s management graffiti, you'd be sure to see:

Empowerment!
Participation!
Self-managing teams!
Down with hierarchy!

These phrases proclaim a new era in management, where control is out and cooperation is in. As Gloria Steinem so aptly puts it, "There's no human being who's going to do what I say. . . . The only power I have is the power of persuasion, or inspiration."[17]

Years ago, Douglas McGregor coined the terms *Theory X* and *Theory Y* to describe different styles of management.[18] In the "Theory X" past, executives just told people what to do. But in the new era, even in the uppermost echelons of an organization, this usually doesn't work anymore. Organizational life is simply too complex for the Theory X approach. An executive cannot be everywhere at once, telling people what to do and making detailed decisions from the top down. Both to leverage their scarce time and tap the creativity of people throughout the organization, executives are empowering people at lower levels of the organization. By empowering people to make operational decisions, executives can focus on leadership rather than control.

True empowerment goes far beyond delegation of authority to one's subordinates. It involves systemic change, which has a dramatic effect on people throughout the organization. Because of its highly leveraged impact on all levels of the hierarchy, empowerment goes well beyond one's abilities as a supervisor. Empowerment represents a change in corporate culture.

In passing through the Theory X phase and into the Theory Y phase, executives learned that total laissez-faire also had its limitations. With power must come accountability. Somehow, executives must maintain enough control to allow them to guide the organization toward its strategic goals, and yet trust their people to exercise distributed authority wisely and in keeping with corporate strategies.

Rosabeth Moss Kanter eloquently states the management paradox: "Speak up, be a leader, set the direction—but be participative, listen well, cooperate."[19]

How can executives guide the firm without actually controlling all the decisions? By sharing access to information and teaching people how to use it, executives have given people an opportunity to make more operational decisions on their own, thus freeing the executives to make decisions that are strategic and directional in nature.

The profiles showed two ways in which information tools are being used to empower people in an organization:

- Information tools mitigated hierarchy by opening new channels of communication.
- Information tools allowed the sharing of information throughout an organization and sharing empowered employees to do their jobs.

Mitigating Hierarchy by Communicating.   Differences in positional power in an organization can constrain communication. Overemphasis on the formal organizational hierarchy as a communication and power map tends to disempower people by reinforcing top-down authority. By giving people at all levels of the corporation better access to people at the top, changes in the perception of the hierarchy occur. Positional power is to some degree displaced by the power of one's expertise. This, in effect, flattens the organization chart.

Information systems can be powerful conduits of informal communication. By their nature, they tend to deemphasize hierarchy and give everyone a basis for feeling empowered. Thus, they provide an excellent vehicle for making an open-door policy real.

By creating new communication links between people at different levels of the organization, executives can reduce the communication barriers that hierarchies often create.

Information Sharing.   Information sharing is another path to empowerment. Tom Peters writes: "There are few greater liberating forces than the sharing of information. There is no such thing as "delegation" or "motivation" without extensive information. Knowledge is power —it always has been, and it always will be. Power—at the front line—is one more "must-do," not a "nice-to-do.""[20]

Frito-Lay executives took advantage of this phenomenon and constructed feedback loops, permanent forces in the organization that guide people toward the right autonomous decisions. Designing feedback loops is using the computer as a medium for the expression of leadership.

One of the most dramatic examples of the power of sharing information comes from Robert Wallace. He led a dramatic turnaround at Phillips 66. At the heart of this management engineering feat was a decentralization strategy. Wallace changed organization structure, and, in parallel, put information into the hands of the front-line managers.

Note that Wallace does not overlook the fact that executives who want to decentralize a company still need controls. As Peter Drucker explains: "Control" is the ability to obtain information.[21] Though Drucker says that information can be obtained through methods other than data processing, it is difficult to argue against the effectiveness of the solution described by Wallace—a solution in which live operating information is distributed throughout the organization on a continuous basis.

Decisions about how and when to share information are made at the top of an organization. Executives who want to empower people will share information with them. They can accelerate these efforts through the use of information systems. By assisting in the formulation of electronic information systems that are designed to share information, executives can maintain "control" of their businesses while simultaneously empowering the people who work there.

Enhance Personal Thinking

The demands of managing a corporation are almost unfathomable. Executives must make sense out of chaos, come up with creative solutions to a myriad of problems, balance intuition and logic, find a time and place for reflection, improve the clarity of their analyses, and "link" their minds with those of others. These pressures tax the limits of executives' thinking and illustrate the paramount importance of the executive intellect to the functioning of an organization. Organizations need executives for the quality of their minds. Anything that extends an executive's ability to think, reason, and be creative will enhance that executive's value to the corporation.

In the classic text, *The Functions of the Executive,* Chester Barnard foresaw, over 50 years ago, the need for increased executive mental capacity to deal with the complexities of modern business:

> That the increasing complexity of society . . . will more and more require capacity for rigorous reasoning seems evident; but it is a super-structure necessitating a better use of the non-logical mind [intuition] to support it. "Brains" [logic] without "minds" [intuition] seems a futile imbalance.[22]

It is important to note that the computer is not strictly a device for calculation or "rigorous reasoning." In Barnard's vernacular, executives are using computers to develop their "minds" as well as their "brains." For example, information systems may help executives keep an eye on the competition or make better decisions by considering more alternatives. Computers can take something that was one-dimensional and make it multidimensional by permitting rapid what-if analyses.

Executives are using computers to manage complexity, think creatively, balance logic and intuition, clarify their thoughts, make use of time in reflection, and hold more effective group meetings.

Manage Complexity

One of the best descriptions I've seen of the requirements placed on the executive mind comes from Thorton Bradshaw, former president of ARCO. I first saw this quotation in Warren Bennis's book on leadership.

> Every decision at my desk is influenced by some, and at times many, of the following: the possible impact on public opinion; the reaction of environmental groups; the possible impact on other action groups—consumers, tax reform, antinuclear, prodesert, prorecreational vehicles, etc; the constraints of government—DOE, EPA, OSHA, ICC, FTC, etc., etc.—and the states and the municipalities; the effect on inflation and on the government's anti-inflation program; labor union attitudes; the OPEC cartel. Oh yes, I almost forgot, the anticipated economic profit, the degree of risk, the problem of obtaining funds in a competitive market, the capability of our organization, and—when there is time—the competition.[23]

As Sandy Sigoloff (Wickes) points out, the complexities of modern executive life demand intellectual assistance. "There's a revolution occurring in the world. We are seeing the evolution of what I call a no-boundary, global economy. . . . It's pretty hard to keep up with [the complexities of a global environment] just by reading prepared reports."

Indeed, executives often mention the value of the computer in helping them deal with complex thinking challenges. Sigoloff used a computerized master calendar to help him and his management team "control 800 to 2,000 events that were time-related and time-phased." He also used external databases to help him sort through the complexities of acquisitions. In addition, Sigoloff found spreadsheets and word processors to be valuable in sorting through internal information.

Note that the computer extends the mind not only by providing facts, but also by aiding near-term memory and serving as a dynamic scratch-pad for manipulating thoughts.

In some cases, one can even program the computer to do a little bit of "thinking" automatically. Tracking the operations of over 600 stores presents Debbi Fields (Mrs. Fields Cookies) with an enormously complex task. A volume-weighting model designed by Randy Fields helps her leverage her management efforts by pointing out the problems that require immediate attention.

The complex world within an organization is dwarfed by the complexity of the external environment. Executives already do plenty of reading, and yet they still find it difficult to keep up with strategic factors in their global markets. Access to external databases helps executives understand the complexities presented by environmental factors such as competition and governmental regulation. Users can selectively filter through tremendous amounts of information. Not only does this give them better filtered views, but it also allows them to see information that might or might not be found in their traditional reading material. For example, one of the external data sources that Richard Crandall (Comshare) accesses summarizes over 400 newspapers. No executive has the capacity to personally look through 400 newspapers a day.

By accessing information in a highly targeted way, executives can gain valuable information that serves them, not only in the short term, but also in their long-term perspectives.

In *The Information Edge,* Lee Paschall, former CEO and president of American Satellite, explains how he thinks through long-range planning issues:

> When we put together a long-range plan for American Satellite, I used the database to search through two years of information on fiber optics. It would have been hopeless to try and find all of this information by hand. We got a complete story of what has happened in fiber optics; we determined the plans, financing, and actual implementation of various fiber networks. I was able to give the Board a very comprehensive report on where fiber optics is going, and what they should do about it.

Paschall also says that, over time, as he accessed the information on the database, he started to notice trends in the information. "In my 'elder statesman' role [as a member of the Board] at American Satellite, I use the database to track trends in our industry. For example, I went back through the database for one year and keyed in on the term 'joint ventures.' I detected a trend, and was able to quantify the size and magnitude of that trend toward joint venture activities in the telecommunications business."[24]

Mark Edmiston (*The Cable Guide*) has found these thinking aids habit-forming. "You realize that [the computer] is going to provide you with information that you never had before and that it gives you the ability to analyze things that you couldn't analyze before. Once you start doing that, I don't think there's any stopping you. I really don't."

Think Creatively

Another critical aspect of an executive is the quality of his or her ideas. An executive's capacity for creative thinking is critical. Word processing is a popular tool to support creative thinking. In preparing messages and thoughts on a computer, executives can shape or adjust those thoughts as they are created. They can add new ideas by immediately accessing new information, they can change the format in which they present an idea (by adding a graphic representation for example), or they can change the wording as they are working with the thought.

Richard Pogue (Jones Day) explains why he prefers a word processor over dictation:

> I've never liked dictation units. I think in a much more organized manner if I'm writing it or typing it. If I'm doing it orally, I just kind of lose track of what I said, and I don't have the visual impression in my mind as to how the document is organized.
>
> A word processor is much more effective for me than [dictation or] a typewriter. As I write something, I'm constantly changing it. I'll type out a sentence, and then as I look back at it, I decide I want to reword or rephrase it, or change it. If you're using a typewriter, you have to start over or use [correcting fluid] or an eraser, and it just creates a lot of impediments to making continual changes. But the word processor encourages change. It's very easy to rework something. It really affects the quality of the work. . . . With the word processor, I'm more likely to make needed improvements.

This dynamic quality of the computer extends to other tools as well. For example, Bill Gantz (Baxter) interacts with financial information.

> Working with the information on the computer helps me think through things more clearly. I could always get someone from our staff to do it for me. I used to do that. But that takes time, and it also changes the way I work with the information. As the model unfolds, I see things I want to adjust and change, and this gives me insight into problems.
>
> If you let someone else do it, you lose that ability to adjust things. After you've worked with the computer for a while, it becomes part of your normal process of thinking about problems. I still use paper reports for the end of the month. But when I'm thinking about problems, I need the dynamic back and forth the model gives me.

Part of creative thinking includes the need for fresh perspectives on ideas. Debbi Fields (Mrs. Fields Cookies) uses an off-the-shelf tool to enhance her creativity in the brainstorming process. Her "idea generator" challenges her creative process by asking her provocative questions about any topic she wants to examine.

Computers will not replace paper, but they provide executives with an alternative means of working with their thoughts and ideas. Computers can help people hold onto many thoughts at once, they amplify the mind's ability to handle complex equations and calculations, and they display information in a variety of useful forms. By making information "live," computers greatly increase executives' capacity to expand their thinking and reasoning abilities.

As an interesting aside, I noted that much of the use of computers for creative thinking occurred outside the office. The environment most conducive to creative work is often one in which the executive has time for reflection, away from the constraints and interruptions of a regular office environment. Almost all the executives I interviewed said their heaviest use of computers was outside regular office hours. Laptops and home computers can provide the necessary tools for doing creative work in a variety of locations.

Balance Logic and Intuition

Most people consider creative thinking as primarily an intuitive process. In fact, new ideas and approaches to problems require a combination of intuition and logic. It's not enough to simply intuit your way to a solution. Solutions or ideas must be communicated to others, and that requires the application of logic, for the purpose of attaining clarity.

When I asked executives whether they were more logical or intuitive, the answers split the group roughly down the middle. But almost all said that they try to balance whatever orientation they may have.

Some of the interviewees use information tools as a balancing mechanism to enhance their less-natural cognitive style. Computers can be used to help develop both logical and intuitive approaches to problems. You might wonder how a computer could ever help with the development of intuition. In fact, several executives said to me that their computers help them sense problems or trends. They use language such as "smell," or "get a feel for," or "get a sense of," when they talk about using their computers.

Sometimes they refer to the ability to see information in different formats as a way of balancing their styles. One person might want to see graphs, another might want to see numbers.

Ken McCready works closely with the chairman of TransAlta. He says that they each have different analytical styles. "I'm the more logical, analytical type, and Harry's more the intuitive. Harry's type helps us to diverge, and my type helps us converge." Interestingly, the two executives choose ways of looking at information on their computers that are complementary to their normal orientation. McCready (with a logical orientation) likes to view information in graphs, and his associate (with an intuitive orientation) likes to view information in numbers or tables.

Mark Edmiston (*The Cable Guide*) views himself as an intuitive thinker, and he likes to use the computers as a counterbalance. "[The computer] is a logic check, and it doesn't lie. If you put in the right data, it's going to tell you the answer. You may not like it, but it's there," says Edmiston.

In fact, the computer can help executives balance their mental strengths and weaknesses in some surprising ways. Thomas Stephens (Manville) shares a delightful story about how the computer has helped him. "Being an engineer, I'm functionally illiterate," says Stephens, laughing. "I really can't write, I can't spell, and I know nothing about English. All the guys around here tease me about some of the work product I turn out because of the misspellings and the typos. But I found a software package that is resident in your computer. As I type any word and a space, it triggers the computer to go look up the word in a dictionary, and if it's misspelled, the computer goes *beep*. It's there all the time as I type. In addition to warning me about the spelling of the words I type, it also has a thesaurus built in, which I can use automatically to call up synonyms. It's just wonderful."

"But people haven't stopped laughing at me yet," quips Stephens. "Now they laugh because they walk by the office and they say it sounds like John Philip Sousa with all of the *beeps* it's making!" As we both settle down from a hearty laugh, Stephens says: "Seriously, it's really powerful. It's made me a more effective person because it covers one of my weaknesses."

Improve Clarity of Thinking

It is self-evident that executives benefit by being extremely clear in their thinking. They must discern the relevant facts and bases for decisions and properly analyze alternatives. They must also communicate precisely what they think, knowing that a degree of distortion is inevitable.

As Warren Bennis points out, writing is one of the best ways to clarify thinking. "Codifying one's thinking is an important step in inventing oneself. The most difficult way to do it is by thinking about thinking—it helps to speak or write your thoughts. Writing is the most profound way of codifying your thoughts, the best way of learning from yourself who you are and what you believe."[25] Outline editors, word processors, and electronic mail can serve as aids to writing and, hence, to clarification of thoughts.

Ron Compton (Aetna), Thomas Plaskett (Pan Am), Ken McCready (TransAlta), and Richard Pogue (Jones Day Reavis & Pogue) mention that the word processor helps them clarify their thoughts. They say that traditional methods such as dictation are not sufficient for them to sort through and structure ideas. They maintain that the writing they do using the word processor is clearer, more concise, and better organized than their other communication.

Improve Group Thinking Processes

Studies of executives frequently mention the fact that they spend most of their time in meetings with others. Interestingly, when you talk with executives, they frequently complain about the quality of those meetings, often expressing dissatisfaction with group productivity.

Just as information tools can improve individual performance, they can be useful in improving the thinking of groups. Though not a panacea for all meeting ills, information tools can significantly impact meeting effectiveness. Any information tool can be used in a meeting environment with the computer screen projected for all to see. This allows all group members to watch the thoughts of the group unfold, to interject their own thoughts into the process, and to test hypotheses.[26]

When he was at American Reinsurance, Ron Compton held frequent augmented meetings. A large screen was set up at the end of a table in his office, and his co-workers jokingly referred to the set-up as "The Altar."[27]

Now, at Aetna, Compton has set up an even more sophisticated group-meeting environment in the boardroom. A large screen is set up at the far end of the table, and keyboards are nested under the table, allowing executives to take over control of the screen by pulling them out. A computer workstation for a meeting facilitator is located on one side of the room.

Any tool can be used in a meeting setting. For example:

- What-if models, including spreadsheets, can help a group examine a number of scenarios and create better buy-in from group members.

- Graphics packages (particularly those combined with spreadsheets) can allow members of a group who have different cognitive styles to see information in a variety of forms.

- Outline editors can be used to capture the thoughts and ideas of a group and place those ideas in a hierarchical structure.

- Access to internal and external data can facilitate discussions where there are disputes or questions about the facts.

- Project management tools can be used to help the group get a shared idea of the scope of a project and its interdependencies.

- And, in terms of communication tools, all forms of teleconferencing can help extend the meeting to people who are geographically dispersed.

The benefits of augmented meetings that were mentioned in the interviews for this book are caused by two primary reasons: (1) computers encourage the group's creative thinking process; and (2) they help structure or focus a discussion. By providing a logical framework for a discussion and by keeping the facts out in front of a group, information tools can help the group effectively and efficiently arrive at decisions and courses of action. Compared to unaugmented meetings, augmented meetings tend to produce fewer misunderstandings, less repetition, and a better understanding of follow-up responsibilities.

The Information Edge contains a full discussion of the benefits of augmented meetings.[28] A partial list of the benefits follows.

- Augmented meetings help the group stay more task-oriented.
- They increase the degree of participation.
- They bridge differences between cognitive styles.
- They increase the volume of ideas and information that the group can handle.
- They reduce repetition.

Augmented meetings greatly increase the speed and intensity with which a group handles ideas. For this reason, augmented meetings are better suited to task oriented groups under time pressure. They may be inappropriate in the delicate climate of a meeting designed to elicit feelings and emotions (an interpersonal team-building exercise, for example).

The Information Prism

Think of a crystal prism. You can hold the prism up to the light, and each facet of the prism reveals a different color, a different perspective. But if that crystal is anchored to a desk or mounted on a pedestal, it is difficult to examine from all angles. Information on paper is like the anchored prism. Whether the information consists of numbers in a spreadsheet, words in a speech, or components of a graphic, once ideas are committed to paper, they lose their dynamism. The information can't be picked up and examined from a number of angles. It can't easily be changed or rearranged.

Computers loosen the bonds on information. Just as a crystal shows different colors when examined from different angles, computers allow people to gain different views of information. You can change an aspect of a spreadsheet or model and watch the results ripple through; you're not stuck with the one view the analyst gave you. You can rearrange the entire order of your speech at will, or carefully "wordsmith" that tricky part. You can even draw a picture and replace whole parts of it, storing the original. Instead of simply *receiving* or *reviewing* information, executives can *interact* with information and with people. Computers make it possible for executives to use their minds to cast light on the different facets of an "information prism."

The information prism is a metaphor for the way in which computers extend the boundaries on information. This gets to the crux of the reason why information tools differ so dramatically from paper, or static, reports. It also explains why executives must work hands-on to receive the full benefits of information tools. If someone else operates the computer, the executive loses the speed and flexibility with which he or she can formulate, change, and work with thoughts and ideas.

> *If information tools can help executives think, then they can help corporations flourish.*

Each of the executives interviewed for this book is unique. They are different as individuals, and their businesses are diverse in scope and purpose. Nonetheless, they all found ways to use information tools to extend their leadership abilities. And despite their diversity, when faced with similar leadership challenges, many chose similar tools and got similar results. The similarities were summarized in this chapter. These common threads indicate that there are patterns emerging in executive use of computers. These patterns predict how certain tools will match certain leadership challenges.

Only a subset of these applications are applicable to any particular executive and business challenge. But the exploration of even one could produce significant results.

NOTES

1. David Diamond et al., *The Wall Street Journal Book of Chief Executive Style* (New York: Morrow, 1989), p. 13.
2. Peter Drucker, *The Effective Executive* (New York: Harper & Row, 1967), p. 23.
3. Ibid.
4. *The World Book Dictionary* (Chicago: Field Enterprises Educational Corp., 1969).
5. Tom Peters, *Thriving on Chaos* (New York: Knopf, 1987), p. 425.
6. Tom Peters, *A Passion for Excellence* (New York: Random House, 1985), p. 8.
7. Lewis Carroll, *Through the Looking Glass* (London: Purnell Books, 1975), pp. 122–123.
8. Warren Bennis, *On Becoming a Leader* (New York: Addison-Wesley, 1989), p. 195.
9. Rosabeth Moss Kanter, *When Giants Learn to Dance* (New York: Simon & Schuster, 1989), pp. 20–21.
10. Dean Meyer and Mary Boone, *The Information Edge,* 2nd edition (Homewood, IL: Dow Jones-Irwin, 1989), pp. 243–244.
11. Edgar H. Schein, *Organizational Culture and Leadership* (San Francisco: Jossey-Bass, 1986), p. 9.
12. Joseph Campbell (with Bill Moyers), *The Power of Myth* (New York: Doubleday, 1988), p. 85.
13. Edgar H. Schein, *Organizational Culture and Leadership* (San Francisco: Jossey-Bass, 1986), pp. 224–225.
14. For a demonstration of the power of organizational structure in bringing about systemic change, see: Dean Meyer, *I.S. Structural Cybernetics* (Ridgefield, CT: NDMA Inc., 1990).
15. Dean Meyer and Mary Boone, *The Information Edge,* 2nd edition (Homewood, IL: Dow Jones-Irwin, 1989), p. 235.
16. Tom Peters, *Thriving on Chaos* (New York: Knopf, 1987), p. 417.
17. Warren Bennis, *On Becoming a Leader* (New York: Addison-Wesley, 1989), p. 159.
18. Douglas McGregor, *The Human Side of Enterprise* (New York: McGraw-Hill, 1960).

19. Rosabeth Moss Kanter, *When Giants Learn to Dance* (New York: Simon & Schuster, 1989), pp. 20–21.

20. Tom Peters, *Thriving on Chaos* (New York: Knopf, 1987), p. 505.

21. Peter Drucker, *The Frontiers of Management* (New York: Dutton, 1986), p. 204.

22. Chester Barnard, *The Functions of the Executive* (Cambridge: Harvard University Press, 1966), p. 322.

23. Warren Bennis, *On Becoming a Leader* (New York: Addison-Wesley, 1989), p. 200. (Bennis found the quotation in Jim O'Toole's book, *Vanguard Management*.)

24. Dean Meyer and Mary Boone, *The Information Edge*, 2nd edition (Homewood, IL: Dow Jones-Irwin, 1989), pp. 244–245.

25. Warren Bennis, *On Becoming a Leader* (New York: Addison-Wesley, 1989), p. 48.

26. For a more extensive discussion of augmented meetings see Chapter 11 of *The Information Edge* by Dean Meyer and Mary Boone (Homewood, IL: Dow Jones-Irwin, 1989).

27. Ibid., p. 234.

28. Ibid., p. 274.

CHAPTER 20

Don't Go Out and

Buy a Computer

First, Assess Your Unique Needs

Computers, in and of themselves, are worth very little. They deliver value only when the right tools are applied in the right way to a specific business challenge. For this reason I caution you to hesitate before making a decision about selecting and using a computer. It is essential first to think carefully through the reasons for doing so.

Far too many executives think that an Information Systems (I.S.) staff can design an executive information system (EIS) on its own. This rarely works. It is trite but true: Executives receive benefits from a system in direct proportion to their own investment of time and effort in selecting the appropriate problem and tool. To make computers useful, executives must participate in a process designed to delineate their particular business goals and information needs.

Clear articulation of your objectives is a prerequisite to finding the right tool. Only after information needs are clear can tools be selected to meet those needs. As Ron Compton (Aetna) advises: "First, think through your business before applying computers. You need to know the critical success factors of your business, and you need to understand your own business style. At the outset, you ought to know what it is that you need to accomplish as an executive."

Common Problems of EIS Design

With business objectives clarified, the problem of system design is only half solved—making the leap from business objectives to information tools is not easy. At this point executives usually turn to their I.S. staff for help. The I.S. staff knows what technologies are available, and is in a good position to identify the right tools once a business need is clear. The staff has a tremendous amount of knowledge and resources to contribute to getting a system up and running. Also, the staff will be expected to support whatever technology is installed; therefore, it must be part of the implementation process to ensure that the systems are maintainable.

Clearly, both I.S. people and executives must participate in order for the process to work. Unfortunately it is at this point that progress toward an EIS often stalls or becomes misdirected.

Encountering the Language Gap

Many needs-assessment processes start out like this:

> *I.S. person:*   What kind of information would you like to have?
> *Executive:*   Well, I don't know. What can you give me?

This approach is bound to be frustrating and unproductive. When executives have little knowledge of computers, how can they be expected to answer a question such as, "What would you like?" The response is necessarily constrained by what they think computers can do, which in turn is based on what computers have done in the past. This is not likely to lead to innovative new applications.

Unfortunately, the very reason executives and I.S. staff must colloborate may also be the reason why they have trouble communicating: They speak different languages. Quite often, executives don't fully understand the technologies, and I.S. people don't fully understand the business.

The need for a common language between executives and I.S. staff is clear. Many executives share the sentiments of one who described his computer experience by saying: "[I'd] never had any computer knowledge or training, and so the language was very difficult for me. I mean the computer language. I still have a lot of difficulty with it. When our computer people put out memos saying we're going to do this or that or change something, I don't know what they're talking about." When faced with the lack of a common language, it may be tempting to give up or put off consideration of computers or leave the design to the I.S. staff. This, of course, jeopardizes the payoff.

Another approach is simply to persevere. One executive just remained persistent in asking for what he wanted:

> I described what I wanted in terms of business information, and they figured out the best way to deliver it. We've done a lot of modifications to the system. I'd say, "I want to be able to do this," and we'd keep modifying the system. But I don't think they could have thought up those ideas [that I came up with]. They were providing the tools, but they weren't using them the same way I was. I've learned to just keep asking for what I want. If [executives] can't explain what they want [the system] to do, it probably won't be successful for them.

This type of approach puts the burden of explanation on the executive, rather than sharing the burden with I.S., and it demands a lot of the executive's time to get what he or she wants. The burden of translation should be more evenly shared between the I.S. staff and the executive by logically dividing responsibilities:

- The executive should be responsible for thinking through his or her business objectives and should participate in the selection of the information tool.
- The I.S. staff should be responsible for designing the right information tools to address the executive's particular objectives and for procuring and building high-quality systems.

In addition, I.S. professionals can play an even more proactive role. They can smooth the design process considerably by helping the executive "deconstruct" business strategies into leadership requirements and then translate those business problems into information tools.

The following two sections describe common approaches to needs assessment that often fail: the "select-the-system" approach, and the "play-around-with-it" approach.

Using the Select-the-System Approach

In the select-the-system approach, I.S. staff selects a (usually expensive) technology. The selection is based on a very narrow definition of what constitutes an EIS. Then the staff tries to talk executives into using the selected technology.

The select-the-system approach has serious drawbacks. It turns I.S. professionals into technology salespeople instead of business consultants. For lack of a shared understanding of the business problem, the executive is unlikely to trust that the I.S. professional is there to help; therefore, the executive doesn't believe in the payoff of the investment and doesn't take ownership of the project. If an application is discovered, the executive places the onus on the I.S. staff to make it work.

The fundamental problem with the select-the-system approach is that there is no guarantee that the executive has a business problem that matches the selected technology. Even if the technology is of some use, the "technology salespeople" may miss opportunities for real strategic applications—they are too busy pushing their selected technology. All in all, the select-the-system approach is the worst possible implementation method.

Using the Play-Around-with-It Approach

In the play-around-with-it approach, I.S. staff installs a tool kit on the executive's desk (or in his or her home) and then leaves the executive to try out the various tools and see what fits their needs. This might also be called the shot-in-the-dark approach.

If executives are encouraged to simply play around with new technology, they may or may not stumble across a valuable application. This method leaves it to change to determine whether they find computers valuable and continue to use them. Sometimes executives are lucky, and they find a system that meets a particular need. More often, executives say: "Well, I played around with some of those financial programs and balanced my checkbook, but computers really aren't valuable to the kinds of things I have to do at work."

The name of the play-around-with-it approach is descriptive of the attitude it embodies. The approach presents computers as toys to play with, not serious business aids. There is no need to leave the potential for strategic value to chance when it can be ensured.

The Business-Driven Approach

Both the select-the-system approach and the play-around-with-it approach are technology driven—that is, the technology is chosen before

---

FIGURE 6
APPROACHES TO INTRODUCING EXECUTIVE COMPUTING

The Select-the-System Approach

1. Go out and buy the top-of-the-line EIS system (select **technology**).
2. Assume the cost is worth it, because it's for executives (don't worry about the **payoff**).
3. Convince the executives to use it (find **users**).

The Play-Around-with-It Approach

1. Put together a demonstration of several technologies (select **technology**).
2. Give executives temporary workstations to play with. Don't worry about which tools they use; personal applications are fine (don't worry about the **payoff**).
3. Step back and see if they like it (hope for a **user**).

The Business-Driven Approach

1. Talk to the executive who might need assistance (find a **user**).
2. Determine his or her key business objectives (determine the **payoff**).
3. Together, select the appropriate tools (select **technology**).

---

the business problem is diagnosed. They are very different from a business-driven process of needs assessment. Figure 6 summarizes the differences between the two technology-driven approaches and the business-driven approach.[1]

Only the business-driven approach has a high probability of success.

Understanding the Objectives of the Business-Driven Approach

Before describing the needs-assessment method of the business-driven approach, it is worthwhile to clarify the objectives of the method. I do not propose that the needs-assessment process define the ultimate EIS.

Such a comprehensive solution would be difficult to define and even more difficult to build. Furthermore, business needs change. By the time the "ultimate" system was complete, in all likelihood it would be obsolete.

Promises of extremely large or complicated executive systems that can't be delivered for two to three years are likely to lead to disappointments. Besides, executives are tired of hearing about expensive, long I.S. projects. Strategic opportunities call for immediate action. Thus, it is best to take change in small, successive steps. The purpose of the needs-assessment process is to uncover near-term solutions for key objectives.

By taking one small step of change that delivers payback immediately, executives can have successful experiences with information systems—experiences that encourage executives to come back for more. As Bill Gantz (Baxter International) advises: "Crawl before you walk, and walk before you run. Don't start out thinking [a system is] going to solve all the problems of the world. If it can make just a little bit of difference, that's all you really [should] ask for. And you may be surprised at what you find it can do for you."

Vital to the needs-assessment method of the business-driven approach is the executive-support consultant who conducts the needs assessment process. Before moving on to a description of the method, consider the type of training and skills the consultant should have and the ongoing role he or she should play.

Selecting an Executive-Support Consultant

Many I.S. professionals are working with a disadvantage. Most are trained to be specialists in a particular area of technology. It is natural for a specialist to be biased in favor of his or her subset of the tool kit. For example, it is likely that a transaction processing specialist will favor solutions that include operational databases.

However, the person who talks to an executive about an information system must be prepared to implement whatever technology is most appropriate—that is, he or she must be unbiased. Unless the consultant is unbiased, a technology-driven approach is likely, and there is no guarantee that the executive will get a system that meets his or her unique needs.

An executive-support consultant must have a *generalized* knowledge of a broad range of tools. Therefore, executive-support consultants may or may not be selected from the ranks of existing I.S. department managers. Often, the top I.S. executive selects a prospective consultant from a line organization and has that person trained in the necessary technical knowledge. In fact, it is easier to train someone with a business background to have a functional understanding of a broad range of information tools than it is to train someone with a technical background in business strategy and interpersonal skills.

The executive-support consultant must not be expected to be an expert in a particular technology. He or she should have the technological knowledge to select a tool but then should rely on technologists to help implement the solution. This distinction between a consultant and a technologist is critical to maintaining the integrity and competence of both.[2]

Regardless of where they come from, executive-support consultants should have the following attributes:

- Significant business experience, preferably combined with an M.B.A. degree
- Political savvy
- Superb interview and communication skills
- A functional understanding of a broad range of information tools (that is, he or she should be a technology generalist as opposed to a specialist)

Once an executive-support consultant has been selected, he or she should receive training in how to conduct needs-assessment interviews with executives. (The next section describes such interviews.) The translation of business objectives into information tools is a complicated task. Most I.S. departments have not created this type of consulting specialty; therefore, there are very few role models or well-established training methods.

I strongly believe in training by doing. In addition to receiving classroom training, the consultant should, as part of his or her training, conduct actual executive interviews, accompanied and coached by an expert.

Needs assessment is not a static process. One can't go in, interview an executive once, provide him or her with the perfect system, and leave. Executives must continually reevaluate their information needs as their businesses evolve. Just as executive priorities change, so should information tools evolve to meet those needs. It is even possible that a tool might be used for a while in the service of a particular need, and then not used after that need has been met. Therefore, the need for an executive-support consultant is ongoing. Once he or she has received the training and conducted the first round of interviews, the consultant can continue to improve the EIS by interviewing executives periodically, particularly when business priorities change.

Because the needs-assessment process should be ongoing and because the person conducting the interview must have a firm grasp of the business, the executive-support consultant should be a permanent, internal staff person rather than an external consultant. The training of the executive-support consultant may be conducted by an external consultant, but the actual ongoing process of needs-assessment should be done internally.

By working together, executives, executive-support consultants, and I.S. professionals can understand each other. Through the structured needs-assessment interview method, they can help each other arrive at systems solutions that provide real value to executives and, hence, to their corporations.

Using the Needs-Assessment Interview Method

The needs-assessment process involves a semi-structured interview. First, the executive describes his or her objectives; the I.S. professional—the executive support consultant—should have enough business background to be able to easily understand those objectives. Then the I.S. professional helps the executive translate business objectives into leadership strategies and then into information objectives. Finally, the I.S. professional describes one or more tools that meet those needs. Together, the executive and the I.S. person select the most appropriate information tools.

This section describes the needs-assessment interview and contains an interview guide (Figure 7). The step-by-step interview is designed to uncover key business objectives, translate those into information objectives, and then select the appropriate tools. (Appendix 4 shows how a needs-assessment approach might apply to the situations of the executives interviewed for this book. The appendix was developed by "reverse engineering" their case studies.)

FIGURE 7
NEEDS-ASSESSMENT INTERVIEW GUIDE

Define the Business Goal

Describe in a few words the general goal of the company. The goal could be to increase revenues, improve margins, or rebuild financial strength, for example.

Define the Business Strategies

Describe the most important strategies (three to five) that the organization will attempt this year to achieve its goal.

Arrange the strategies in the order of priority.

For each business strategy, define the necessary leadership strategies

What do you personally have to accomplish to meet the demands of each business strategy? In other words, what are the most crucial personal objectives, or leadership strategies, for each business strategy?

Under each business strategy, place the accompanying leadership strategies. Arrange the strategies in the order of priority.

For each leadership strategy, select one or more information success factors

Select the most important three or four information success factors that are related to your leadership strategy. Arrange them in the order of priority.

(See Figure 8, entitled "Information Success Factors.")

For each information success factor, select one or more tools

At this point the interviewer selects one or more tools he or she believes will help and describes them to the executive in functional terms.

The executive says yes or no to additional exploration of each application.

FIGURE 7 *(continued)*

In order of priority, for each tool:

The consultant estimates how long it will take to install the tool. Will it take too long to meet the near-term objective?

The consultant provides a rough estimate of how much each tool will cost. Is it worth it?

The consultant tells the executive how many hours of training and usage are necessary. Is it worth the time?

If the benefits outweigh the costs, you have an application.

If the answer to any of these questions is no, then move to the next task.

It's impossible to fix everything; therefore, the executive and the executive-support consultant must work on the most important problems or opportunities first. By setting priorities at every step in this process, they ensure focus on the few areas of greatest importance.

The executive-support consultant gets a basic understanding of the executive's objectives in the first interview. After that, the objectives are simply modified as time passes. The first needs-assessment interview usually lasts about two hours. Subsequent interviews may last anywhere from 30 minutes to an hour; they are shorter because the executive-support consultant and the executive have already established a rapport and common understanding of the business.

A discussion of each step in the interview follows. To begin the process, assume that you are the executive being interviewed.

Define the Business Goal.   The interviewer asks you to explain in a few words the organization's primary strategic goal. The business goal could be, for example, to increase market share, improve margins, improve financial condition, or maintain quality. The business goal creates a context for the interview. All your business and leadership strategies should be aligned with this goal.

Define the Business Strategies.   The next step is to develop a summary of your organization's strategies for the coming year. Strategies are the key actions that the organization as a whole will take to achieve its goal. They might include initiating acquisitions, reducing costs, or decentralizing decision making. Since time for discussion and analysis is scarce, include only the highest priority strategies.

Define the Leadership Strategies.   The next step is to personalize the business strategies, to fully understand what role you, as leader, will play in their accomplishment. The executive-support consultant might ask a question such as "What key projects do you need to accomplish in order to make the board, the executive committee, or the stockholders happy?" Leadership strategies are specific actions you *personally* will undertake or oversee to ensure that a business strategy is achieved. (Appendix 4 gives examples of leadership strategies for each of the profiled executives.) Each business strategy might lead to more than one leadership strategy. Discuss one business strategy at a time, and the leadership strategies within it. Focus on the most important and arrange them in order of priority.

Define the Information Success Factors (ISFs).   The link between business objectives and information tools has been the most elusive part of EIS applications. To address the gap between business objectives and information tools, Dean Meyer and I designed a list of information success factors (ISFs) to serve as a bridge between business objectives and the selection of information tools.[3] We have expanded and restructured our original chart so that it can better serve top executives. (See Figure 8.)

The ISF list should be used simply as a discussion aid, in moving from leadership strategies to information tools. It should help executives explicitly describe the kind of payoff they need from an information system. The list should also help the executive-support consultant determine the type of information tools that are needed.

Each leadership strategy could lead to a few information tools, although some strategies will not lend themselves to computer support.

Review Appropriate Tools.   In the next step of the interview, you and the executive-support consultant brainstorm various tools, with the consultant giving functional descriptions of the tools and how they would work in the business scenario. (Appendix 1 and Appendix 6 contain information that may assist you in this discussion.)

FIGURE 8
INFORMATION SUCCESS FACTORS

Personal Thinking

- Be well-informed
  Stay up-to-date
  Increase depth of knowledge
  Adjust filters on information
  Absorb information quickly
  About what?
  > Internal activities:
  >> Business operations: status, problems
  >> Business measures: goals, achievements
  >> Projects: status, milestones, due dates, critical path
  >> Commitments, appointments
  > External activities:
  >> Who's doing what?
  >> How do they see us?
  >> Marketplace status and trends
  >> Investments, the economy
  >> Global business and political events

- Think and make decisions
  Enhance creativity, brainstorm, invent, design
  Get the facts
  Organize ideas and information, manage complexity
  Analyze and compare alternatives
  Balance logic and intuition
  Forecast
  Allocate resources

- Leverage time
  Work independently of time and location (asynchronous work)
  Improve responsiveness

FIGURE 8 *(continued)*

Managing Organizations

- Design organizations and cultures
  Pick, promote, and reward people
  Flatten hierarchies and empower people
  Measure performance on selected objectives (feedback loops)

- Communicate with people (inside or outside)
  Know people
  Reach people, be accessible (asynchronous communication)
  Listen to people
  Write with clarity and consistency
  Personalize messages
  Present, convince, negotiate
  Improve teamwork and collaboration
  Improve meeting effectiveness, thinking in groups
  Announce, one-to-many

- Coach people
  Broaden peoples' perspectives
  Focus people on what's important
  Teach critical-thinking abilities
  Balance the need to know and the need to delegate

An extremely broad range of tools is available today in off-the-shelf packages that range from very inexpensive to very expensive. Because there are so many off-the-shelf tools to choose from, it is not always necessary to resort to customized programming (which increases the cost and time of the project significantly).

There are no hard-and-fast rules for matching tools to ISFs. Appendix 2 presents some suggestions concerning which tools might match specific ISFs. Of course, the list of tools in Appendix 2 is by no means exhaustive, and tool selection must be based on the unique situation. Appendix 2 is intended only to spark some ideas for conversation.

Executive-support consultants can be trained to recognize patterns and suggest tools that closely match ISFs. But only you, the executive, can make the final decision as to whether a tool is or is not appropriate. A brainstorming session between you and the consultant is the best way to specifically match tools and leadership problems. The key to continued executive involvement in this step is the consultant's ability to describe quickly, in simple terms, what a computer can and can't do.

The executive-support consultant should be able to explain in simple language exactly what the *function* of the tool is. I stress the word *function,* because the executive should understand what the tool does well enough to know whether or not it will work in the business context. Analogies and metaphors are helpful in simplifying descriptions. Sample functional descriptions for most information tools can be found in Appendix 6.

It is incumbent upon the executive-support consultant to make himself or herself understood. If you do not understand the terms the consultant is using, then simply ask the consultant to speak more plainly. If he or she cannot, see to it that the consultant receives additional training. Or, as a last resort, get another consultant.

In some cases, a tool may be particularly difficult to describe or understand. If you think a tool sounds appropriate but are not completely sure, the consultant may arrange a brief demonstration of that particular tool. (Too often, executive demonstrations are technology-driven instead of needs-driven. Once executives have set priorities on their business strategies, leadership strategies, and ISFs, well-targeted demonstrations have much greater value.)

Evaluate Informal Estimates.   Once a tool is found that seems to relate to an ISF, and hence to a leadership strategy, discuss whether it would really be worthwhile.

First consider the time it would take to develop and install the system. If the business situation is very short fused, there may not be sufficient time to implement the system.

Financial return is another important consideration. The consultant should provide a rough estimate of costs, although these should not be taken as commitments until the consultant has consulted with technical experts. You, as the executive, must make a value judgment as to whether the system is worth its cost.

For most executives, the real cost of information tools is not the price of the hardware and software. Rather, most executives perceive costs in terms of the amount of their time required to make a system work. In other words, they want to know how much time it will take to learn the system and to use it. This question provides the acid test. If you do not believe that it is worth your time to learn and use a tool, then the selected problem is not of real importance or the tool does not meet your needs adequately.

If the time needed to learn and use a tool is not offset by the benefits it will provide, then go on to examine the next priority.

Executive Training

Once a tool has been selected, the next step is training. Most of the executives I interviewed said that current off-the-shelf software is reasonably easy to learn. Nonetheless, executives must be willing to make an investment in learning how to use the tool and in making the new tool part of the normal way of working.

Different executives prefer different modes of training. Videos, manuals, and "stumbling around" were the most frequent methods of learning, followed by one-on-one training.

A surprising majority taught themselves how to use the tools. Consider the following quotations:

> I never took any courses in how to use the computer. I wouldn't have time. I find it more productive to learn the packages and machines by *doing*. I use it on real problems when I'm learning. I play with it and use the manual.
>
> —KEN McCREADY (TransAlta)

> Over the holidays, I got the flu, and I couldn't ski with my kids. So I got out the computer, and *boy*, I know how to use 1-2-3 now! I set up some models and watched a videotape about it. The great thing about the way software is designed now is that you push a button and the instruction manual is built in.
>
> —THOMAS STEPHENS (Manville)

A variety of self-training methods are available. Many vendor companies provide videotaped primers or computer-based tutorials.

One-on-one training can be extremely effective and time-efficient if it is conducted by competent, "business-literate" I.S. staff. However, everyone learns differently, as evidenced by the following quotations:

> "I never took any classes. . . . I go through the manuals fairly quickly. There's probably some very esoteric uses that I don't bother with because I'm in a business, I'm not a rocket scientist [laughter]."

> "I never took any courses in how to use the computer. I wouldn't have time to do it. I find it more productive to learn the packages and machines by doing. I like to learn how to use [the computer] by using it on real problems that I have. I play with it and use the manual. I'm no expert in any one package. I'll just go as far as I need to go."

> "One-on-one training is best for me."

> "Well, I started off using the manuals and reading through, figuring out how to do it. But then I found out that we have a staff here that is really outstanding. When I've had problems, I've called them, and they come up here quickly. I get a lot of help."

My experience has been that most executives appreciate personal training in how to use various tools. However, executives must experiment with their own learning styles.

Ongoing Support

After the first application is up and running, the executive requires ongoing support. This ranges from the need for answers to questions and additional training to the need for modifications and enhancements to the system.

The executive-support consultant serves as a single point of contact for all the executive's information systems requirements, both prior to and after training. The consultant will "contract" with the appropriate technologists and trainers throughout the company to make sure that all the executive's needs are met.

To uncover new applications and opportunities, the executive-support consultant will also periodically conduct needs-assessment interviews with on-line executives. By treating needs assessment as an ongoing process, tools for executives can continue to be selected in a flexible and opportune way.

Chapter Summary

All too often, the process of executive needs assessment is either handled incorrectly or ignored altogether. When needs assessment is handled incorrectly—through simplistic demonstrations, by playing with tools, or by guesswork—the results are often disappointing. Technology-driven change, in which executives have systems force-fed to them, usually follows. In this situation, no one wins. The executive is unlikely to find the system useful, and the IS staff is blamed for a (usually expensive) failure.

As a result, many executives are rightfully jaded about the willingness of I.S. to help them. The answer is not more technology or easier-to-use interfaces. The answer is the needs-assessment process undertaken by executives and I.S. staff, who must collaborate on a business-driven approach. With the executive's full participation in the process of understanding and selecting an information tool, the chances of finding a strategic application are greatly increased.

NOTES

1. Based on Dean Meyer and Mary Boone, *The Information Edge*, 2nd edition (Homewood, IL: Dow Jones-Irwin, 1989), pp. 307–311.
2. N. Dean Meyer, *Structural Cybernetics* (Ridgefield, CT: NDMA Inc., 1990).
3. Based on Dean Meyer and Mary Boone, *The Information Edge*, 2nd edition (Homewood, IL: Dow Jones-Irwin, 1989), p. 320.

VII

WHERE

FROM HERE?

Part VII

This book is a snapshot in time—an early time in the birth and growth of executive computing. Part VII looks to the future and imagines the evolution of both information technology and its application to business.

Why bother with conjecture about the future? Part VII should be useful for two reasons:

- The scenarios may further spark your imagination as to how you might use computers today.
- The comments of the executives about what they want, and the scenarios described in the latter part of the chapter, may help guide those who design systems to move in the direction of tools that extend the capacity to think, reason, and manage complexity.

I hope Part VII will influence those who are thinking about using or developing executive information systems to move toward tools for thinking rather than just tools for convenience.

CHAPTER 21

Imagining
the Future

Though this chapter is entitled "Imagining the Future," a great deal of it is concerned with the present.

Technological availability and technological usage are often out of synch. The state of the art always precedes the state of practice. For example, VCRs were commercially available in 1970, but it took much longer for them to be widely adopted. Similarly, there was a decade between the introduction of cost-effective (Group III) facsimile devices and widespread usage.

With regard to executive computing, technology seems to be ahead of usage by about 5 to 10 years. Even the executives in this book, who are by far some of the most sophisticated users of information systems, have only begun to tap the potential that today's tools offer. Conducting the interviews for this book brought this home to me. As these executives described their objectives and concerns about their businesses, my mind often raced to potential applications. It became apparent that there are technological capabilities already available that many of them consider futuristic. There are quite a few more ways in which available tools could be applied to their needs.

One executive recognized this same potential, and said to me: "The limitation is me. At this point, the limitation is my ability to invest the time to learn more, to set up more support systems. And generally, that's been the case with computers. The limitation is not the hardware or the software; it's the imagination."

This chapter begins with a description of what executives say they want. Their wishes, along with a compendium of their discoveries as described in the profiles, provide the basis for forecasting the future of executive computing.

Given that there is so much unused technological capability, some of "tomorrow's" applications will inevitably be based on today's technologies. This makes near-term forecasting easy. The first "futuristic" scenario contained in this chapter consists of technologies that are already commercially available.

In the second scenario, I imagine a more distant future—one not constrained by the technologies available today. Forecasting new technologies can be dangerous business—especially for those of us who do not regularly view the computer industry's laboratories. Perhaps some of the imagined capabilities will never emerge; no doubt, many other unimagined possibilities will.

But my emphasis is not on technology, but rather its application to the work of executives. Even without an accurate technology forecast, one can learn a great deal by examining what executives do and how they think. Indeed, one would hope that the future of executive computing is determined to a greater extent by business needs than technology for technology's sake. For this reason, I have chosen to imagine the future based on the requirements inherent in Dean Meyer's phrase, "tools for thinking."

But first, what did the executives themselves say about what they wanted from computers in the future?

What Executives Want

I asked the executives profiled in this book how they might use computers in the future and what improvements they would like in their information tools. Their intriguing answers fell into six basic categories: portability, voice input, maneuverability, nonprogrammer programming, the information hologram, and the electronic consultant.

Portability

Executives truly appreciate the ability to access information and computer-based tools away from the office. They believe that, in the future, information will become even more convenient, and that computers will be designed for portability:

Right now, I look like a Sherpa guide when I'm hauling around my computer and my portable phone. But this problem is quickly being solved, and this is important when you travel 180 days a year.

—THOMAS STEPHENS (Manville)

I really want a small notebook-sized computer, if it had a big-enough screen. I'd like to keep one in my briefcase. But right now, I can barely walk with my briefcase because it's so heavy.

—ELLEN GORDON (Tootsie Roll Industries)

[In the future] I'll be writing my memoirs on a two-pound laptop that goes 23 hours between battery charges.

—RON COMPTON (Aetna)

What will they do with portable computers? They talk about access to both information and tools that help them work with their ideas. For example, consider the following quotes:

After a five-day trip, I'd like to be able to cast my notes into the computer. You can write them on the back of an envelope, but then you can't find them or read them.

—MARK EDMISTON (*The Cable Guide*)

[Information] will be more portable. Sometimes when I travel, I say, 'Gee, I wonder. . . .' It would be nice to have that information available [to help me answer those questions when I'm thinking about them]. A great deal of information will be provided in very convenient form so you never have to carry routine documents. You'll just unplug your widget, and away you'll go.

—MICHAEL JORDAN (Frito-Lay)

Ultimately, you're going to be carrying things like a little newspaper on your pocket computer. And in due time, you'll have a small piece of equipment that will translate instantaneously as you talk to someone speaking another language.

—BURNELL ROBERTS (Mead)

A number of executives mention improved use of computers on airplanes:

In 10 years, I think there will be screens on the back of airline seats. You'll have something like a floppy disk with your whole system on it that you can just load into another machine—everything will be standard. I also think you'll find them in your hotel room.

—BILL ESREY (United Telecom and US Sprint)

In the future, I think there will be continual, virtually uninterrupted access to computers, irrespective of where you may be. I think you'll see massive interconnection. There will be lightweight portables that communicate via satellite in real time. You'll be able to communicate on a wireless basis to [your main computer in the office]. Airlines will have such demand [in the future] that they'll have special antennas, and you'll be able to broadcast out of an antenna external to the plane to the satellite and into your [main computer]. You'll be doing your business while you're on the airplane, and talking directly with your staff.
—SENATOR HUMPHREY

Senator Humphrey believes that accessibility will extend into congressional committee rooms in the future. "One of the biggest wastes of time around [Congress] is committee meetings. Of course, they're absolutely necessary because you have to get input from diverse points of view, but testimony is often terribly redundant and long-winded. Some day, of course, the Senate committee hearing rooms will have a keyboard in front of each senator so that he can be keeping up with other things while listening to redundant testimony hour after hour."

The accessibility and portability of future computers will have a great deal to do with executives' ability to perform asynchronous work. Because time management is so important to executives, many envision a future where they will be able to use a computer wherever and whenever they wish.

Of course, we are already moving closer to this scenario. Powerful new portables weigh less than five pounds and fit into a briefcase. Telecommunications standards allow these portables to plug into any telephone. And airline telephone service is now being expanded and its quality improved with a new satellite system. The realization of most of the executives' visions does not seem far off.

Voice Input

There are some rudimentary applications of voice-input technology today, but sophisticated voice-input technology is still a long way away. Current state-of-the-art systems can recognize about 5,000 words (enough to capture virtually all business communications), but the machines are speaker-dependent—that is, they respond only to the sound of one particular person's voice. They are also noncontinuous, which means the speaker must pause briefly (and unnaturally) between each word. Today, it is difficult to speak precisely enough for a computer to recognize words with a satisfactory degree of accuracy.

So far, there are very few executive applications of speech recognition technology, perhaps because of its limitations. Speech recognition is primarily used for jobs that require the use of the hands for other activities, such as sorting mail or assembly-line work.

Although keyboards do not seem overly intimidating to the interviewed executives, some of them envision a future for voice-based technologies. Many recognize that the keyboard is likely to be faster and more effective for giving commands; however, they would like to be able to annotate information with voice attachments:

> Ideally, I'll be able to look at a chart or a memo, and I could speak to the computer and annotate the chart or memo. Then I'll push a soft key that sends it to the right person. What will come up on his screen is this chart, tied with a voice message that says, "Jerry, this is really exciting, can we get it to market sooner?"
>
> —BILL ESREY (United Telecom and US Sprint)

> I'd like to be able to communicate through my computer. I'd like to send a chart to someone and have a [voice] message attached saying "Jim, here's the report. Why is this happening?"
>
> —BILL GANTZ (Baxter)

Beyond voice annotation, executives talk about speech recognition for text input. For example, Richard Crandall (Comshare) says: "I'd like voice-input, text-output technology. . . . You would speak to it, and your speech would show up as a piece of text. You would touch the text and attach it on the screen to the image you want to send. Then you would tell it to send the message and the image to somebody."

Even though they like the idea of being able to input information via voice, many executives would still want a keyboard or some other mechanism that would allow them to edit the information once it had been entered:

> I'd love for the computer to be able to capture my voice. Certainly for word processing and the outline editor, it would be much faster to talk to it than to type. I'd like to be able to blither at it and then revise it with a keyboard or some other controlling mechanism.
>
> —KEN McCREADY (TransAlta)

> I'd like to be able to talk to it like I'm talking to you, and have it produce the first draft. But I'd still want to get in there and edit [with the

keyboard]. Because you know, even as I'm talking to you, I'm thinking back on different ways I might have said something. So I'd like to be able to speak my stream of consciousness into it and then modify it.
—THOMAS PLASKETT (Pan Am)

In the future, I expect that many executives will use voice input to enter their first draft or to annotate text and data, but I expect that those same executives will still need a device that allows them to give the computer detailed commands and do precision editing.

Voice recognition, no matter how accurate it may become, is likely to remain slower than a keyboard for this sort of work. For example, imagine simply trying to delete a word in a document by voice: "Delete the word 'the.' No! Not that one. The one in the third paragraph in the second sentence after the word 'are.'" The human voice may never be precise enough to do this type of work efficiently and effectively.

The interactive nature of the editing process demands a user interface that lends itself to jumping around in information and editing pieces of text. This interactivity is the same factor that causes many of the executives to prefer word processors over dictation.

Maneuverability

Getting where they want to go with a computer is of importance to executives. Some executives would like to see improvements in the ability to navigate between, and within, applications. As Richard Pogue (Jones Day Reavis & Pogue) says: "You ought to be able to punch one button to go from word processing to e-mail." This capability is already available in many windowing (graphical) user interfaces, although new user interface software is only beginning to be used.

Also, I think that executives will become increasingly interested in the ability to maneuver not only between applications, but within applications. Thomas Stephens (Manville), while talking about user interface design for rapid thinking, says: "It should get easier and easier to get from point A, I've got an idea, to point B, it pops up on the screen."

Already, hypertext is designed to permit people to move quickly through complex relationships between information and ideas. Outline editors allow people to sketch their thoughts quickly, and then restructure them fluidly. (One example of this type of software is called a thought processor.) But right now, the user interface on most computer systems moves much more slowly than human beings can think. The interfaces are designed to make learning easy for the novice, not to support high-performance thinking for the expert.

In the future, executives will demand applications that move at the speed of thought. This involves more than simply increasing the speed of the machines. It involves creating user interfaces that are highly intuitive and designed for performance thinking. Executives will want applications that help them structure their thoughts, pursue a line of analysis, or stimulate the creation of new ideas.[1]

Nonprogrammer Programming

One executive mentions that he would like the ability to do some rudimentary programming, without having to learn programming skills. Mark Edmiston (*The Cable Guide*) says: "I am not a programmer, but I would like to have the ability to customize things a little more . . . to sort of nonprogrammer program it. As quick and useful as some of my software packages are, I still have to work within a sort of box that the programmers built for me. I'd like to make those boxes more flexible. I'd like some ability to customize the standard boxes."

Executives can already build macros—that is, combine existing commands into programs—within many tools. There are programs that allow computer users to replay predesigned keyboard sequences with the touch of a single key. For the future, there is work being done in an area called object-oriented languages. This research may result in the type of rudimentary programming that this executive desires.

The Information Hologram

One executive presents a wonderful, distant-future scenario in which person-specific information would be contained in a three-dimensional hologram. Richard Crandall (Comshare) speculates:

> There will be a multidimensional hologram of your information floating above your desk. You'll be able to reach out and touch things and rotate it around. Other people will also be able to walk around it and touch different parts of it. It will contain information in both graphical and analytical forms. There will be no screen, no computer . . . just you and your information. The response will be instantaneous, and the interface will be your hand and your voice.

Today, there is a software package that allows people to plot data in three dimensions and then rotate the plot on the (two-dimensional) screen to see it from different angles and look for graphical patterns.* This may be a small hint of what's to come. Whether or not holograms can provide three-dimensional desktop displays, the vision of complete flexibility, maneuverability, and accessibility of information is intriguing.

The Electronic Consultant

Other executives mention that they would like to have an electronic consultant or "coach" with artificial-intelligence capabilities. They speculate that this on-line consultant would stretch them to think about ideas from different perspectives. Here are a few of their wishes:

> In science fiction terms, you'd almost have a companion—really a complete extension of your memory—that you'd have extremely ready access to.
>
> —KEN McCREADY (TransAlta)

> It will have built-in artificial intelligence so that a lot of what you're already thinking about will have been built in. You'll have an intelligent companion.
>
> —SANDY SIGOLOFF (Wickes)

> I'd like for the computer to push the limits of my thinking. I can envision sitting down with a terminal and having a dialogue with the computer. Rather than the computer being a slave to my keystrokes and demands, it would prompt me. It's like chess. My daughter and I play a game of chess on the computer that has all the classic chess moves of all the masters programmed into it. When Ann and I were playing last night, we started to move the rook and the computer asked, "Are you sure?" It prompts me and takes its power and my creativity and builds the two together. That is what I'd like in a business scenario as well.
>
> —THOMAS STEPHENS (Manville)

This is an area with enormous untapped potential. Though "artificial intelligence" or "expert systems" have received a great deal

---

*This product is called MacSpin.

of hype over the past few years, their potential has barely been tapped. There are many new ways in which advanced expert systems could contribute to the capture and distribution of knowledge and expertise. Today, most expert systems are being used as a medium for publishing what an expert knows about a particular subject. More generalized systems in the future may actually coach a person how to think—perhaps about a topic on which no expert exists.

We may already have seen a glimpse of the future in Debbi Fields's (Mrs. Fields Cookies) use of the computer as an electronic consultant. Not only has she passed along her own expertise in this way, but she also uses The Idea Generator to facilitate her own creative thoughts and ideas.

Similarly, Ron Compton's expert system at Aetna will capture his AMP planning technique. It is not content specific; rather it will coach Aetna's managers in a method for thinking about their own unique problems. In both these cases, the expert systems are not the experts, but they help people improve their own skills.

Two Scenarios: Realistic and Fantastic

In this section, I attempt to put together what we have learned from leading executives' speculations about the future. I imagine the future in the form of two scenarios. Both examine a day in the life of an imaginary executive in imaginary companies.

The first scenario is based on currently available technologies. What makes it futuristic is the fact that, even though the technologies are available, very few executives take advantage of them in the ways that our imaginary executive, Robert, does.

The second scenario is based on technologies that may or may not ever be available. But, if they were created, they might contribute substantially to executive effectiveness. Unlike many technology forecasts, I have been careful to project the business needs, not just the technologies, of the future. In this way, I attempt to illustrate the notion of tools for thinking as opposed to tools for convenience.

For purposes of story-telling, I have packed a great number of applications into a single day. Executives certainly may use the computer less in a single day than I have indicated, but I take a bit of literary license to examine a number of tools in each scenario.

Realistic Futurism

Yesterday was not a good day for Robert Ludwig, CEO of LASCO. His worst suspicions were confirmed: LASCO's two biggest competitors finally signed a merger agreement.

LASCO had been, until yesterday, one of the two largest consumer-packaging companies in the world. But, with the announcement of this merger, LASCO immediately fell down the list in terms of size. Worse yet, the merger gives First Packaging International (FPI, the new company) distinct competitive advantages because of its improved ability to serve the customer. The trade press called it "a merger made in heaven." FPI can offer the customer a more complete product line, more options within each product segment, leading research and development facilities, and the latest in advancements in packaging machinery and related technologies.

Robert is deep in thought about FPI when his wife, Janet, asks him if he wants a second cup of coffee. He nods, and she asks why he is looking so gloomy.

"It's this damned FPI merger," he answers.

"But what have they got that LASCO hasn't got?" asks Janet, surprised at the vehemence of his response. She is accustomed to LASCO's market leadership position. Robert has rarely looked so troubled about his work.

"For starters, they can support our customers start to finish. They can assist with everything from design all the way through production—glues, inks, even printing services! And that's not all. Within each product segment they've got a variety of different kinds of paper and plastic in all shapes and sizes," says Robert, obviously just getting heated up. "Then, to top it off, now FPI has the best technology in the business. Each of the separate companies had a technology specialty. One was tops in adhesive chemistry, and the other was on the leading edge in terms of laminating techniques. Now they've got both—not to mention the fact that the merger gives them a variety of international locations and the largest sales force in the business."

"Doesn't sound good," says Janet sympathetically.

"It's not," mutters Robert.

"So what are you going to do?" she asks.

"Good question. I'm not sure yet. We have a strategy meeting scheduled first thing this morning."

"Will you be home for dinner?"

"Yes, but it'll be late, so don't wait for me. I want to check into WBSI tonight with you. I'd like to see what's going on in that conference on European monetary unification," replies Robert. "I'll get home around 9:00, and we'll take a look together. How does that sound?"

"That'll be fine. I've got plenty to do here," says Janet. "You should finish your breakfast. Dave will be here any minute." Dave chauffeurs Robert from their Connecticut home to LASCO headquarters in New York City each day.

On the drive into work, instead of reading *The Wall Street Journal* as he normally does, Robert is once again deep in thought. He pulls a pad of paper and his Mont Blanc pen out of his briefcase and starts jotting down notes. He lists two categories on the yellow-lined paper. On the left he scribbles "Strengths" and on the right he scribbles "Weaknesses." Under "Strengths" he writes:

- Name recognition, long-standing reputation
- International sales force, long-standing customer relations
- Structure of organization (highly independent divisions) makes it easier to respond to specific customer needs
- Well-capitalized, liquid (plenty of cash on hand), profitable (for now!)

Under "Weaknesses" he writes:

- Structure of organization (highly independent divisions) results in lack of coordination on strategy, making it hard to fill in product matrix
- Too bureaucratic, not well coordinated in response to complex international customer needs that require work across divisions

As he writes the second item under "Weaknesses," Robert thinks back to a recent problem. One of LASCO's best customers was introducing an innovative new product that had complex packaging requirements requiring new manufacturing technology. The customer wanted to announce the product simultaneously worldwide. LASCO had a number of problems with this large project. Robert received weekly phone calls from the CEO of the customer company, complaining about LASCO's lack of coordination. This is particularly worrisome to Robert because large projects compose the high end (most profitable) part of LASCO's business.

Dave, the driver, sees Robert look up from his work and tells him, "The traffic looks great! We shouldn't have any problems getting you into the office a bit early today."

"Well, it's nice to have some *good* news for a change," says Robert, smiling.

A half hour later, Robert puts away his pad of paper and says, "Since the weather is so beautiful today, why don't you just drop me off out front."

Dave obliges, and Robert steps out of the limousine and into a crisp, sunny autumn day in New York. He bemoans the fact that he won't see much more of it. Today is going to be busy.

Robert takes the elevator to the 31st floor, where he is greeted by the receptionist. Robert returns the greeting and continues on down the hall to his office. Robert's secretary, Alice, greets him, and asks him if he wants coffee. "Decaf, please, Alice. I've already had two cups of the real stuff."

She smiles and disappears down the hall to the kitchen. When Alice returns with a steaming cup, she tells him that everyone has been informed of the strategy meeting and will be there at 9:00 sharp. Robert thanks her and then takes a moment to glance through the pink "While you were out" slips that are piled on his desk.

At 9:00 Robert strides toward the boardroom. People are just arriving, and those who are already in the room turn to look at Robert, trying to read his face for a reaction to the news about the merger. Robert opens the meeting with a review of the strengths and weaknesses that he jotted notes on in the car. As he finishes delineating these, he turns to the group and asks, "Is there anything to add to these two lists?"

After a wandering discussion in which people restate Robert's points in a variety of ways, the general consensus among the group is that Robert has captured the most important points.

"Well, now we've got to think about what we're going to do about all of this. Any ideas?"

One executive vice president responds, "Well, it's pretty obvious that we're going to have to look at some synergistic acquisitions to quickly broaden our product segments, fill in the product matrix, and acquire some new [packaging] technology that's already up and running."

"I agree," says Robert. The group launches into a discussion of some potential acquisition candidates. The discussion starts to wander, and Robert reins it back in by describing to the group one of his own ideas.

"I'm really concerned about getting some teamwork going around here across divisions. They're like islands," Robert asserts. "I'd like to see more cross-fertilization across the divisions so that we could offer some of our existing product lines worldwide. You all know that there are products invented in Europe that have never even made it to the U.S., and vice versa."

Robert's comment sparks another group discussion about whose fault this lack of coordination between divisions is. Robert cuts this debate off: "Let's not worry about whose fault it is. It's just part of our culture, and our divisionalization served us well when we were dealing with smaller customers who always wanted us to tailor things to their requirements. We still have to maintain that strength. But we also have to satisfy the large customers to compete internationally. Somehow we've got to improve coordination across functional areas and dispersed locations, without losing our ability to respond to specific requests. So how are we going to have our cake and eat it too?"

After a bit of brainstorming about projects that might be coordinated on an international basis, the meeting starts to slow down. Robert figures that, at this point, he has gotten most of the ideas that the group has to offer. He calls a close to the meeting and returns to his office.

In his own mind, Robert knows that a few acquisitions and shared projects are not enough. He is after a change in the culture—a change toward an organization that not only permits local autonomy and responsiveness, but also takes advantage of synergies, can coordinate international projects, and pursues a common strategy.

He looks down at his yellow pad. He has scribbled notes in the margins and on the next page. The paper is covered with arrows that now seem intertwined, and thoughts are abbreviated when his scribbling ran out of space. The mess reminds him that there's a better way to do this.

He decides it's time to sort this stuff out and get it in a format that he can understand better. He turns on the PC in his office and loads the outline editor-word processor. He enters all of the notes on strengths and weaknesses, as well as the strategies that the group discussed. He sorts the information into a hierarchical structure by using the outline editor. He realizes that there are two basic strategies: acquisitions and improved internal collaboration.

For each of these business strategies, he must take responsibility in the form of a leadership strategy. In the outline, underneath each of the two strategies, he enters a heading labeled, "Personal leadership strategy."

Under the business strategy "Encourage international collaboration," Robert asks himself, "What can I do to inspire everyone to cooperate?" He enters the following leadership strategies:

- Build into management incentive plan some recognition of teamwork across profit centers
- Personally set an example by staying in close touch with key worldwide activities
- Personally point out opportunities for collaboration, and (in very important situations) get personally involved in forming project teams across organizational boundaries
- Build awareness of the corporate product matrix and strategy
- Encourage lateral communication and cooperation

Robert knows that he is going to need all the help he can get from all parts of the organization to respond to this competitive threat to LASCO. Several months ago, he and his Information Systems executive-support consultant, John, had their first interview, and it was a terrific success. Robert wonders if John will have any more ideas about how information tools might help him with his new objectives. Once he has the information entered into the computer, he places a call to John. Moments later, John arrives in his office.

"John, I'm under a lot of pressure right now. I'd like to see if you can help me think of any ways in which computers could help with some of these objectives."

John pulls a chair up beside Robert, and together they review his personal leadership strategies. Under each entry in the outline, they start a new category for Information Success Factors (ISFs). Robert decides there are three basic ISF "themes," and he adds these to the outline:

1. Leverage time: Be everywhere at once in order to stay on top of all activities and serve as the convergence point to make LASCO feel like one firm.

2. Be well-informed: Keep up-to-date with internal and external activities so that I can spot opportunities for collaboration.

3. Communicate: Get all divisions to understand the importance of filling in the corporate product matrix and developing a shared strategy. Also, build cross-organization communication patterns.

"Let's take them one at a time," says John. "First of all, you want to leverage your time. Within that theme, what do you need to do?"

"Well," says Robert, "I'm going to be the focal point for a single company-wide vision and strategy—at least until the organization starts to work more as a team on its own. So, to guide projects all over the company, I've got to respond quickly to the people who need my input. Also, if I want to start encouraging people to be more reponsive and communicate better with each other across divisions, then I'm going to have to set an example."

"What are the obstacles to doing that?" asks John.

"Time zones," responds Robert quickly. "Staying in touch with people in a global organization takes some doing. With some of the Asian offices, it's almost impossible to have any type of informal communication. Sometimes it takes me a week to answer a question they've asked me. I feel like I should be spending 24 hours a day in the office!"

"Well, you're already on the electronic mail system domestically and to Europe. Would you like for me to get you hooked up with the Asian offices as well?"

"Great idea. That way we can get around all of this time-zone stuff. I don't know why I didn't think of that myself. I've been sending faxes, but the interim step of getting something typed up just makes it so much less convenient. I'd like to zap all that stuff to a bunch of people right away. That way, I'm more likely to communicate the things I'm thinking about."

"What else can we do to leverage your time?" asks John.

"This is going to be a pressure-cooker situation until we get some things under control," responds Robert. "But I can't just respond with firefighting. I'm the one who's supposed to do a lot of strategic and tactical thinking about how we are going to pull all of this together. Somehow, I've got to find some more hours in the day. For example, this morning on the drive in, instead of reading the paper, I started outlining all of this stuff."

"Would you like to use that time in the car even more effectively?" asks John.

"Absolutely," replies Robert. "That's an extra two hours a day I could use for planning."

"Well, you've been talking about that laptop you saw in the airline flight magazine," says John. "Maybe it's time for us to get you one."

"It sure would be nice to be able to do some electronic mail from the car while I'm driving in. I could hit some of those time zones I'm missing. I also could've used the outline editor this morning to sketch out my thoughts."

While they are talking, the speaker phone buzzes and Alice says, "Mr. Ludwig?"

"Yes?"

"It's almost time for your meeting on R&D. They're in the marketing conference room."

"Alice, you're right. Thanks." Robert invites John to join him at the meeting, to understand his situation better.

The meeting is under way by the time Robert and John arrive. The topic, new product development, has certainly gained importance since yesterday's FPI merger, and the discussion is animated. As Robert joins the group, there is disagreement as to whether or not two important R&D projects are redundant. A polite but emotional argument ensues between two vice presidents, each defending the merits of his project. John whispers something to Robert, and Robert interrupts the debate.

"I've got a suggestion here," says Robert. "As a group, could you give me some help building a matrix of our most important products? I think it would help us see where we come up short and where we have some redundancies."

The group agrees that this would be useful. Robert asks John to operate the computer, which is connected to a large screen in the conference room. John uses a spreadsheet to build the matrix, and all the members of the group contribute to its development. Again the debate ensues when they get to the cell that contains the R&D projects over which they were arguing earlier.

Robert points out that the debate centers on whether or not one of the projects will investigate a particular new manufacturing technique along with the new adhesive it is developing. John suggests that the group access the internal database of international R&D projects to help sort out exactly what the project includes and where the overlap may be. The group agrees, and they find that a small segment of one project should be replaced by the results of the other.

After an hour and a half of building the matrix, the group decides to take a break and come back to the project after lunch. Since the matrix has guided the discussion in a constructive direction, Robert feels comfortable leaving the group to continue without him. As he walks back to his office with John, Robert says, "I wish my 9:00 meeting had been that productive. Thanks, John. You did a great job there."

Robert invites John to have lunch with him to continue their earlier discussion. Alice orders lunch from the executive cafeteria, and the meal is served in Robert's office.

"We were just about to talk about being well-informed when we were interrupted for the meeting," notes Robert, preparing to take a bite of salad. "And as a matter of fact, what we worked on in the meeting gave me some ideas. That matrix we built might help me track R&D projects," he continues. "I'd like to use it as a guide to see where we've got redundancies or where we need to fire up a project to fill an empty cell. If I check into the database of R&D projects and keep cross-checking with the matrix, it'll give me a good feel on a continuous basis for where we need to consolidate our R&D efforts."

"I can make that a bit easier for you if you'd like," says John. We can have the R&D database automatically update your spreadsheet every day. Would that help?"

"Sure would. Expensive?"

"I can find out for you by tomorrow. I doubt it will be more than $30,000."

"It would take only one consolidation like the one we found this morning to pay for that ten times over," responds Robert. "Do it. And, I've got three more things to put on the list for being well-informed. Here's what I've got to know. . . ."

As Robert talks, John types the points into the outline editor on Robert's computer.

"I need to increase my depth of knowledge of my biggest customers and their activities, and I also want to develop better overseas contacts," Robert says. "Then I want to get a better feel for how we're compensating people around here. What are we paying them to do? Are we giving them an incentive to do the kinds of things I want to have happen? Finally, and I hate to admit this, but I'm going to have to do more reading. I've got to absorb more information about what's going on in the marketplace. God knows when I'll find time for this one. . . ."

Again, John suggests that they take the items one at a time. He asks Robert to elaborate on what's wrong with the way things are working today.

"Well, in terms of knowing my customers, I'm already tracking the worldwide sales and service activities for our largest customers. Every day I check into our system for that. It automatically shows me customer requirements that cut across divisions. But I haven't really done much with those observations, I guess. I think I'll keep my e-mail handy as I'm browsing the data, to make sure all our people working the same account know about each other and know that the whole is more important than their part," says Robert.

"A few messages from you should wake them up!" says John. "But then, aren't you likely to be a bottleneck? How about suggesting in your messages that they look at the same data, so that eventually they'll start to see the synergies for themselves?"

"Super idea!" says Robert enthusiastically. "If the account execs don't have terminals now, they'd better get them. What's next?"

"How are you doing at developing your international contacts?" asks John.

"Well, the idea for that shared phone book database among executives was excellent. In fact, the other day I was looking through our Spanish contacts. We need to do an acquisition over there to supplement our manufacturing operations with some product-development facilities. It just so happened that our European sales VP knew someone at a company we were interested in, and he had put the name into the database. When I found this guy's name, I gave him a call just to introduce myself and touch base. It paid, because we hit it off right away. I started feeling him out about selling his company, and before I knew it we were talking about getting together to design a deal. We got a move on that one before it ever came on the block," explains Robert. "I'm really excited about it, and I'm going to meet with the guy over there next week."

"Good, so the database worked just the way we thought it would."

"Absolutely," replies Robert. "I think we just need to keep building that phone book."

Robert continues: "Now this compensation thing is a problem. I was taking a look at the financials in the system the other day, and I noticed something very disturbing. Just for the hell of it, I did an informal correlation between bonuses and increases in salary expense and division performance. For that, I got a pretty good correlation. But when I cut it by product area across all geographies, there was no correlation. I was struck by the obvious: We're paying people *not* to collaborate!"

"So, I've decided to shift the management incentive plan from being based 100 percent on divisional performance, to basing payouts on 50 percent division and 50 percent corporate performance," explains Robert. "I think that's going to make a big difference. I'd like to get even more performance and compensation information into the databases so that I can catch more anomalies like that one."

"Should we talk about that now?" asks John.

"No, I think that can wait," answers Robert.

"It looks like you've got things pretty well covered on your first three items under 'Being well-informed,'" notices John. "What about your reading?"

"That's the one I'm worried about," replies Robert. "I've just got so much stuff to absorb."

"What kinds of stuff?"

"Well, I've got the R&D information under control by tracking the internal database, but I need to know more about what's going on in that area outside the firm."

"How are you getting that information now?" asks John.

"Industry reports, newspapers, and summary reports from the clipping service," replies Robert.

"And that's not enough?"

"Well, the clipping service missed a few related items that came back to bite me the other day, and I realized I needed to pay more attention to this stuff myself," replies Robert.

"Have you tried an external database?"

"What's that?"

"Well, there are huge databases that track thousands of periodicals on just about any topic you can imagine. What you do is establish search criteria. In other words, you tell the computer what you want it to look for," explains John.

"You mean I could tell it to look for certain aspects of the packaging industry?" asks Robert.

"Sure," replies John. "You can give it very specific instructions as to what you're looking for, and then you can modify your search and feel your way as you go."

"Wow," says Robert. "Sounds like something I should look into."

Robert and John make plans to get together in two days to start Robert's training on the external databases. Robert and John do not have time to go into Robert's third area, communication, but they decide they'll talk about it more after they finish the external database training session.

It is now 1:30 in the afternoon, and Robert is due to meet with his Human Resources vice president on his ideas for the incentive compensation program. John and Robert have barely touched their lunches, so they both take a couple of minutes to finish their sandwiches.

Robert goes to the meeting and John returns to his office. The remainder of the day is filled with phone calls and other internal and customer meetings.

At 5:30, a number of offices are empty, and the phone finally quiets down. As Alice leaves for the day, Robert decides to take advantage of the quiet time to think through some more of his objectives. Robert recalls his two overall comunication objectives: (1) get across the idea of the corporate product matrix and communicate a unifying organization strategy and (2) to encourage people throughout the organization to build cross-divisional communication patterns.

"I've got a direction I want this company to go in. How am I going to communicate that direction?" Robert asks himself.

Clear and consistent messages are essential to his ability to pull the company together across divisions. If Robert's vision is not clear, then people won't know what to do. If it is not consistent, people might go in opposing directions. The best possible situation, especially for kicking off the new culture, would be to get to everyone at once with the same message. Robert decides that a simultaneous organization-wide announcement of his new vision for the company is in order. But how can he reach all the international locations as well?

Robert remembers something that John described to him several months ago, when he was talking about the customer who had made an international announcement. "That's it!" he says to himself. "We'll hold an international videoconference to announce our new vision for the company and our competitive strategy." He makes a note to ask John more about videoconferencing.

Robert then turns his attention to the meeting that he has next week with the executive from the Spanish acquisition opportunity. He has an idea about how to be more persuasive in this negotiation. He will work through several scenarios on his spreadsheet and present Mr.

Rodriguez with a variety of ways of putting the deal together. Robert sketches out the approaches by using the spreadsheet, and then he sends them to an analyst via electronic mail to fill in some of the missing information. Robert also sends the spreadsheets to LASCO's Spanish office, asking one of the executives there to send back his ideas before Robert's flight next Sunday.

It is now 7:00 P.M., and Robert is getting tired. He calls Dave, the driver, and tells him he is ready to leave. Dave picks him up out front. Robert's mind is still reeling with ideas from the day's activities, and he can't relax until he writes them down. As he pulls a pad of paper out of his briefcase, he thinks longingly of the laptop that John will get for him. He sure could use it right now.

When he arrives at home, Janet has already eaten, but she has kept some dinner warm for him. They pour two glasses of wine, and Janet slowly sips hers while Robert eats his dinner.

They then turn to the computer and check into WBSI, a global network of executives who are linked by computer conferencing (a group-oriented version of electronic mail). Some time ago, Robert, wanting to learn more about a broad range of global issues that might affect LASCO, had begun looking for an interdisciplinary environment that would expose him to any issues he would not normally think about.

He heard about the WBSI computer-conferencing community from another executive. It met both his intellectual needs and time constraints. He joined the group two years ago. Spouses are fully included in the group's activities. Janet and Robert have taken particular interest in two of the WBSI conferences. One is titled "Monetary Issues Raised by the EEC Community for 1992" and the other is "Market Economies and Democracies."

For obvious reasons, the conference on 1992 is important. But tonight Robert is particularly interested in the market economy discussion, because he sees parallels between national economies and those that naturally exist inside the corporation. It strikes him as odd that international markets seem better coordinated than his various divisions.

Tonight, Robert and Janet find several fascinating comments from other executives, academics, and political leaders. One particularly astute comment is made by a senior executive from the U.K. who, it turns out, is also currently involved in an acquisition in Spain. Robert and Janet discuss the conferences for half an hour, add a comment to each, and then decide to retire for the night.

Six weeks later . . .

Robert has had great success with his computer. He began juxta-posing the internal R&D data with the external database information. When the information showed him a cell of opportunity not yet covered by either LASCO or the competition, he expanded the product matrix. Robert used this new opportunity to get a project started; of course, the project team is composed of people from several different divisions in different countries.

There was another benefit from the use of the computer. One afternoon, while Robert was checking into the external databases, he found information on legislation that had made it out of committee. The legislation would affect many of their largest customers. Robert asked his vice president of governmental affairs to send a voice mes-sage to all locations, explaining the legislation and how it would impact LASCO. The simultaneous voice message met his need for consistency in communication.

The product matrix allows Robert to stay on top of the key pulse points of new product development. In addition, for key cells in the matrix, Robert wants people to start communicating and developing ideas across divisions. Therefore, he selected groups of people from different divisions and put them together in computer conferences formed around those key cells.

The videoconference to announce his vision for an integrated company is scheduled for next week. In keeping with his objective of creating clear and consistent messages, Robert has been using his word processor-outline editor to structure and "wordsmith" the speech. He has also been working with the product matrix, pulling portions of it into a graphics tool to modify it for display during the conference. He feels ever more confident of his ability to explain his vision.

To encourage cross-organization communication, Robert has taken several steps. First, he has made the worldwide customer sales and service activities database available to everyone in the corporation. This led people to start viewing their projects in the context of all the other activities going on in the firm. As people have seen where their projects fit in and discovered the potential synergies across projects and divisions, they have already begun consulting each other more often.

Second, Robert has become a better listener. Not only has he made numerous face-to-face visits to manufacturing facilities, but he has also set up special electronic mailboxes for people to give him feedback on specific areas of importance. For example, he set up a mailbox labeled "Strategic rumors" as a channel of communication from the sales force. The sales force has been sending him information they have picked up regarding customer needs and rumors of competitive moves.

The negotiations with Mr. Rodriguez were successful. In Rodriguez's recent visit to the United States, they completed the agreement in the LASCO boardroom. During the meeting, the spreadsheet model that Robert had originally designed was displayed. John operated the spreadsheet, as Rodriguez asked many what-if questions. Rodriguez was very impressed by the fact that the team could work dynamically with the information, and he felt his company would be in the hands of good managers. The back-and-forth process made both parties feel comfortable with the assumptions underlying their agreement.

So far, LASCO has been holding its own against FPI. The FPI merger has been somewhat rocky, as the company struggles to meld two very different corporate cultures. Of course, Robert has used this to LASCO's advantage. Wall Street analysts have been very complimentary about LASCO's efforts at expanding its product line and improving international coordination.

It's still too early to tell, but it looks as if Robert has made the right moves.

Fantastic Futurism

Parts of the following scenario are fanciful, although all of it has some basis in fact. Some of these technologies are already available, some are being prototyped in laboratories, and others may never exist. The purpose of this scenario is not to predict future technologies, but to give readers an idea of the future executive. Given these caveats, I think this scenario may provoke some creative thinking about the direction in which we can take the technology of the future.

Meet Maria Esteban. As of January 2020, Maria was appointed CEO of the retail clothing manufacturer, Vitesse. Vitesse mass-manufactures boutique clothing.

Vitesse grew spectacularly from 2000 until 2015. But as it grew, it lost its creative edge. It has, since 2015, been drifting downward toward mass-market discount stores and lower margins. Maria was appointed one year ago to fix Vitesse financially and repair the company's reputation, which has shifted from avant-garde to passé.

She was recruited because she has a solid background in both finance and design, with degrees from a major design school as well as one of the world's top business schools.

As she thought through the decision to take the job, Maria was concerned by the complacence and lack of creativity she sensed among Vitesse employees. When she interviewed for the position, she not only visited the New York location, but she also flew out to Los Angeles to talk to the designers. They told her that Vitesse had become bureaucratic and that the company no longer appreciated the contribution that designers made to success.

Another problem was that shareholders had become antsy. Overreacting to market conditions, they didn't want to do any more investing in new products or ideas. Slumping profits were not going to sit well with them any longer.

However, despite these problems, Maria decided to take the job because of four primary factors working in the company's favor. First, the company has a very flexible manufacturing process. Over the past five years, it has made sizable investments in computer-aided manufacturing, and that investment is paying off in very fast retooling capabilities. Second, the company has well-established channels of distribution, with direct sales to major retail chains and distributorships for brand labels to small stores. Third, the financials are in adequate shape. And fourth, the Vitesse name is recognized by leading designers worldwide.

Maria sees her job as one of totally revamping the Vitesse culture to encourage risk taking and openness to new ideas. By restoring a feeling of entrepreneurship and creativity, Maria feels that Vitesse can regain its reputation as a design innovator and recapture the high-margin, upscale retail business.

To revamp the culture, Maria has a clear-cut leadership strategy. Her first priority is to make all the Vitesse designers feel pampered and appreciated. Symbolic of her commitment to this goal was Maria's decision to move to Los Angeles immediately after her appointment as CEO. Vitesse corporate headquarters are in New York, but the majority of the Vitesse designers are in Los Angeles (which by 2020 has surpassed New York City as the design capital of North America). Maria felt that, by moving to L.A., she could get closer to the design side of the business while showing everyone in the firm how committed she is to this critical area.

Another prong in Maria's leadership strategy is to set an example for creative, innovative thinking. She believes that she can personally mentor and challenge others to follow her example. In addition, Maria wants to forge more strategic alliances and joint ventures to build excitement and bring new ideas into the firm.

The final aspect of her strategy is the most challenging. Maria is determined to shift the Vitesse culture toward entrepreneurship and risk taking by moving from a centrally planned internal economy to a "market" economy within the firm. Instead of handing out the budget from the top down each year, Maria wants each group to earn its keep by charging other internal departments for its services. She is convinced that this internal market for services will ensure strong horizontal links, and make the whole company more entrepreneurial and customer-focused.[2]

Maria and her husband, John, are native New Yorkers, so the move to Los Angeles was not an easy one. Maria laughingly says that she doesn't feel at home yet because the people are too nice and the city is too clean, a credit to the residents' radical environmental protection laws. Maria and John have two children, both in grade school.

It is a bright, sunny morning in early April as Maria heads to work in downtown Los Angeles. She commutes with her husband from their new home in the hills overlooking the city. On their way to work, they drop off the children at school. Then she and her husband have approximately an hour's commute in the snarled L.A. traffic.

John offers to drive, and Maria is glad because she needs to get some work done before she gets into the office. Maria steps into the back seat. The children have already turned on the computer that is attached to the back of the front seat. The screen is glowing with a video game entitled Middle-Aged Mutant Mollusks. Maria smiles and changes the program.

One of her up-and-coming young designers, Fifi, has asked Maria to take a look at some of her latest work, "to get her opinion." Maria is highly flattered and gratified. She wants the designers to see her as a coach instead of simply a boss, and this is a sign that her efforts are working. Maria wants to take a look at the designs before she gets into the office, so she accesses the Vitesse internal database of design projects.

She asks the computer to search for "Fifi, March 21 through March 31." Instantly, a menu fills the screen. Does Maria want to see

Fifi's leisurewear, activewear, or eveningwear? She presses a button for eveningwear.

A three-dimensional holographic figure appears in front of the screen, modeling a stunning evening dress. Maria touches an accessory on the model and six other designs for that type of accessory are displayed. Maria is gratified because she has been trying to encourage the designers to think of more accessory options. The fact that so many accessory designs are included in Fifi's portfolio shows that Maria's personal interest in the area is having an impact.

Maria browses through several other areas, carefully considering all of Fifi's work. In response to Fifi's request for Maria's input, Maria decides to send Fifi her comments in electrophonic mail. Electrophonic mail is distributed via computer and contains voice, text, video, interactive graphics, and holographic images. Electrophonic mail has been critical to Maria's ability to stay in touch with the New York office and her large staff of designers.

Maria wants to add value with her comments. Therefore, before composing the electrophonic message, Maria thinks carefully about the designs. What is it that is familiar about them? She realizes that they bring to mind a fashion show she attended last year in Beijing. Perhaps some of the ideas she got from that show would be useful to Fifi to spark further creativity.

Maria directs the computer to find in external databases information on Beijing fashion designers. A menu appears, and Maria scans it for familiar names. She selects one and makes the eveningwear selection. Again, a hologram appears in front of the screen. Maria looks at several designs, occasionally touching them to view alternative accessories.

She touches another point on a hologram and the picture disappears, leaving behind on the screen textual information regarding Maria's query. She adds the relevant textual information to her electrophonic message, including a three-dimensional graphic display annotated with a voice-over by Maria, describing what she likes and dislikes about the Beijing designs. Having invested time in this message, Maria decides to send it to all their eveningwear designers rather than just to Fifi.

Maria also does voice annotation on her favorite holograms by Fifi. She encourages her to continue the good work, praising her for the range of accessories, and asking Fifi's opinion on the Beijing designs. This private electrophonic message also includes a 3-minute videotape from the Beijing fashion show that Maria attended.

John calls to the back seat and asks Maria if she needs to keep the car today. She answers no and asks him if the automobile recharger is working at his office. (John has a tendency to forget to charge the car, and this is a joke between them.) He laughs and says yes, and then drives straight to Maria's office. John drops Maria off in front of her building and promises to call later in the afternoon to see when she will be ready to return home.

Vitesse's West Coast offices occupy half an office building in downtown Los Angeles. Maria's decision to move to Los Angeles prompted several other executives to transfer with her, and the new executive offices now occupy the top floor of the building. Maria takes the elevator to the executive suite and is greeted by the receptionist for the floor. Beautiful holograms of Vitesse designs adorn the lobby, and the wall behind the receptionist is a changing kaleidoscope of Vitesse fabrics. Maria gives the receptionist a cheery good morning and continues on to her office.

Maria's secretary, Alicia, is not in today, but she has left extensive instructions for Maria. Maria should have no problems surviving the day, since Alicia is a good planner. Also, another executive secretary down the hall, David, is available to help Maria today. He will screen her phone calls and has access to her electronic calendar.

As she walks into her office, Maria switches on the wall screen behind her desk. She turns on her computer and pushes several buttons to load the priority organizer program. Her computer sorts through all the information she has received since she last logged on. The wall screen begins to fill up with several different windows, each representing a topic of importance to Maria. In each window there is a menu of information (messages, news, and operational data) about that topic, waiting to be examined. Maria's categories are operational information, internal commitments, press information, buying patterns, design trends, and new internal designs.

One window on the wall screen is entitled "Top Priority." It contains a message from Alicia in electrophonic mail. Maria pushes a few buttons and a video image of Alicia fills the screen. "Good morning, Maria. I'm off for two days of surfing. I'll be back on Monday. I've asked your computer to give you your phone messages in priority sequence and to update your calendar as it tracks you through the day. Everything should be in order. I'll call in later today. Just leave any messages for me in electrophonic mail."

The screen darkens and the original wall of windows appears. Under "Operational Information," Maria sees that there are two external database articles, three electrophonic mail messages, and one aberration. Maria checks the aberration first. Aberrations are automatically generated messages that report manufacturing or operational deviations.

The computer reports that a cutting machine is down in Indiana. There is a message from the plant manager following the notice, containing a two-minute video showing Maria the machine and indicating the problem. The message also has textual information that tells Maria what happened and what will be done to avoid the problem in the future. Two three-dimensional spreadsheets are included in the message from the plant manager. One shows how the outage will affect the plant manager's individual P&L statement, and the other shows his estimate of the impact on the entire organization's P&L statement.

Maria smiles. Already her efforts at creating a culture of entrepreneurship are working. Last year, soon after she was appointed CEO, Maria had the financial reporting system changed. First, she had the software changed so that it would reflect individual profit-and-loss performance. Second, she made sure that every person in the organization had access to these numbers in a dynamic fashion, so that they could ask what if's about their profit center and the company as a whole.

Needless to say, this has had significant impacts on the way people view their work. Now they understand their individual contributions to the profitability of the firm. The message from the plant manager is indicative of the ways in which the culture now supports individual initiative as well as proactive thinking about people's broader role in the company.

The change in the financial information has impacts at Maria's level, also. Because she can periodically check individual performance, she can better fulfill her coaching role. A slip in performance shows her who needs the most help. Like the internal database of designs, the on-line operating information allows Maria to balance her need to obtain information with the need to delegate and give people room to move.

Satisfied that the plant situation is under control, Maria retrieves the external database articles suggested by the computer. As she is scanning one on computer-integrated manufacturing, the computer asks her if she would like to see more information on a related topic. The external and internal databases are linked by a neural network that does the initial sorting of information and then automatically suggests related topics and areas of interest that may be found in any of thousands of external databases or internal documents. Maria pushes the Y button, and the link automatically takes her to the exact paragraph in another related article on the topic.

Maria then views the internal commitments window, a summary by person and time of the commitments within each topic window. Two of the commitments are things she owes others. The remainder are actions that are owed to her.

One of her commitments was to review Fifi's designs. Since she already finished that in the car, Maria deletes it from the list. The other commitment she has is to call Mr. Avalon of Petite Chic this morning. (Mr. Avalon is very important to her joint venture strategy.) She compares the remaining commitments with a summary of her electrophonic mail. It looks as though everyone who owes her a commitment today has sent her an electrophonic message. Good. Since she sees there is something from everyone on their designated topics, she decides to wait until later to review the actual messages.

As she continues to review her priorities in each category, the phone rings. Maria pushes a button on the speaker phone, and the voice of David, the executive secretary standing in for Alicia, emerges. "Good morning, Ms. Esteban."

"Good morning, David."

"I have Mr. Avalon on the phone for you in video and in voice as scheduled. Are you ready for him?"

"Certainly," replies Maria. "Thank you, David."

The image of Mr. Avalon appears on the wall screen behind Maria's desk, accompanied by two windows of textual information in the lower corners. The textual information in the lower-right corner contains Mr. Avalon's profile, reminding Maria that Mr. Avalon's wife's name is Françoise, along with the fact that tomorrow is the 10th anniversary of the founding of Mr. Avalon's company.

The lower-left window is empty, and Maria pushes several buttons to bring up the commitment-tracking application. It appears in the window, and she types in Mr. Avalon's name. Immediately it provides a summary of all the questions she has for Mr. Avalon.

While she is talking with Avalon, Maria brings up a third window in the top-left corner of the screen. This window is connected to external databases. Maria pushes a function key that is preprogrammed to do a database search on Mr. Avalon's name and the name of his company. As they continue their discussion, the headline of an article appears, announcing that Petite Chic's top designer received an industry award this morning in Paris.

Mr. Avalon speaks to Maria in French, and his words appear in English as subtitles at the bottom of the wall screen. He and Maria discuss a joint venture they are considering in the design area. Mr. Avalon's company, Petite Chic, is small, but up-and-coming. Maria hopes that the deal will help improve Vitesse's lapsing reputation for innovative design, and Mr. Avalon hopes that the size and venerability of Vitesse will improve his company's status in the international retail world.

As they speak, Maria accesses several charts through her computer and displays them for Avalon, showing him how she sees the deal from a financial perspective. She also pulls in the information she extracted from the external database on the drive in to work. Avalon remarks favorably on Fifi's Chinese-style designs.

They make plans to meet for dinner when Maria is next in Paris, a month from now. (Maria's calendar automatically optimizes her travel schedule, immediately showing her the location and time of the next available slot.) Mr. Avalon teases her about missing April in Paris, and she says, "The Pacific Ocean isn't so bad right now, either!"

"By the way," she continues, "congratulations on your company's 10th anniversary. And also, please convey my congratulations to Jacques (the award-winning designer)."

Avalon thanks her warmly and seems impressed that she knows about the award already. He asks, "Don't you ever sleep?"

She laughs and tells him that she tries to keep up with him and his company, but that it is a challenging job. Half an hour has elapsed when the two executives take their electronic leave.

Maria returns to her priorities wall screen. Under "Press information," there is an important article comparing Vitesse designs with those of their closest competitor. Maria quickly reads, and decides that she will send an electrophonic message about it to all her managers. As part of her coaching role, Maria has been trying to get everyone in the company to focus on the importance of improving the Vitesse image. Getting everyone to understand the importance of press coverage is an important part of broadening their perspective.

Maria prepares the electrophonic message, including the actual article, several holograms comparing the designs side by side, and a voice-over from her. She dictates textual information about the significance of the press response and then edits her words with a keyboard until they carry the right tone.

Maria would like to expand on the information included in the article. In particular, she believes that the reporter has not accurately assessed the market for the Vitesse line of activewear. Vitesse activewear is very different from the competitor's, and the reporter has not expounded on this at any length. To help bolster her opinions, she decides to consult a marketing expert.

She pulls up her database of electronic consultants. A menu of different topics appears in a window on her wall screen. Each item on the menu represents an expert system that has been built by an authority on that particular topic. Therefore, Maria has at her fingertips access to the world's leading thinkers on a wide range of subjects. Some of the newer expert systems are linked to external databases, so she can get the opinion of the consultant as well as the lastest written information on the topic. She asks the consulting system several questions about the activewear market and includes its answers in her message. Finally she is satisfied with the message. She sends it to the entire company, including the manufacturing plants.

Maria glances at her slender gold watch. It is almost time for the daily executive committee meeting. She buzzes David and asks him if the coffee is ready, and he assures her a cup will be waiting in the boardroom.

Executives in both Los Angeles and New York are just entering the videoconference room as she walks in. Maria was never a proponent of videoconferencing until she moved to Los Angeles. In the past, the system simply didn't reach the places she needed to go. Now it has become a critical part of her routine, since half of her executive committee is in New York and half is in Los Angeles. They all chat convivially as they enter.

The far end of the room is filled with another wall screen. An assistant operates the computer to which it is connected. Since a number of people in the room will be speaking at once, he has turned off the voice-activation mechanism. (The wall screen in New York simultaneously displays the same information that is on the L.A. screen, and the assistant in New York can change both screens easily.)

Maria begins the meeting by asking the assistant to display the meeting agenda. He does so, and what appears on the wall screen is an outline of the meeting. The outline is in neo-hypermedia. Neo-hypermedia is a means of storing information in hierarchical form across various media. Therefore, a node in the outline contains textual, visual, graphical, or audio information.

As people make contributions during the meeting, the assistant types a brief summary of their comment and places it under the appropriate node in the outline. The meeting participants can also ask the assistant to attach other pieces of information to back up their meeting comments. When they come to the topic of Chinese designers, Maria asks the assistant to display the designs she was reviewing with Fifi and Mr. Avalon. The assistant does so and then stores a link to the holograms under that node in the outline.

Everyone is pleased with the progress of the daily meeting as they reach the last item on the morning agenda. The meeting is adjourned for lunch, and Maria hurries off for a lunch meeting with a famous designer she is trying to woo away from the competition.

The meeting reconvenes at 2:00. The afternoon's agenda is an important one. Maria explains to her executive committee how she wants to continue to roll out the plan for reshaping the Vitesse culture. She begins by talking about the steps she has already taken to reshape Vitesse. She mentions that she has had the financial information changed to report and track individual P&Ls, and she reminds them of how she has distributed that information company-wide. She tells them of how successful electrophonic mail has been in putting her directly in touch with the people responsible for results. As an example, she mentions today's message from the plant manager in Indiana.

There are two more important steps that Maria wants to take, and she would like the executive committee's input and support. First, she thinks it would be a good idea to increase the topics tracked by the internal operational database. In addition to tracking budgets, she would like the database to track the number of design ideas generated or handled in some way by each group.

Second, she wants the committee to discuss the lack of designers at the top of the corporation. There is one position open on the executive committee, and Maria is interested in filling it with a designer. Also, she wants to discuss what the company can do to ensure a line of succession among designers.

There is very little debate regarding tracking the number of design initiatives. A few of the staff executives broaden the concept to include their initiatives, and the committee makes it clear that standards must be determined separately for each group. With that said, everyone thinks increased tracking is a good idea.

But on the second point, filling the seat on the executive committee with a designer, there is more discussion. Several of the committee members would like to know who Maria is considering and why. Maria turns to the assistant who is operating the wall screen and asks him to pull up the internal personnel database. He does so, and she gives him three names. The profiles for those people are loaded into the computer, and the screen splits into three windows. Each contains information on one of the candidates.

First, a brief video of each person is shown. In the videos, the designers describe their personal goals and how these goals fit with the overall goals of Vitesse. A video profile is included in everyone's standard personnel file, and it is updated twice a year.

Next, the screen displays measures of each designer's performance so that comparisons can be made across windows. Finally, Maria asks the assistant to display the international working experience of each of the three people. One has worked extensively in Israel and speaks fluent Hebrew, another has spent considerable time in China, and the third is a native of France. The committee asks the assistant for more information on the people in different categories. After a long discussion, Maria thanks her fellow executives for their input and tells them she will make the announcement within two weeks.

The meeting is adjourned, and Maria returns to her office. It is 5:00 P.M. and she decides to use the remainder of the day to do some creative thinking. All day long an idea has been nagging at her, and she wants to think it through. Her idea is to introduce a line of cosmetics carrying the Vitesse label. A major factor in the cosmetics industry is package design, and Maria believes that Vitesse could produce some of the most innovative packaging in the industry.

While she was reviewing the Beijing accessories designs this morning in the car, she got an idea. One of the belt buckles was a spectacular design done in cloisonné. Maria believes cloisonné should be included in the cosmetics package design.

Maria starts with a database search in the area of cosmetics, narrowing her search to packaging. Several interesting articles pop up, and Maria files them in neo-hypermedia. Then she tries her hand at a few rough sketches of the products. She goes into her graphics hologram package and uses a wand to draw the product in three dimensions, experimenting with different colors. She files these sketches in her neo-hypermedia file titled "confidential." Her idea must remain top secret until the time is right.

Finally, she takes a few minutes to think through the financials. Using her three-dimensional spreadsheets, Maria examines a few alternatives. What would happen if they tried to manufacture the cosmetics themselves? Too expensive, she decides. Then she considers several joint ventures. Two of the scenarios she puts together look plausible. She is engrossed in this project when the phone rings. Her husband is waiting for her in the car downstairs.

Maria joins John in the car. It is her turn to drive, and John makes several calls on his cellular phone while they head back into the hills. About half an hour into the trip, John hangs up the phone and they discuss their respective days. They pull into the driveway of their house, which commands a gorgeous view of the city lights below.

The lights are on in the window as they put the car in the garage. John plugs the car in to charge overnight. They make their way inside and are greeted by the children and their nanny. The children beg their parents to play one computer game with them before they go to bed. John and Maria assent. Nanny takes her leave, asking if they want her to pick up the children after school tomorrow. John says that he will be working from home tomorrow, and that he will pick them up.

After a thrilling game of Middle-Aged Mutant Mollusks, the children are tucked into bed. Maria and John pour two glasses of wine; kick off their shoes; and sit on the couch, talking for another 20 minutes. Maria reminds John that there is a vegetable casserole that has been in the computerized slow cooker all day, and he agrees that just a quick bite would be perfect. They go into the kitchen; grab some small plates; and sit at the counter in the center of the room, looking out over the valley.

Why Imagine?

These two scenarios represent an available present and a wished-for future. I include them in order to stimulate your own imagination for applications of computers in your setting, both today and tomorrow.

The scenarios displayed a variety of personal thinking tools. Some of them also demonstrated the use of computers to enhance group effectiveness, both asynchronously (collaboration through electronic mail and writing, for example) and face-to-face (augmented meetings, for example).

It doesn't take much technological advancement to join Robert and Maria's world. All of Robert's tools are commercially available. Much of what Maria used is running in today's laboratories; some of it, such as outline editors with hypertext links, was operational 20 years ago.

The first scenario mentioned WBSI. Though the scenario was imagined, WBSI is very real. The Western Behavioral Sciences Institute runs an ongoing educational development program for top executives. This high-level group gets together once a year, face-to-face, in La Jolla, California, for a week-long series of seminars, speeches, and group discussions on a broad variety of social, political, business, and intellectual topics. After the executives leave La Jolla, the forum is continued via computer conference. Participants can participate in these conferences asynchronously, and they can send each other personal electronic messages.

Consider the comments of Richard Farson, president of WBSI and originator of this innovative executive program:

> What executives want, what they are constantly seeking, is the advice, the interpretations, and the opinions of their trusted colleagues. . . . Executives want the dynamic databases that exist in the minds of their trusted colleagues. And they need instantaneous access to those databases in a fluid, easy way.
>
> What WBSI provides is the opportunity for executives to communicate on a global scale about issues that pertain directly to the new requirements of leadership. . . . [Computer conferencing] permits many-to-many communication. It permits us to create communities, to network people. For the first time, executives can . . . come together with [peers] on a global scale that in the past might never have been available to them.

Computing and communications tools are enabling possibilities today that we might only have imagined in the past. I hope this combined glimpse into the present and the future has stimulated creative, fresh ideas for how to better apply computing and communications technologies to today's unique business and leadership challenges.

NOTES

1. Douglas C. Engelbart, *High Performance Knowledge-Worker Teams*, Report AF30602-80-0260-F (Cupertino, CA: Tymshare, Inc., 1981).

2. Instead of the corporation collecting revenues and then distributing them, the sales force would "own" the customers' dollars and purchase internally the needed goods and services. Therefore, in an internal market economy, budgets are based on the internal demand, and people adjust them dynamically as conditions change. For more information, see N. Dean Meyer, *The Internal Economy: A Market Approach*. (Ridgefield, CT: NDMA, 1990).

CHAPTER 22

Conclusion

Isn't all this rather obvious?

Not very many top executives use computers, but what about everyone else? Don't people already know all this? Interestingly enough, as I talk with friends and business acquaintances about the topic, I discover that a large percentage do *not* use computers. Even many of those who do have not gone beyond some very basic applications for convenience. I marvel at how this could possibly be. As an ardent computer user myself, I can't imagine how I did without the machine all those years.

Writing This Book On-line

The process of writing this book is a perfect example of the criticality of computers to my work. I started my research by conducting a massive literature search using external databases. I used my organization's database of contacts to help me locate research sponsors and interviewees. An electronic calendar kept our sales and administrative staff from double-booking me for consulting on the days I had executive interviews. A piece of software designed for qualitative research helped me sort through a six-inch stack of interview transcripts. A combination outline editor-word processor helped me create, write, restructure, and revise the entire manuscript.

Throughout the project, I kept track of all my interviewees' addresses, phone numbers, secretaries' names, fax numbers, and other details in my organization's database. I used facsimile to send information to executives and to my publisher. A spreadsheet helped me develop a work plan that coordinated the interdependencies of the editing process and helped me set realistic milestones for completion of the manuscript.

I sincerely doubt whether I would have taken on such a huge project without the assistance of my computer. In fact, I recently told someone that I'd rather share a telephone than share my computer, and I meant it.

The Cost of Ignorance

The vast majority of people who use computers for meaningful aspects of their work share my feelings, and executives are no exception to this rule. Given the strong feelings most avid users have for their computers, how could it be that so many others have no idea of the computer's power and payoff?

In Chapters 1 and 18 I gave a variety of reasons for why this could happen. But still, on some level, I find it hard to believe. It seems trite to say computer appreciation is a matter of education. But I suppose, to some degree, that's true. Perhaps it is more accurate to say, appreciation is a matter of translation—translation from personal objectives to computers.

I recently read an article about computing in the Soviet Union. Apparently, as of 1990, personal computers were extraordinarily expensive and scarce. A PC XT, which sold for as little as $1,000 in the U.S. at that time, cost the ruble equivalent of between $70,000 and $90,000 in the USSR. A PC AT cost approximately $250,000. A 80386 machine cost the ruble equivalent of approximately $300,000. Because they were so expensive, instead of using the computers, a considerable number of Soviets kept them as they would rare jewels or works of art![1]

In my mind, the unused computers that sit on executives' credenzas are worth far more than the cost of a PC in the Soviet Union. The ways in which these computers could be used to improve the effectiveness of executives and organizations are so significant and so extraordinary that the numbers would dwarf even shocking Soviet price tags.

What's the Next Step?

This book has explored myths about executive computing, examined the business contexts that are the foundation of high-payoff appli-

cations, discussed ways of thinking about goals and objectives in relation to computers, and peeked into the future of executive computing.

I suppose the answer to the question What's the next step? rests
with the reader. I hope that I have been convincing in demonstrating
the potential connection between leadership and information tools.
Where I hope you will go from here is to follow your imagination and
find that connection by thinking about how computers can enhance
your performance in some critical aspect of your work.

I'd like to close with a thought on ethics. Computers are a tremendously powerful human invention. It is clear from the cases that I
described that they have the power to transform the workplace in
significant ways. They amplify the aims and objectives of executives.

I have not as yet expressed the other side of the equation. The
same powerful tools that can deliver impressive benefits can also be
used in the service of less laudable goals. Computers can be used by
highly controlling executives to increase their centralized power in
negative ways.

As Shoshanna Zuboff so clearly points out in her landmark book,
In the Age of the Smart Machine, it is all too easy to create a monster
when designing information systems that touch other parts of an organization. Zuboff describes the panopticon, an architectural innovation
of the late 1700s. This device allowed prison guards in a tower to track
every movement of the inmates without the inmates' knowledge. A
structure of glass and mirrors, the panopticon provided surveillance
capabilities unachievable through the use of conventional building
materials. The structure provided what its inventor, Jeremy Bentham,
called universal transparency. In other words, the panopticon allowed
greater control; no one could hide.

Zuboff uses the idea of the panopticon to construct a brilliant
metaphor: "Information systems that translate, record, and display
human behavior can provide the computer age version of universal
transparency with a degree of illumination that would have exceeded
even Bentham's most outlandish fantasies."[2]

There is an alternative to this Orwellian specter. The same machines that can be used to enslave can also be used to empower. In the
past, when we automated a process, we had to break the process down
into its component parts to replicate it with a "dumb" machine. But
Zuboff points out a distinct difference in the new, "smart" machines
that represent information technology: Computers not only allow us to
replicate processes, they allow us to reflect on those same processes.

Thus, Zuboff explains, there is a difference between *automating* and *informating*.

> [Technology] simultaneously generates information about the underlying productive and administrative processes through which an organization accomplishes its work. It provides a deeper level of transparency to activities that had been either partially or completely opaque. . . . The word that I have coined to describe this unique capacity is *informate*. Activities, events, and objects are translated into and made visible by information when a technology *informates* as well as *automates*. . . .
>
> An emphasis on the informating capacity of intelligent technology can provide a point of origin for new conceptions of work and power. . . . The questions that we face today are finally about leadership. . . . Will they be able to create organizational innovations that can exploit the unique capacities of the new technology and thus mobilize their organization's productive potential to meet the heightened rigors of global competition? Will there be leaders who understand the crucial role that human beings from each organizational stratum can play in adding value to the production of goods and services?[3]

Computers don't set the goals; they just make human goals easier to reach. Computers aren't inherently good or evil. Rather, the people who use them are responsible for the results they seek. Because computers constitute such a powerful leadership medium, it is essential that leaders assess their motives for designing and using them.

Computers give executives the opportunity to empower or oppress. If executives are truly interested in expanding their own minds and the minds of their people, they will use computers in ways that are consistent with that philosophy.

I believe most executives want healthy working environments for their employees. In an age where computers can provide unprecedented levels of detail and information about employees, executives face a moral imperative to consider the ways in which they use and share information. If executives take advantage of the power of computers to informate their environments, truly momentous and unprecedented benefits are bound to follow.

Is computer use worth the risk? I think so. The combination of enlightened, ethical leadership and powerful technology brings with it incredible possibilities.

I hope we are headed for a future in which computers will be used to enhance the potential of people and organizations in ways far beyond my most optimistic projections.

NOTES

1. Gary Chapman, "Perestroika to the Tenth Power: The Computerization of the Soviet Union," *Visions,* Fall 1990, pp. 36–37.

2. Shoshanna Zuboff, *In the Age of the Smart Machine* (New York: Basic Books, 1988), p. 322.

3. Ibid., pp. 9–11.

A Comprehensive

Listing of

Information Tools

Tools to Work with Information

Ideas
Outline editors
Expert systems (with process expertise)

Text
Word processing packages
Electronic publishing packages
Text comparison packages
Grammar and spelling checkers
On-line thesaurus
Language translators

Numbers
Statistics packages
Modeling packages
Decision-support systems
Spreadsheets

Images
Graphics packages
Line-drawing systems

Painting packages
Computer-aided design
Animation packages

Time
Calendars
Commitment-tracking systems
Project management systems

Sources of Information

Local database management systems
Access to MIS data
Live MIS operational data
Videotex
Bulletin boards
Records management tools

External databases
Programmed learning
Computer-based instruction
Expert systems (with content expertise)
Multimedia systems

Tools to Communicate with Others

Information dissemination
Facsimile
Videotape
Audiotape

Personal message systems
Electronic mail
Voice message systems

Teleconferencing
 Full-motion video
 One-way video
 Freeze-frame video
 Audiographic
 Audio
 Shared screen
 Computer conferencing

Matching Tools

to ISFs

Personal Thinking

- **Be well-informed**
    Stay up-to-date
    Increase depth of knowledge
    Adjust filters on information
    Absorb information quickly
    About what?
    Internal activities:
    —Business operations: status, problems
    [Access to dynamic internal operating data, PERT or
    Gantt charts, computer conferencing, electronic mail,
    graphics]
    —Business measures: goals, achievements
    [Access to dynamic internal operating data, access to
    performance information, commitment-tracking sys-
    tems]
    —Projects: status, milestones, due dates, critical path
    [PERT or Gantt charts, commitment-tracking systems]
    —Commitments, appointments
    [Commitment-tracking systems, electronic calendars]

External activities:

—Who's doing what?

[External databases]

—How do they see us?

[External databases]

—Marketplace status and trends

[External databases]

—Investments, the economy

[External databases]

—Global business and political events

[External databases, networked international communities of top executives (for example, WBSI.)]

- **Think and make decisions**

  Enhance creativity, brainstorm, invent, design

  [Commercial expert systems (for example, Debbi Fields's The Idea Generator), outline editors, word processors, external databases, teleconferencing (to add members to group), graphics packages, drawing packages]

  Get the facts

  [External databases, internal operating data, electronic mail, teleconferencing]

  Organize ideas and information, manage complexity

  [Outline editors, word processors, spreadsheets]

  Analyze and compare alternatives

  [Spreadsheets, corporate models, text-comparison software]

  Balance logic and intuition

  [Outline editors, word processors, graphics]

  Forecast

  [Spreadsheets, corporate models, external databases]

  Allocate resources

  [Spreadsheets, corporate models, internal operating databases]

- **Leverage time**
  **Work independently of time and location
  (perform asynchronous work)**

  [Electronic mail, voice message systems, internal databases, all tools on a portable computer]

  Improve responsiveness

  [Electronic mail, commitment-tracking systems]

Managing Organizations

- **Design organizations and cultures**
  Pick, promote, and reward people

  [Access to internal personnel data, spreadsheets, broadcast of positive results through teleconferencing or electronic mail]

  Flatten hierarchies and empower people

  [Shared access to all types of information (including dynamic internal operating data and external databases), electronic mail]

  **Measure performance on selected objectives
  (feedback loops)**

  [Shared access to all types of information (including dynamic internal operating data and external databases), spreadsheets]

- **Communicate with people (inside or outside)**
  Know people

  [Personal phone book, external database search, networked international communities of top executives, personnel information]

  **Reach people, be accessible (communicate
  asynchronously)**

  [All forms of teleconferencing, electronic mail, computer conferencing, videotape, facsimile, voice messaging]

  Listen to people

  [All forms of teleconferencing, electronic mail, computer conferencing, facsimile, voice messaging]

Write with clarity and consistency

[Outline editors, word processors, grammar and spelling checkers, commercial expert systems, internal operating databases, external databases, electronic mail, teleconferencing (to solicit opinions on policy)]

Personalize messages

[Outline editors, word processors]

Present, convince, negotiate

[Spreadsheets, graphics packages, desktop publishing, internal operating databases, external databases]

Improve teamwork and collaboration

[All forms of teleconferencing, electronic mail, voice messaging, computer conferencing, facsimile, shared access to dynamic internal operating data, shared access to performance measures]

Improve meeting effectiveness, thinking in groups

[All forms of teleconferencing; use of any of the tools in a meeting environment, including spreadsheets, outline editors, or corporate models]

Announce, one-to-many

[All forms of teleconferencing, voice messaging, electronic mail]

- **Coach people**

Broaden peoples' perspectives

[External databases]

Focus people on what's important

[External databases, internal databases, electronic mail]

Teach critical-thinking abilities

[All forms of teleconferencing, expert systems, desktop publishing, access to dynamic internal operating data]

Balance the need to know and the need to delegate

[Outline editors, commitment-tracking systems, sharing access to dynamic internal operating data, spreadsheets]

Examples of

Organizational

Fine-Tuning

Create Channel

Create communications channel to all offices.

Electronic mail

Pogue, Humphrey, Sigoloff, Roberts, Esrey, Crandall, Fields, Compton, Wallace

Videotape

Stephens (to sales force regarding rumors)

Expert system

Fields (to stores), Compton (to employees)

Voice messaging

Fields (to employees), Gantz (to employees)

Create communications channel to different levels of the organization.

Electronic mail

Pogue, Gordon, Fields, Compton, Wallace

Expert system

Fields, Compton

Voice messaging

Fields

Add channel of information coming into the brain.

Access to external data

Esrey (competitive information), Wallace, (competitive information), Gantz, (competitive information), Crandall, (competitive information), Sigoloff (acquisitions), Jordan (competitive information)

Access to internal data

Edmiston (editorial content, financials, performance information), Wallace (financials, performance information, personnel information), Esrey (financials, performance information), Jordan (financials, performance information), Compton (financials, performance information), Fields (financials, performance information), Sigoloff (financials, performance information), Gantz (financials, performance information), Roberts (personnel information)

Create communications channel to selected groups.

Computer conferencing

Compton (to internal groups)

Teleconferencing

Esrey (external speech)

Create communications channel to customers.

Electronic mail

Wallace

Adjust Filter

Remove filters on operating information.

Access to selected internal operating data

Compton (performance information), Wallace (operating information)

Access to selected internal operating data manipulated in live models

Edmiston (performance information), Gordon (operating information), Sigoloff (operating information and financials), Plaskett (operating information), Crandall (operating and financial information), Fields (operating and performance information), Jordan (operating information)

Adjust filters on external information.

Targeted access to external databases

Sigoloff (acquisitions), Crandall (competitive information), Jordan (competitive information), Wallace (general business and political news)

Create Amplifier

Amplify message to internal audience.

Videotape

Stephens (bad press), Gantz (quality), McCready (quality)

Augmented meetings

Gantz (focus on the facts)

Voice messaging

Gantz (rumors), Fields (how to run a store)

Internal databases

Esrey (importance of competitive information), Crandall (importance of quality), Compton (the quick, flexible, and right message), Wallace (importance of teamwork)

Electronic mail

Fields (how to run a store)

Expert systems

Fields (how to run a store), Compton (the quick, flexible, and right message)

Expand Capacity of Brain

Manage complexity.

Spreadsheet

Pogue (compensation determination), Edmiston (planning process), McCready (negotiations), Plaskett (financial analysis), Stephens (negotiations and thinking through acquisitions), Compton (message preparation)

Word processing

Pogue (message preparation), Humphrey (message preparation), Sigoloff (message preparation), McCready (message preparation), Plaskett (message preparation), Compton (message preparation)

Personal database
  Edmiston (tracking key sales prospects)
Access to internal data
  Sigoloff (bankrupcy proceedings)
Access to external data
  Sigoloff (thinking through acquisitions)
Outline editor
  McCready (quality-of-service program)
Graphics
  Stephens (negotiations), Compton (message preparation)
Augmented meetings
  Stephens (group discussions), Crandall (group discussions), Compton (group discussions)
Commitment-tracking system
  Crandall, Fields
Volume weighting model
  Fields (knowing which stores to fix first)
Extend group knowledge base.
  Group database
    Roberts (international contacts)
Expand capacity to respond to employee communication.
  Word processing
    Plaskett, Stephens
  Electronic mail
    Compton, Roberts, Pogue
Stimulate creative thinking.
  Expert system (The Idea Generator)
    Fields (management strategies)
  Word processor
    Compton (personal communication, management strategies)
  Spreadsheet
    McCready (personnel issues, negotiations)
  Augmented meetings
    Stephens (group discussions), Crandall (group discussions)

Leadership

Strategies

Part II: The Leader as Commander

Pogue (Jones Day Reavis & Pogue)

Business goal: growing an integrated, global firm

Business strategies: carefully assimilate acquisitions, implement functional organizational structure

Leadership strategies: act as a strong managing partner, maintain strong central control of business content, and personnel

ISFs: inspire confidence through listening, avoid becoming a bottleneck for decision making, construct a fair and equitable means of handling compensation

Tools: electronic mail, spreadsheet

Humphrey (U.S. Senate)

Business goal: high throughput of consistent communications

Business strategy: administrative efficiency

Leadership strategies: channel high volume of communications through him for consistency, respond quickly to requests, network all offices to be geographically independent

ISFs: maintain accessibility to keep personal in-basket clear

Tools: electronic mail, word processing

Edmiston (The Cable Guide)

Business goal: revenue growth

Business strategies: expand production, improve editorial content, attract advertising revenues, expand to other formats

Leadership strategies: stay personally involved in planning and selling, delegate but stay informed

ISFs: stay up-to-date on internal activities, know people

Tools: access to internal operating data, spreadsheet, personal database

Gordon (Tootsie Roll Industries)

Business goal: maintain quality and margins

Business strategy: cost control

Leadership strategies: maintain personal involvement in operations—that is, purchasing, marketing and sales, employee motivation

ISFs: track internal business operations, maintain accessibility

Tools: access to internal operating data, electronic mail

Sigoloff (Wickes Corporation)

Business goal: restructure without dissolution

Business strategies: manage cash, complexity, and communication

Leadership strategies: maintain personal involvement in managing complex operations, coordinate events carefully, build teamwork, promote fact-based thinking

ISFs: track business operations, track projects, work independently, reach people, maintain accessibility, manage complexity

Tools: access to internal data, PERT charts, electronic mail, spreadsheet, word processor

Part III: The Leader as Communicator

Roberts (Mead Corporation)

Business goal: maintain global market position

Business strategy: compete better internationally to counterbalance American business cycles

Leadership strategies: establish a global network of contacts, encourage global team building, pick the right team members

ISFs: know people, pick people, maintain accessibility

Tools: group database, access to personnel data, electronic mail

McCready (TransAlta Utilities)

Business goal: improve customer satisfaction

Business strategy: implement quality-of-service program

Leadership strategies: track priorities and commitments, track employee performance, work with the provincial government

ISFs: pick people, analyze and compare alternatives, organize ideas and information

Tools: spreadsheet, outline editor

Plaskett (Pan Am)

Business goal: recover financially

Business strategies: reduce costs, improve morale

Leadership strategies: communicate openly and consistently with all employees to build personal credibility and rebuild trust in management

ISFs: produce high-volume correspondence with personalization and consistency, improve the clarity and consistency of messages

Tools: word processor

Stephens (Manville Corporation)

Business goal: restructuring without dissolution
Business strategies: design organization to compensate victims and still survive, then grow through acquisitions
Leadership strategies: educate parties while negotiating, lead strategic planning exercise, build widespread involvement in planning, design acquisition offers
ISFs: organize ideas and information, negotiate, improve thinking in groups, manage complexity
Tools: spreadsheet, graphics, word processor, augmented meetings

Part IV: The Leader as Coach

Gantz (Baxter International)

Business goal: diversification
Business strategy: implement strategic acquisition with merged culture
Leadership strategies: establish unifying theme of quality, coach by personal example, create an open, fact-based environment, gain credibility as a leader
ISFs: be well-informed, improve group thinking, communicate consistently
Tools: internal databases, spreadsheets, external databases, voice message system, facsimile, augmented meetings

Esrey (United Telecom and US Sprint)

Business goal: increase growth rate
Business strategy: start up venture in fiber-optic long-distance network
Leadership strategies: coordinate start-up activities, focus people on priorities, broaden people's attention, set external benchmarks

ISFs: work with people, work independent of geography, be well-informed, implement feedback loops

Tools: videoconferencing, electronic mail, internal databases, external databases

Crandall (Comshare)

Business goal: increase market share

Business strategies: block moves by the competition, manage internal product development priorities, focus on customer satisfaction, focus on quality, create strategic partnerships in the sales process, retain top people, develop alliances with other vendors, create an effective environment for collaboration.

Leadership strategy: implement feedback loops

ISFs: be well-informed externally and internally in regard to competitive announcements, internal product development, customer complaints, quality, customer visits, and turnover; keep in touch with customers and suppliers; communicate regularly

Tools: external databases, internal databases, electronic mail, augmented meetings

Fields (Mrs. Fields Cookies)

Business goal: maintain quality with rapid growth

Business strategy: invest in store procedures

Leadership strategies: coach, measure performance, be "present"

ISFs: maintain accessibility, coach, implement feedback loops, get the facts, organize ideas, manage complexity, think creatively

Tools: voice message systems, electronic mail, expert systems (both process and content), volume-weighting model, access to operating information, spreadsheets

Part V: The Leader as Culture Change Agent

Compton (Aetna)

Business goals: retain competitive position, gain advantages of size without disadvantages

Business strategies: teach "quick, flexible, and right" management method; align people with corporate direction

Leadership strategies: track performance on key objectives, teach the AMP, be a role model, do an excellent job of picking and developing people, develop precise expectations of employees, communicate expectations clearly, be a superb listener and analyzer

ISFs: reach people, teach people, measure performance, be accessible, make decisions, communicate clearly, listen well, leverage time

Tools: expert system, objectives database, access to internal financial data, word processor, graphics, spreadsheets, electronic mail, computer conferencing

Jordan (Frito-Lay)

Business goal: become more responsive to niche-market opportunities

Business strategies: decentralize, teach entrepreneurship

Leadership strategies: coach, develop strategy, build teamwork

ISFs: implement feedback loops, stay informed, track operations and commitments, allocate resources, share information

Tools: shared access to internal operating data, external database

Wallace (Phillips 66)

Business goal: avoid bankruptcy

Business strategies: trim staff and improve margins, decentralize control

Leadership strategies: immediately improve top management's understanding of the business, focus others on the bottom line, build a culture of teamwork

ISFs: track operations, empower people, communicate with people, pick people, stay informed externally and internally

Tools: internal operational databases, external databases, electronic mail

APPENDIX 5

For More

Information . . .

For more information regarding this research, you may contact the author at the following address:

NDMA Inc.
641 Danbury Road, Suite D
Ridgefield, CT 06877
phone: 203-431-0029

For other information on the subject of executive information systems, see these two books:

John Rockart and David DeLong, *Executive Support Systems: The Emergence of Top Management Computer Use* (Homewood, IL: Dow Jones-Irwin, 1988.)

Alan Paller with Richard Laska, *The EIS Book* (Homewood, IL: Dow Jones-Irwin, 1990.)

Executive Glossary

AI *See* Artificial intelligence.

Amplifier Used in cybernetics to mean a method for expanding a simple (low-variety) message throughout a complex (high-variety) working environment. For example, one person, such as the president of a company cannot direct the day-to-day efforts of everyone in the organization (which embraces an immense amount of variety), so he or she may employ an amplifier to extend the effect of a message. A policy statement and a telecommunication tool for announcements are examples of amplifiers.

ANSI American National Standards Institute, a standard-setting organization for many industries, including the computing industry.

Application An information tool that addresses a particular business problem.

Application software A computer program other than an operating system. Application software is what the user works with directly to accomplish actual tasks. An example of application software is Lotus 1-2-3.

Artificial intelligence (AI) A variety of types of information systems that emulate human thinking.

ASCII The industry-standard code used to represent textual characters. If someone creates an ASCII file, it means the file has been translated into a format that is easily transferable across different types of computers.

Asynchronous work Work accomplished independently of time, location, and centralized prescribed access to resources.

Audiographic teleconferencing Audio teleconferencing (a high-quality conference call) complemented by interconnected graphics devices such as slide projectors, telewriters, or electronic blackboards. The graphics devices can be viewed from all locations.

Audio teleconferencing   Teleconferencing involving speaker phones and telephone bridges that connect more than two telephone lines. This is a high-quality version of a conference call. The conference can be set up in two ways: an operator can dial all parties, or all parties can dial a specific number at a specified time. Allows for special services, such as the playing of prerecorded audiotapes.

Audiotex   *See* Voice processing.

Augment   Experimental software invented by Dr. Douglas C. Engelbart; one of the first end-user computing systems that integrated a broad range of tools. Included an outline editor, hypertext, electronic publishing, document management, decision support, graphics, image handling, database management, links to MIS and external databases, electronic mail, and shared-screen teleconferencing; incorporated cooperative processing, consistent user-interface, the first mouse, a keyset, and a variety of levels of help facilities. Operational at the Stanford Research Institute in the 1960s, used as a design model for many of the products now commercially available.

Augmented meeting   A meeting that uses information tool(s). All participants can see the screen, which is often displayed by a video projector. The tools can be used as a group-discussion aid—for example, notes on the meeting may be recorded in an outline structure, or participants may build a PERT chart of a project. Augmented meetings are most effective when they employ a trained "chauffeur" who operates the tools on behalf of meeting participants.

Automated factory   *See* Computer-integrated manufacturing.

Batch system   A computer system that is run by a computer operator for the benefit of the organization. Typical examples of batch systems include general ledger, payroll, and order processing systems. *See also* Data processing.

Bibliographic library database   An external database that provides bibliographic references to journals, magazines, and newspapers. Typically organized by industry or discipline and accessible by a keyword in title. *See also* External database.

Bit   A unit of binary information (either a zero or a one). Instructions to computers are composed of bits.

Bridge   Used in teleconferencing, a device to connect more than two telephone lines; or, a device used to link two networks that may have different protocols.

Business chart maker   *See* Graphics.

Business graphics   *See* Graphics.

Business television   Television programs designed for business purposes, generally requiring payment of a fee for reception. May use only broadcast television technologies or may utilize one-way video with two-way audio teleconferencing. May also include videotapes.

Byte   A series of bits that together represent a number, letter, or machine instruction.

Cable   A set of wires bundled together to permit the transmission of various types of information. Different cables are used to connect different devices—display screens, keyboards, mice, printers, plotters, etc.—to a computer. You must be sure the cable was designed for the purpose for which it is used.

CAD/CAM   *See* Computer-aided design and Computer-aided manufacturing.

Calendar system   Tools to manage a calendar or schedule of events; often provides features to schedule meetings by automatically comparing multiple calendars.

Causal database   A database contained within an expert system; simulates events by representing an expert's thought processes. A causal database is more precise, more robust, and more expensive than a rules-structured database.

CD   Compact disk; an optical disk read by a laser that can hold voluminous amounts of information. Most commonly in the form of CD-ROM (read-only CDs), although new technologies permit erasing and rewriting.

CD-ROM   Compact disk-read-only memory, a nonmagnetic optical disk read by a laser. A CD-ROM can hold voluminous amounts of information. Once a master disk is created, manufacturing costs per disk are very low. Once manufactured, the information it contains is permanent and cannot be changed or erased. Used for high-volume publishing of information databases.

Change analyzer An information tool that takes two versions of a document and highlights the differences to identify what has changed across revisions. Particularly useful in legal or legislative environments and in collaborative writing projects.

Chart-book A book of charts and graphs that describe business operations; produced periodically in place of routine MIS reports. *See also* Graphics.

Chauffeur A consultant who operates information systems on behalf of an executive or participants in an augmented meeting.

CIM *See* Computer-integrated manufacturing.

Circuit-switched network A telecommunications network of computers or telephones; functions as a dedicated line between two points (in contrast to a packet-switched network, which shares lines). For example, a telephone call constitutes the equivalent of a dedicated wire between two locations.

Cognitive styles Several typical patterns in which people think; generally refers to a framework developed by Carl Jung that differentiates structured from intuitive thinkers and fact- from concept-oriented people. Jungian cognitive style is measured with a test called the Myers-Briggs Indicator.

Commitment-tracking system An electronic reminder system used to track commitments other people have made, reminding the user when work is due. Can also be used to track and set priorities regarding the user's commitments and responsibilities, or the priorities of others. Used to encourage a culture of responsiveness and reliability, may be as simple as a database of reminders, or it may sort entries by person, project, due date, priority, etc.

Communicating word processor A word processor that can send documents to another word processor via telephone lines or networks; now generally replaced by a word processing package on general-purpose computers, that can, via modems and phone lines, transmit documents.

Compatibility The ability of two different computer systems to work together. When used to describe hardware (for example, "This board is compatible with IBM PCs"), it means that the two types of hardware can be attached to form a single system. When used to describe software (for example, "This program is compatible with IBM PCs"), it means that the software can be used on the specified hardware. When used to describe data (for example, "The files are compatible with Lotus 1-2-3"), it means that the data can be read by the specified hardware or software.

Computer-aided design (CAD)   Tools to aid in design work. CAD software defines physical objects numerically and portrays them on the screen graphically. Because the objects are defined numerically, they can be easily manipulated. CAD systems typically consist of a database, which describes the design; decision support tools to manipulate the data; and graphics tools that portray the data (as a three-dimensional object or a schematic, for example). Often linked to computer-aided manufacturing (CAM).

Computer-aided manufacturing (CAM)   Tools to convert the output of computer-aided design (CAD) tools into manufacturing specifications and machine-control programs.

Computer conferencing   A personal message system that sends text messages to a group's (or a person's) computerized "in-basket(s)." Messages are sent and read using terminals or personal computers. Groups are formed around particular topics. When the user checks in to the conference, the computer remembers where he or she last left the dialogue, and lists all messages since the user last checked in. Also, the software allows the user to add a new message to the dialogue.

Computer-integrated manufacturing (CIM)   Tools that collect information from the factory floor and combine that information with operational databases. Often used by management for decision support. This includes everything from digital machine-tool control (Level 1), to real-time management of the factory (Level 2), through inclusion of information in administrative and operational databases (Level 3). Robots are Level 1 devices which are controlled by Level 2 devices. Levels 1 and 2 are reported on in Level 3 (the operational and administrative databases reviewed by managment).

Cost-avoidance benefits   The use of information systems to avoid costs such as future hiring; assumes costs otherwise would have been incurred, e.g., people otherwise would have been hired.

Cost-displacement benefits   The use of information systems to replace costs such as administrative time.

CPU   Central processing unit; in every computer, the portion that reads the instructions in a program and performs the designated functions by adding, subtracting, comparing, changing memory, and determining which instructions in the program should be executed next.

Cursor   A pointing mark on a display screen. Usually appears as a blinking square or blinking line underneath a character on a computer screen. The cursor tells you where you are on the screen. Think of the cursor as the top of a pen or pencil on a page of paper. The cursor can be moved by using cursor keys, mouse, joystick, etc.

Cursor keys   Keys on a personal computer or terminal keyboard; allow the user to move the cursor on a display screen. Cursor keys typically includes the up-, down-, right-, and left-arrow keys.

Cybernetics   The science of how systems are organized, regulated, and reproduced. The word *cybernetics* originates from the Greek word for steersman. A leader in applying cybernetics to organizations is Stafford Beer. Concepts of cybernetics (such as feedback loops, regulators, filters, and amplifiers) may be used to design organizations or to design information systems that motivate and guide organization performance by providing the right kind of feedback.

Database management system   A tool that stores information in a series of records, each of which is in the same format. Because of the way databases are structured, it is easy to retrieve information in highly specific ways. For example, a database could print a list of all a company's customers who live in a certain zip code or of all who bought a particular product last year. A database can quickly scan thousands of records containing any type of information.

Data processing (DP)   Computerized processing of routine business transactions such as payroll, bookkeeping, orders, and inventories. Generally, DP applications are well-structured, periodic, and centrally managed.

DBMS   *See* Database management system.

Decision support system (DSS) A tool with which to build models, either in the form of a spreadsheet or a set of equations and relationships. DSSs are often linked to a database that provides numbers as input to the model.

Desktop publishing Relatively low-cost publishing tools designed for use by a single person. *See* Electronic publishing.

Disk A magnetic medium used to store computerized information. Disks come in many sizes and hold varying amounts of information. A disk is analagous to a computerized file cabinet. Information on disks is stored in files. There are two types of computer disks: floppy and hard. Floppy disks currently come in two sizes, 5.25 inch or 3.5 inches. Hard disks are rigid, and they hold much more information than a floppy. Hard disks are stored inside the computer and are not normally removed by the user; floppy disks are frequently removed and inserted by the user.

Disk operating system (DOS) A brand name for two types of operating systems. One runs on older generation mainframes; the other runs on personal computers. *See* Operating system.

Document Any combination of text, data, graphics, and images.

Document archive A library of computerized documents for long-term storage; provides an index of documents and automatic retrieval.

Document interchange The ability to send a document created on one system to another (different) system. The receiving system can change as well as view the document. Document interchange is easier when the two systems can send and receive files through a network and can translate their files into and out of a common format.

Document management Archival facility for text files. Often makes powerful indexing and tracking functions available.

DOS *See* Disk operating system.

DP *See* Data processing.

Drawing *See* Line-drawing system.

DSS *See* Decision support system.

Dumb terminal *See* Terminal.

Econometric model A quantitative model of future economic conditions and their impact on an organization. Usually linked with decision support tools and may be linked to models of the organization's performance or simulations of market demand and customer buying behavior.

EDI *See* Electronic data interchange.

EIS *See* Executive information system.

Electronic blackboard An imaging device that allows people in one location to write on a blackboard (or whiteboard) and have the image printed on paper or appear on a television screen in other locations. Generally used in conjunction with audio teleconferencing for one-to-many applications such as teaching.

Electronic data interchange (EDI) The electronic exchange of data in predefined forms that are the electronic equivalent of paper business forms. Typically, EDI occurs between companies and is related to business transactions such as purchase orders and invoices. Requires that the two systems "agree" on the format of the data they send and receive.

Electronic mail A personal message system that sends text messages to a person's (or a group's) computerized "in-basket(s)." Messages are sent, stored, and read using terminals or personal computers.

Electronic mail with forms An electronic mail system that allows the user to send a person or a group a message that contains a form and then allows recipients to fill out the form and return it to the originator. Some systems can take the data from the form and automatically enter it into a database.

Electronic publishing A text-formatting tool that prints the output of a word processor or outline editor in a range of type fonts, often with automatic document-wide formatting and page layout.

End-user computing (EUC) The broad range of interactive tools for thinking. Distinct from data processing and computer-integrated manufacturing. (See Appendix 1.)

ESS (Executive support systems.) *See* Executive information system.

EUC *See* End-user computing.

Executive information system (EIS) Any application of computer or communication tools to executive objectives; the executive directly participates in the selection of the problem and the selection, design, or use of the tool.

Expert system   A computer system that questions a user and guides the user's decision making; based on a database that represents the knowledge and judgments of an expert. The knowledge database may be either rules-structured or causal.

External database   A database maintained by a company or government organization and made available to other users, generally on a per-hour or per-unit-of-information basis. An external database can be accessed via telephone or computer network from a terminal or personal computer. Thousands of commercial databases are available, and they offer news, market prices, bulletin boards, or bibliographies of major publications in virtually every field. Library scientists are trained to find the appropriate databases and to search them effectively. External databases can also be accessed by users.

Facsimile   A device that scans an image on a piece of paper, converts it to data, and transmits it over a telephone line or network. A similar device on the recipient's end prints the image.

Fiber-optic cables   Telecommunications lines made of a glasslike cable that is flexible and bends the light within it. With bursts of light from a laser, sound and data is transmitted through the cables. Fiber-optic transmission is very fast, immune to noise from magnetic motors and transformers, and secure from electronic eavesdropping.

File   An orderly arrangement of information. Information on disks is stored in files. Some types of files are created by the user; others reside inside the software. A file on a disk is analogous to a file in a filing cabinet.

Filter   In cybernetics, a means of reducing complex (high-variety) information into a simple (low-variety) message. A summary report or a secretary who screens telephone calls are examples of filters.

Firmware   One or more computer programs and supporting data stored permanently within a computer or its component parts.

Floppy disk   A small, flexible disk enclosed in a flexible jacket; limited in capacity and speed, but very portable. Most common are the 5.25- and 3.5-inch disks used in personal computers.

Freeze-frame video teleconferencing A device which captures an image of a person, a document, or an object from a video camera and transmits it as a still photograph at slow speed over a conventional (voice-grade) telephone line. Generally, the other location also has a device for returning an image. Freeze-frame teleconferencing is often used in conjunction with audio teleconferencing. Although the devices may use a bridge for multipoint conferences, they are most commonly used between only two locations. This type of teleconferencing combines the flexibility of a video image with the low cost of standard telephone lines.

Full-text search A search that scans an entire document (or set of documents) for a word or combination of words. Used to identify passages of text (or references) in a large document or library.

Function keys On a computer keyboard, keys (typically labeled "F1," "F2," etc.) that are used to tell the software to perform certain functions. Each software package uses them differently, although quite often F1 accesses on-line help.

Gantt chart A project management chart that shows tasks as bars covering time periods; particularly useful to review resource requirements over time. Certain types of applications software allow the user to create electronic Gantt charts, which are easily alterable.

Grammar checker A text analyzer that identifies problems in grammar and writing style. Typical problems are punctuation errors, incomplete sentences, passive voice, hackneyed or convoluted phrases, vague terms, and jargon. May also include reading-level analysis, that is, the analysis of the educational level required to read the document.

Graphics Depictions of data, such as line, bar, and pie charts; distinct from image-handling displays, which are not driven by data. More powerful systems (such as those on mainframe computers) allow the intermixing of various types of graphs along with tables of numbers and text on each page. Booklets of charts and graphs (instead of MIS reports) may be produced automatically to document business operations.

Group database A database designed for a small group (for example, a department or project team) and accessible to and maintained by the group. For example, a group might create a database of a department's work orders. *See also* Database management system.

Group editor   A text-editing tool designed to support groups of people collaborating on a single document. Features may include the ability to track who wrote what, or the capacity to add comments to other people's text.

Hard disk   An inflexible disk enclosed in either its access machinery (and not removable) or in special hard casings; much faster and with a greater capacity than a floppy disk, but not portable.

Hardware   Computer- and telecommunications-based equipment. Software runs on hardware.

Host computer   *See* Time-sharing computer.

Hypertext   Text documents which are structured hierarchically in which each node may be a word, a line, or an entire paragraph. Allows views of the text—for example, a table-of-contents-style overview—or filters based on the content ("Show me every paragraph that contains . . ."). Within the text, one may include links (pointers, or references) to views of other places in the same or other text documents; the reader may follow the link (such as a footnote) and see the specified view.

IEF   International Executive Forum. *See* WBSI.

Image editor   A tool to work with images—that is, drawings represented in the computer as a set of dots (as distinct from graphics, which are generated from data). For example, image editors allow a user to create and edit drawings on the screen; the tools typically include a variety of image-manipulation features, such as rotation, shading, enlarging, reducing, distorting, etc.

Image handling   *See* Image editor.

Information system (IS)   Computer and telecommunications technology that stores, manipulates, and transfers information. Includes three major types: data processing and management information systems, process automation, and end-user computing.

Joystick   A device that allows the user to move the cursor or point at characters or points on the computer screen by moving a lever up and down and from side to side. Most often used with computer games.

Keyset   A device that allows the user to enter characters (as on a keyboard) by playing "chords" with one hand; invented by Dr. Douglas C. Engelbart to work with the mouse and allow high-speed interactions with a computer, without having to look away from the display screen.

Knowledge-based system   *See* Expert system.

LAN   *See* Local area network.

Large-scale integration (LSI)   A technology that permits the combination of a large number of transistors on an integrated circuit. The result is that each chip can perform a complex set of functions. For example, an entire computer CPU can be put on a single chip because of large-scale integration.

Library database   *See* External database.

Light pen   A device connected to a personal computer or terminal; allows the user to select a point on the display screen by touching the device to the screen. Commonly used in computer-aided design or image-handling tools where drawing is involved.

Line drawing system   An image-handling tool that allows the user to draw and edit images on the screen; typically includes a variety of image-manipulation features such as rotation, shading, enlarging, reducing, distorting, etc.

Local area network (LAN)   A device that connects personal computers, typically providing shared access to data and printers and sometimes providing communications with other computers. Shared information is frequently used for local databases, file archives, and electronic mail.

LSI   *See* Large-scale integration.

Mainframe business graphics   Graphic displays including line, bar, and pic charts that are not data driven and so are distinct from those produced by image-handling tools. Some business graphics packages allow the mixing of various types of graphs, along with tables and text, on each page. Since the package resides on the mainframe, data processing systems can run it automatically to produce books of charts and graphs rather than numerical reports.

Mainframe computer   A large computer designed for high-speed information processing; generally for high-volume data processing or to support the use of a centralized tool by many people.

Mainframe graphics   *See* Graphics.

Management information system (MIS)   A database of recent and historic business transactions that results from data processing. MIS is used primarily as a basis for future data processing and as a source of historic operating data for tracking the organization's performance. Operating managers receive regular MIS reports, and the MIS is available for ad hoc query by analysts and senior managers.

Management science (MS)   Mathematical techniques applied to simulating, optimizing and guiding management decisions. Generally applied to less-structured processes, as distinct from operations research.

Merge lists   A list often generated by a database management system which allows for the automatic creation of personalized form letters for every person on the list.

Microcomputer   A computer processor (CPU) on an integrated-circuit chip. A microcomputer may be combined with other electronic components that provide memory, storage, input/output, and other peripheral functions to create a personal computer or minicomputer.

Minicomputer   A medium-sized computer, generally one that does not require special air-conditioning and cooling facilities.

MIS   *See* Management information system.

Model   A set of equations that simulate real processes—for example, physical processes, such as the flow of parts through a manufacturing assembly line; financial processes such as future cash flows or budgets; market processes such as shifts in market share; or buying patterns, such as price elasticity. Optimization models take as input a set of objectives and determine the ideal solution; they are used for well-understood processes, such as plant scheduling or mixing chemicals. Simulation models take as input a set of assumptions and forecast outcomes; this allows decision makers to ask what-if questions.

Modem   A device connecting computers and terminals to telephone lines for the purpose of sending and receiving information; converts digital information to beeps for transmission and converts incoming sounds to digital information for reception.

Mouse   Connected to a personal computer or terminal, a device whose movement on a flat surface allows the user to select a character or point on the display screen. Generally, a mouse includes up to three buttons, which (like a keyboard) provide input to the computer. Invented by Dr. Douglas C. Engelbart, the mouse has proven a fast and accurate means of pointing to items on a computer screen.

Multimedia systems   Systems that integrate standard data and text processing with graphics, animation, speech synthesis, audio, or text.

Multitasking   The ability of a computer operating system to process more than one task at a time. Used by a personal computer to perform some tasks automatically while the user is working on another task, by all time-sharing computers to serve multiple users at once, and by large data processing systems to support complex transactions.

Network   A series of devices and telecommunications lines that link computers together. One type of network links computers and another type links telephones. Networks connect different locations and allow them to send information to each other. *See also* Server.

Neural networks   An AI-based technology for finding patterns in large databases. For example, neural networks might look at customer data and tell who's likely to have a lot of insurance claims or default on loans. Neural networks allow the user to search databases with search parameters that are less precise than those normally required for database searches.

News library database   An external database that provides the full text of consumer and business news stories from newspaper publications, news-wire submissions, or industry-oriented news-gathering services. *See also* External database.

Object-oriented languages   High-level programming languages that are particularly useful for programming database applications.

OCR   *See* Optical character recognition.

One-way video teleconferencing   A system which transmits live video images from a central studio to many locations and also provides multilocation audio teleconferencing for questions and discussions. Popular for one-to-many announcements. Setup is analogous to that of a TV talk show with call-ins. *See also* Business television.

On-line   On a computer. When applied to data (as in "The data is on-line"), *on-line* means the information has been entered into a computer and is stored there in an accessible form. When applied to information tools (as in "an on-line calendar system"), it means that the tool is computer-based and accessible by the user.

On-line database   A database available for interactive access and ad hoc inquiries.

Operating system   The program that provides functions to manage computer files and hardware and allows access to other software. When you turn on a computer, it automatically loads your operating system. Then you give it a command telling it to load whatever applications software you want to use. Operating systems help you manipulate all the files stored in your computer. For example, if you want to copy a file from one disk to another, you give the operating system a command to do it for you.

Operational databases   *See* Organizational database.

Optical character recognition (OCR)   A device which scans a piece of paper and converts typed (or in some cases written) words into computerized textual data.

Order-entry system   A data processing information system that allows people to enter orders for fulfillment by another group elsewhere in the company.

Organizational bulletin board   A database accessible to people throughout an organization; makes company news and reference information available. Specific topics are generally selected through a series of menus rather than a keyword search.

Organizational database   A database accessible to and maintained by people throughout an organization; distinct from MIS databases, which are accessible to everyone but maintained automatically by data processing systems. Electronic versions of the corporate telephone book, policies, and publications are organizational databases. *See also* Database management system.

Outline editor   A text-editing tool that treats the text as nodes in an outline; designed for authors to use in brainstorming and organizing ideas in addition to word processing.

Packet-switched network   A telecommunications network connecting computers that send information in "packets" so that people and computers can share telecommunications lines; distinct from circuit-switched networks.

Painting system   *See* Line-drawing system.

Parallel processing   A computer system that combines more than one CPU so that, to work more quickly, it can perform more than one task at a time.

PC   *See* Personal computer.

Personal computer (PC)   A microcomputer small enough to fit on the user's desk; designed for use by a single person. Generally, a PC includes disk drives for information storage. Through a network, a PC may be connected to other personal computers.

Personal database   A database designed for, accessible to, and maintained by an individual. An executive's electronic telephone book is an example of a personal database. *See also* Database management system.

Personal message system   A tool that sends messages to a person's (or a group's) computerized "in-basket(s)." Messages can be read via any terminal that can be linked to the computer supporting the personal message system. Includes electronic mail, computer conferencing, and voice-message systems.

PERT   Program evaluation and review technique, a project management technique or computer-based tool that portrays a project as a series of interrelated tasks. Shows the critical path of tasks that constrain the pace of the project.

PIMS   Product Impact of Marketing Strategies, an external database of the operating results of a range of companies and business units. PIMS allows comparison of a company's operating statistics with those of others in the same industry.

Plotter   A printing device that draws charts and graphs, often employing a range of colored pens. Simple plotters are small enough to fit on a desktop; larger plotters handle more colors, larger paper, and finer detail.

Printer   A device that takes information from a computer and prints it on paper. The information from the computer can be graphic or textual. Printers range in quality from a dot-matrix printer to a laser printer. Laser printers produce extremely high-quality output and allow the user to print text in different fonts.

Process analyst A consultant who participates in a meeting to ensure an effective process of communications but who does not participate in the content of the meeting. Also sometimes called a process facilitator.

Process automation The use of real-time computers to control machines. Process automation is found in automated factories and warehouses, computer-controlled buildings and appliances, and laboratory instrumentation.

Productivity Outputs divided by inputs, a measure of throughput or efficiency; used to measure administrative time savings produced by information systems. Productivity does not apply to the unstructured work of managers and professionals.

Program A set of instructions that tell a computer how to perform a function. *See also* Software.

Project management system A tool that helps people manage projects by storing data about planned and actual tasks, dates, responsibilities, and costs. Data is portrayed in PERT and Gantt charts as well as reports.

Protocols Technical specifications detailing methods of communication, interaction, etc.

Records management Archival facility for paper documents; often includes computer-based indexing and tracking functions.

Reminder system A tool that tracks data by time and automatically notifies the user when a specific date and time arrive. Used to track commitments and deliverables.

Rules-structured database A database that matches inputs with outputs or situations with outcomes, without attempting to understand why the relationship occurs. Used in expert systems; distinct from causal databases.

Server On a network, a computer that provides services to other computers (rather than directly talking to a user). A server links computers together to allow them to share software, files, and access to such devices as printers and modems.

Shared-screen teleconferencing Software that allows two or more people in different locations to simultaneously use any information tool and view the same computer screen. If adjustments are made to the information by any of the participants, those adjustments appear at all locations. Generally used in conjunction with the telephone or audio teleconferencing to allow for discussions of the information on the screen. Useful for collaboration such as co-authorship, negotiations or training.

Slide maker A hardware and software system to make 35mm slides and overhead transparencies. Slides may include text, graphics, and images. Inexpensive slide makers use the image on the computer screen; more powerful machines provide much higher resolution.

Software A computer program that performs a function. Hardware is the machinery; software tells the machine what to do. An analogy can be made to a stereo system: Your stereo system might be considered hardware, and your CDs and records might be considered software.

Speaker phone A telephone device that broadcasts incoming sound on a loudspeaker and, with one or more microphones, captures outgoing sound so that a group in one location may participate in a telephone call or teleconference.

Speech recognition An input device which takes the sound of a person speaking (via a microphone) as input and converts it to computerized text.

Speech synthesis An output device which accepts as input computer-based text and reads it aloud, often through a telephone.

Spelling checker A text analyzer that identifies misspelled words. Some also suggest one or more correctly spelled alternatives and automatically edit the document as the correct spelling is identified.

Spreadsheet A tool to work with numbers in the form of a table—that is, in rows and columns. Any cell in the table may contain a text label, a number, or a formula that combines other cells. This allows the tool to be "programmed" to automatically add up columns or calculate numbers based on other numbers. Spreadsheets are used for budgets, numeric analysis, decision models, and simple forecasting models.

Statistical package A set of interactive statistical tools to support data analysis—correlations, regressions, and cluster analysis, for example. Some systems offer a wide variety of advanced analytic techniques. Some can be linked to database management systems or run automatically by data processing systems. Statistical packages are used in market research, forecasting, and scientific research.

Stock/commodity prices library database   An external database that provides current prices of currencies, equities, and commodities. Typically organized by industry or market. *See also* External database.

Strategic information system   Any information system that directly contributes to the strategic business objectives of an organization.

Strategy tree   A planning methodology developed by Dean Meyer and Mary Boone for mapping the strategic business activities of an organization and then identifying opportunities for strategic information systems.

Systems theory   *See* Cybernetics.

Teleconferencing   Real-time electronic communication between three or more people at two or more locations; may involve speaker phones and "bridges" that link more than two telephone lines. May include audio, audiographic, freeze-frame video, two-way video, one-way video with two-way audio, business television, and shared-screen.

Telewriting device   An image device which allows people in one location to write on a digital pad and have the image appear on a television screen in another location; the other location can edit the same image using a similar digital pad. Essentially shared-screen teleconferencing with an image handling tool. Generally used in conjunction with audio teleconferencing for collaboration among a few people on drawings.

Terminal   A keyboard and display designed to be connected to a computer—generally, a minicomputer or mainframe that supports many users. A personal computer may be used as a terminal when connected to other computers.

Thesaurus   A program that suggests synonyms for words. Some word processors, grammar checkers, and spell checkers give the user automatic access to a thesaurus.

Thought processor   *See* Outline editor.

Tickler system   *See* Reminder system.

Time-sharing computer   A computer that supports more than one user at a time; users are connected through terminals and telecommunications lines.

Tool   A related set of information-handling functions designed for interactive use by users (different from batch systems, which are run by computer operators). A tool is made of technologies. For example, a spreadsheet or electronic-mail tool is made of technologies such as microcomputers, minicomputers, mainframes, networks, etc.

Track ball   A device attached to a personal computer or terminal; allows a person to point at a spot on the display screen by rolling one's hand over a fixed ball. A track ball is used in place of a mouse where desk space is extremely limited.

Two-way video teleconferencing   A system which sends live video and audio to another location. Portrays motion and generally requires very high-speed telecommunications lines, such as microwave and satellite links, although some telecommunications costs may be saved by sacrificing image resolution or clarity of motion. Usually used only between two locations.

UNIX   A brand name for a type of operating system. Of interest because it is an industry standard that runs on many different types of hardware.

User   A person who uses a computer.

User interface   The conventions used by the computer to communicate with the user, including how the user specifies commands and points at the display screen and gets help and how the computer portrays information and feedback on the display screen. Ideally, a user interface should be both easy to learn and easy for experienced users to use.

Value-added benefits   The impact of information tools on an organization's effectiveness; distinct from simple time savings.

Videotex   A database in which items of information are selected by choosing from a series of tree-structured menus. Selecting an item from one menu leads the user to a submenu or to more information. A common application is seen in kiosks at airports or hotels, where users touch a screen to gain information. Organizational bulletin boards are often run on videotex systems.

VMS *See* Voice message system.

Voice annotation A tool to attach brief recordings (such as a person's voice with a message) to a computer-based document (such as a textual document or message).

Voice mail A brand of voice message system.

Voice message system (VMS) A telephone-based personal message system that sends recordings of a person's voice to a person's (or a group's) computerized "in-basket(s)." VMSs are generally attached to a telephone PBX, and typically allow broadcast of a message to a group, forwarding, answering, and limited storage and filing. A voice message system is analogous to an extremely sophisticated network of answering machines.

Voice processing Using the telephone as an interface to provide access to information systems such as voice message systems, bulletin boards, or electronic mail. May incorporate speech synthesis or speech recognition.

WBSI Western Behavioral Sciences Institute. Sponsors the International Executive Forum (IEF). The IEF is a network of leading businesspeople and intellectuals connected by computer conference. The group meets face-to-face once a year in La Jolla, California. Topics covered by the group range across a broad array of business, political, and social issues. WBSI is located at UCSD, 90500 Gilman Drive, La Jolla, California 92093-0055. Phone: 619-534-0904. Fax: 619-534-2333.

Windows Division of a workstation screen into multiple areas called "windows," each portraying different information. Windows may be overlaid, one on top of another. Windows allow the user to view and simultaneously work on a number of different pieces of information. MicroSoft makes a specific product for windowing, which is called Windows.

Word processor A text-editing tool that treats the text as a stream of characters. Word processors allow extremely flexible manipulation of textual information. They also allow the user to format information in preparation for typesetting output.

Workstation   An appliance used to communicate with a computer, including an input device (such as a keyboard) and an output device (such as a display); may be a personal computer or a terminal.

WORM   Write once read many; an optical disk read by a laser. WORM disks can hold a great deal of information. Information can be stored on the disk by a local device but, once written, the information is permanent and cannot be changed or erased. Used for low-volume publishing of information databases.

WP   *See* word processor.

INDEX